D1319858

Survival in the Executive Jungle

by CHESTER BURGER

THE MACMILLAN COMPANY, NEW YORK

The author wishes to thank Wm. Collins Sons & Co.
Ltd., London, and G. P. Putnam's Sons, New York,
for permission to quote from *The Path to
Leadership,* copyright © 1961 by Bernard Law,
Viscount Montgomery of Alamein.

THE MACMILLAN COMPANY, NEW YORK
Collier-Macmillan Canada, Ltd., Toronto, Ontario

Library of Congress catalog card number: 64-12542

To My Wife

Contents

Introduction

When I showed the manuscript of this book to a young college graduate student of business administration, I was hardly prepared for his reaction.

"It's very interesting," he told me, "but too bad you had to mix fiction with fact. Some parts of it I liked very much, but Chapter One spoiled the whole thing. Nobody would believe those things really happened. Why can't you leave out the stories and just stick to the truth?"

Well, as I told the college student, every line of the book is true. Each incident actually happened. I have neither created nor embellished the incidents described. The only liberties I've taken are to change names, places, and industries, to preclude the possibility that you might be able to identify someone you know—perhaps the executive in the office next door.

For almost a quarter of a century, I've had the opportunity first to observe, and then to participate in corporate life at the executive level. My experience has been that of an insider. I haven't had to imagine what went on inside the executive offices because I was behind the closed doors, participating actively.

Of course, this has given me a different perspective, and

this book reflects it. All of it is derived from my personal experience. Before you incorrectly assume that these incidents occurred in a particular company with which I was associated, let me explain that I spent more than eight years as a public relations consultant to more than a hundred corporations, large and small, in all parts of the nation. This gave me the rare opportunity of working closely with their senior managements on a wide variety of business problems.

The experience, and the responsibility for this book are totally mine, but I'm grateful to my superiors over the years who gave me the opportunity to acquire that experience. In particular, I want to thank Marion Harper, Jr., chairman of the board of Interpublic, Incorporated; the Honorable William Ruder, formerly Assistant Secretary of Commerce and president of Ruder & Finn, Inc., Nathan W. Picker and Sidney W. Picker, chairman of the board and executive vice-president, respectively, of Echelons Office Temporaries, Inc.

A number of my business friends and associates were kind enough to offer suggestions and comments based on their own experiences. They include Jesse G. Bell and Peter A. Dolan, Jr., of the American Telephone & Telegraph Company; Harold Bixler, of Boyden Associates, Inc.; Marshall Graham, of Cresap, McCormick, and Paget; Miss Mitzi Morris, of Jerry Fields Associates; Lawrence Gardiner of The Coca-Cola Export Corporation; and Wallace Wohlking, of Cornell University's New York State School of Industrial and Labor Relations. My appreciation also to Maximilian Becker and Robert Markel, who suggested that my observations might interest others.

The problems which I describe could occur only in a dynamic and vigorously competitive economy. Anyone who knows American industry intimately must be impressed with its vitality and energy. In this atmosphere, the executive who can handle himself with skill and objectivity will thrive.

Chester Burger

To be great, to be a person of stature, a man must have character, judgment, high intelligence, a special aptitude for seeing his problems whole and true—for seeing things as they are, without exaggeration or emotion—and above all the ability of decision, the right decision, of course.

—Field Marshal Montgomery

Jungle Warfare

YOU'VE JUST MOVED to a new executive position, but already somebody wants your job. The higher your position, the more certain it is that you'll have to fight for it. The hunter who is stalking you as his prey may be one of your subordinates, a "friendly" colleague, or even your boss. In the carpeted upper floors of Executive (Bitter) Suite the new executive is fair game, without benefit of fair play. The jungle tactics you'll face were never dreamed of by the Marquis of Queensberry. The cost of defeat is loss of your livelihood, even though it may be concealed by the polite phrase, "voluntary resignation."

Don't rely for protection on the illusion that your company is different, that your management wouldn't allow such things to happen, that office politics are absent.

Office politics exist in every company, and at every corporate level. They're the inevitable concomitant of a competitive economy. I've known more than one hundred corporations from the inside, but never one where office politics were absent. So don't expect to escape it in your own company. The innocent young man who wishes he could simply concentrate on his job, and ignore his personal relationships, is daydreaming. Such a situation simply does not exist at the executive level.

One new executive, who held such illusions, was shocked

1

on his first day on the job when a colleague advised him jocularly to "sit with your back to the wall, to protect yourself against a knifing. They happen pretty often around here." The company was notorious for its savage practice of office politics, and it was untypical only in degree.

Even well-managed companies know they can't eliminate office politics, but they do try to minimize them. They encourage competition, but always seek to keep it in constructive channels. They measure executives regularly in comparison with others, but the yardsticks are those which benefit the company. They may be volume of sales, or reduction of costs, or improvement of service. Whatever they are, they do not include an executive's ability at office politics or his score on the golf course. In these companies, insofar as able management can make it possible, promotions are made only on the basis of reasonably objective standards. Devices to eliminate or minimize personal favoritism are incorporated into the company structure. International Business Machines' famed Open Door policy is such a device.

The Open Door began when IBM was a much smaller company. Thomas J. Watson, its president, invited any dissatisfied employee to visit him personally if the employee could not secure satisfaction at a lower level. Today, the company employs more than 127,000 people, and it would be manifestly impossible for the president or the chairman of the board personally to meet more than a few complainants. Yet, the Open Door policy continues. The reason, one IBM executive told me, is that it forces executives throughout the vast enterprise to make certain they have solid and reasonable grounds before disciplining, demoting or dismissing an employee. The Open Door allows employees to challenge such action directly to the head of the corporation. Even though the president may not overrule the action, employees know that he will investigate their complaint. If the action was arbitrary, he will personally discover it. Such a policy effectively minimizes office politics. It does not eliminate competition, but only arbitrary abuse of executive power.

In companies known for internal instability, the picture is different. Senior executives battle juniors; junior executives war against each other; and not infrequently, employees battle for the junior executive's job. No Geneva Convention exists to outlaw inhuman executive warfare.

The first attack on your outpost may come from your fellow executives, your colleagues of equal rank. Each of them wants to win promotion, but perhaps there is room for only one at the next higher level. These men are circumspect in their tactics of warfare. The division manager might not respond kindly to an overt attack on you. So, instead, they try to provoke you into an unwise course of action in which you will destroy yourself.

They may simulate friendliness, aiming at your naïveté and inexperience. They invite you to lunch, feign good will, and gently seek to misguide you. If they've learned that the division manager demands their monthly reports promptly, one will remark, "I'm going to be late again with my monthly report. I don't like to be late, but I'm busy working on our new sales plan, and I know the boss considers that more important."

Just two sentences; then the conspirator moves on to other topics. Of course, he'll turn in *his* report promptly on the first of the month when it's due, but hopefully, he has suggested to you that lateness is acceptable. If, gullibly, you swallow the idea and hand in your own report a few days late, because you were busy with something "more important," you have damaged your reputation with your superior.

Or perhaps the modern-day Machiavelli has learned of a higher-level opening, for which several junior executives will receive consideration. He has been tipped off that top management wants a dynamic man to upset the department's *status quo* and institute thoroughgoing reforms. Out of professed sheer friendship for his competitor, the conspirator will take his would-be victim aside.

"Have they told you about the opening?" he asks Peter Mack, his target. "I just heard about it on the twenty-fifth floor. They're looking for someone to replace Mr. Kastenholz. He's being transferred elsewhere. They want someone who can go in there without rocking the ol' apple cart. Someone who can just keep things rolling along without change. I'm going after the job myself, and I guess you will too. I hope I get it, but the best of luck to you."

His unsuspecting colleague swallows the bait. When called for his interview, Mr. Mack follows the suggested line.

"You know the department, Mr. Mack," says the divisional manager. "How would you handle things if we gave you the job?"

"I'd change as little as possible," Mr. Mack promptly replies. "Those people are very loyal to Mr. Kastenholz. He has things running smoothly. I'd try to pick up where he left off, with a minimum of changes. I don't want to disturb the operation, and I think I can take over quickly and win their confidence."

The divisional manager listens a few minutes more, but his mind is already made up. Mr. Mack has just knocked himself out of the race. An hour later, Mr. Schramm, the conspirator, will come along, say the right things, and get the job.

In the executive jungle, the plotters seldom operate as lone wolves. Usually, they form into packs, ready to pounce on an unwary victim. They never assemble openly in the clearing but prefer to conceal themselves in the corporate underbrush.

The cliques may consist of scattered individuals in a dozen departments, bound together as closely as a German collegiate dueling society. The British "old school tie" does not surpass them for bonds of brotherhood. The tie that binds can be almost anything: religion, place of origin (I once saw a group of Minnesotans form such a clique), or even homosexuality. These cabals never organize more formally than as a mere thought in the minds of their members. They operate under the banner of "An injury to one is an injury to all." Antagonize one member and you will bring down on your head the wrath of all for the remainder of your career in the company. Top management seldom breaks up their smooth functioning, because, all too often, their tentacles have already extended into top management.

Members of the clique spread destructive rumors as part of their psychological warfare. They feed the rumor mill which already exists in most large organizations, especially in those where prompt and accurate channels of information don't exist. The large organization provides fertile ground for the rumormonger, because its vast size makes it difficult to trace down the original source of a false report.

"Did you hear about Casey?" the rumormonger will ask in whispered tones. "Somebody told me about him in the cafeteria this morning. He must be in trouble. Somebody ran into him at an employment agency looking for a new job. Did you hear anything about it?"

No, the other man hadn't. And couldn't have, for the rumor was totally false. No one saw Casey at an employment agency, because Casey hadn't visited an employment agency. He wasn't in trouble. But he soon will be, when the rumor gets around.

His loyalty to the company will be questioned. When the rumor finally reaches him, and he promptly denies it, the perverse logic of the gossipers will construe his denial as further confirmation, for of course he would be expected to deny such a report. What management would promote a man who's already looking for another job? The rumor has killed his chances for promotion.

The conspirator who plots to destroy an executive seldom

flashes a knife openly. His murder weapon is more apt to be a casual remark, repeated from time to time under circumstances which ensure that it will eventually reach the victim's supervisor. "Lipton is a fine young man, but more ambitious than able." A few such comments, and the assassin has spun his spider's web around the victim. The remark is never explained or elaborated on, but the seed has been planted. Henceforth, others in the company who have heard the comment will begin eyeing poor Mr. Lipton suspiciously.

Or a remark may be dropped at a cocktail party. "Yes, Mr. Cott works in my office. He's a very able fellow. Too bad he gets into so many controversies." A moment before, no one knew Mr. Cott was controversial, because, in fact, he was not. But one sentence has made him so. When the office gossip finally gets back to him, and he finds it necessary to deny it in self-defense, he will be halfway toward his own firing. His very denial will make him more controversial.

Another weapon in the office arsenal is the smokescreen. It serves the purpose of blinding you to new developments in the company, thus preventing you from doing your job properly. The man who wants your job will calculatingly withhold necessary information from you. It may be information about internal administrative changes which normally would be communicated to you by memo. But one day, the memo does not arrive, and instead, the villain chooses to inform other executives verbally. By some "accident," he neglects to tell you. Later, when the matter comes up for discussion at a management meeting, you find yourself unprepared when your superior asks your opinions on the matter.

When you embarrassedly maintain that nobody told you about it, you have already gone onto the defensive, and your antagonist has moved one step ahead. He may insist that he did tell you. If his story sounds sufficiently convincing to the boss, you are additionally convicted of a bad memory. Or he may calmly apologize for having accidentally failed to notify you. If he speaks with sufficient *savoir faire*, the boss may drop the matter, but you should consider it a clear warning that a plot to oust you is afoot.

Variation No. 1b on the smoke-screen tactic is even more devious. It's so effective that three highly placed executives I know personally have fallen victim to its poisoned darts. This method does not withhold information, but transmits it so casually that the victim never hears it, and subsequently finds himself in serious trouble because he failed to act on it.

It usually begins with a guerrilla skirmish in the men's room. Conspirator and innocent victim pause to pass the time of day. They talk about the weather, or their weekend golf scores. In the middle of the conversation, the assassin remarks quickly, "By the way, management wants your report some-time next week." The sentence has hardly passed his lips when he moves on to discuss a beautiful shot he made on the green early Sunday morning. Or maybe it's a dirty joke. Whatever it is, he distracts the victim by discussing something else. Hopefully, the request for the report is forgotten in the torrent of words.

When next week comes, and the report has not been received, the cannibal knows he's succeeded. "I told him very specifically the report was due," he insists. When the victim is brought in for a verbal flogging, he denies having been asked. But in vain. The plotter is prepared. "We were standing in the men's room last Monday morning. I told you about it very specifically. Remember when we were talking about golf, and I mentioned it to you?" The victim reacts like a lamb ready for the slaughter. The casual remark recalls itself dimly. But it's too late. The damage has been done.

Your boss himself may be the villain. He may be an expert in the Rules of Executive Warfare. A favorite technique is to undercut you with your own staff. He plots his tactics with the skill of a Royal Commando on reconnaissance patrol. Ignoring company channels, he asks one of your subordinates about a particular assignment you've given. The staff member, knowing nothing of the impending treachery, repeats your instructions.

"No, better not do it that way," your superior instructs your staff man. "It won't work. Kusiak didn't know what he was doing when he told you that. Do it the other way."

This method is doubly effective, for it disrupts your own management planning (you lose control of the activities of your department), and simultaneously it signals to your staff members that your own position is in danger. Unwilling to tie their fate to your uncertain future, they shift their allegiance away from you and to your boss. After a period of time, you find yourself a captain without a crew.

At the same time that your superior is campaigning to oust you, he is simultaneously claiming credit for the very things he denies you have accomplished. Your progress reports are neatly retyped by his secretary with his name substituted for yours, and the plural substituted for the singular, "we" for "I." "We accomplished this; we did that." When his superiors at a higher corporate plateau read his reports, they are impressed by his fine accomplishments, for the "we" is construed to mean him, expressed modestly. Your name is never mentioned.

There's nothing wrong in helping him to "look good." A competent employee should always make his superior "look good." But there's a difference between making him look good because of your work, and using your own reports to destroy you. Only an exceptionally alert top management would probe beneath the surface, and discover that his personal contribution to the division's progress is minimal.

The attack on your position may even come from a top executive, a corporate autocrat who thirsts for absolute power. The hard-hitting columnist of *Women's Wear Daily*, Samuel Feinberg, painted a word-picture of such executives.

Certain of them are absolute monarchs; others, benevolent despots. As a class, they know more about every phase of the field in which they are engaged—or think or say they do—than anyone who works for them. By words and action, they make clear their conviction they are infallible, inviolable, indispensable. They don't encourage free exchange of ideas and opinions and are particularly leery of any underlings who appear to be challenging their leadership. They frequently insist on conformity, on "yes men."

They are sarcastic and curt except when it suits their purpose or fancy to turn on the charm and curry favor with someone. This one-man rule often takes the form of government of faceless creatures by crisis. Everybody is expendable but themselves. Under the self-induced hynotic spell of such egotism, they give the impression they have either found the elixir of eternal life or accepted the awful truth, "after me, the flood."*

Mr. Feinberg cited the late Sewell L. Avery of Montgomery, Ward & Co., whose name was abbreviated by employees into the single word "SLAvery." During his reign, Mr. Avery fired or forced the resignation of more than sixty-five vice-presidents. Their fault, says Mr. Feinberg, was that they questioned his infallibility.

Another was Charles H. Revson, chairman of the board of Revlon, Inc., "a classic example of modern-day business autocracy in action. Mr. Revson has forced or encouraged resignation of a long roster of executives. During the late 1940's, the casualty list was about 130 percent a year."

These dismissed executives knew exactly why the boss wanted them out. But your superior may be after your scalp for a different reason. Perhaps he regards you as a threat to his position. Maybe you are. Or maybe you're nothing of the sort, but he's a crochety gent who's been with the company for nineteen years and doesn't look kindly on rising young upstarts. Now in his late forties, he's entered what Dr. Harry

* Reprinted by permission of *Women's Wear Daily*, issue of March 25, 1963. Copyright 1963, Fairchild Publications, Inc.

Levinson of the Menninger Foundation's industrial mental health division calls "the executive's anxious age." Writing in the magazine *Think*, Dr. Levinson aptly described his state of mind:

Middle age is for many men an acute psychological loss period. The losses are made even more painful by the recognition that there are aggressive rivals who threaten to dethrone them. In almost any field, younger men bring new skills and techniques which will ultimately displace the old. The older men fear to lose their self-respect if they admit what they have been doing is no longer adequate. To accept the newer ways, for some, is to make that admission. If they do change, they admit the younger men are right. If they fail to change, they run the risk of seeing younger men move rapidly ahead of them. Rapid technical changes may even make their experience of limited value. They are stimulated to defensive competition at the very time when, in their careers, competition would seem to offer the least rewards in the form of advancement, and when they are already coping with severe psychological stress.

Some withdraw from the competition. These are men who have reached a plateau. "We can't do anything to budge our middle-aged engineers," said the president of an engineering firm. "I don't know what gets into them, but they seem to stop at dead center." A college president made the same complaint about his faculty. "We give them early promotions to encourage them to produce," he said, "but it doesn't seem to do any good. They coast along comfortably in ruts, and you can't force a man to be creative." Like a wounded animal who seeks the protection of its cave, a man in such a position may well build a psychological cocoon around himself.

Others become hostile to possible competitors as well as to superiors. They may refuse to train younger men in ways which are difficult to see. They may use the younger men as flunkies, or criticize them harshly, all in the name of giving them good training.*

* Reprinted by permission from *Think* magazine, published by International Business Machines Corporation. Copyright 1962 by Harry Levinson.

Such executives, driven by personal insecurities, try to destroy promising young "comers" in the junior ranks. Often advancing years induce their terror. Woe to the aggressive young man who tries to push his way upward as they did a dozen years before.

All their working lives, they have struggled up the corporate ladder to reach their present positions. By ability and artifice, by competitiveness and cunning, they have succeeded. Now they are tired. They have always looked forward to the day when they'd have it made. Now, they discover they must struggle to hold what they have. The fear of being ousted terrifies them, for their personal financial responsibilities have become greater than ever. Support for children in college, membership in the country club, maintenance of a lavish home in the suburbs, require a high income. They cannot slip backward, unlike the young executive whose modest financial needs are limited to support of a small apartment and two young children.

The threatened executive will stop at nothing to preserve his way of life, which is, as he sees it, his life itself. If he feels you menace his job, he may try to oust you for reasons which have nothing to do with your own record of performance.

One young man in the hardware industry told me of his own experience. He had, so he thought, done his job reasonably well, and had previously received several commendations from his superior, Frank Gordon. But one Friday afternoon, he was unexpectedly summoned into the executive's office for a calling-down.

"You've been doing your job well, Mr. LeCount," Mr. Gordon began, "but I want to give it to you straight. You don't get along well with people. You handle people poorly, and you seem to arouse them against you."

Young Mr. LeCount listened open-mouthed.

"I don't care how well you do your job if you can't work well with others. If you can't show some quick improvement,

I'm going to have to let you go. That's all." With that, he
arose and bluntly escorted the young man to the door.

Mr. LeCount left in a state of shock. He had been totally
unprepared for the blast. He could not cope with it. At home
over the weekend, he tried to figure out where he had failed.
Had his work been criticized, he could have sought to improve
the unsatisfactory aspects. Confronted, however, with a vague,
all-encompassing charge of inability to get along with his
associates, he did not know what to do or where to begin.
Handicapped by inexperience and relative immaturity, he was
paralyzed by fear. On Monday, he returned to the office tense
with anxiety, too upset to pay attention to his associates.

On Tuesday morning, when Mr. LeCount entered the
office, the corridor buzzed with animated conversation. Frank
Gordon himself had been fired the afternoon before!

Only then did the real story emerge. Mr. Gordon's superior, a vice-president of the company, two weeks earlier had
severely criticized Gordon himself for poor performance. Mr.
Gordon's job was "on the line." Out of panic, Mr. Gordon
had reacted by threatening, in turn, each member of his own
staff. Somehow, two of them had gotten together, compared
notes, and discovered that Mr. Gordon had told each the same
thing, that they didn't know how to work with people. Further
investigation revealed that all their colleagues had received
the same sermon, in almost identical language, always sufficiently vague so that they would be unable to correct their
alleged deficiencies. When the vice-president heard their
stories, he immediately guillotined Mr. Gordon out of his
job. It was one of those rare occasions when an executive
plot backfired against the plotter.

In companies ruled by the law of the jungle, subordinates
as well as superiors threaten the executive. To protect himself
from below, a retailing manager, who bore the scars and
bruises of previous engagements, made it a rule to lay his
cards on the table whenever he hired a new employee.

"I've decided to hire you," he would tell a newcomer, "but I want you to know there's only one way you can get a promotion here. The only way you'll get my job is when I get a promotion. If you work with me, I'll do everything I can to help you, and when I move up, you'll move up. But try to play politics behind my back, try to knife me, and I'll cut you dead so fast you'll never know what happened. Now do we have a deal, or don't we?"

They did, and the new man joined the staff. The executive kept his end of the bargain, and the employee kept his. It was a disturbing way to begin a new job, but it worked, the executive told me, because each of them knew exactly where the other stood.

Threatened from above and below, and by enemies who call themselves friends, it's no wonder that the executive leads a jittery, insecure life. But the careers of thousands of executives testify that survival is possible. If you become the target of an ouster drive, don't despair and don't panic.

The first rule of survival is to see things exactly as they are. If the facts indicate that someone is out to get you, then he probably is. If you've made an honest error, and your supervisor shatters you with intemperate and destructive criticism, it's a clear indication that he's gunning for you. You're in for a fight.

Don't close your eyes to the fact that you've become a target simply to avoid facing a painful state of affairs. The danger won't disappear because you pretend it isn't there.

You have only one effective weapon for self-defense: your ability to keep icy calm and objective. If you've mastered the talent of seeing things exactly as they are, you'll probably survive all the attacks and emerge as an outstanding executive, a credit to yourself and your company.

2

Tribal Customs
for the Executive

IN THE EXECUTIVE JUNGLE, your job title may be more important to you than the work you do or even the size of your paycheck. In your office lair, the prestigious title often earns wall-to-wall carpeting on the floor and an attractive private secretary outside. At home, it carries prestige among your neighbors and friends. In today's society, the right title is "executive."

If you're an executive, you may not be called an executive, but instead, a manager, or president, or vice-president. You may be called a foreman, supervisor, or just "the boss." We want to look at the man who's really an executive, not the building janitor who is designated as "Manager of Building Services."

The United States Government officially defines an executive as a man who earns at least $100 a week; supervises at least two full-time employees; has discretionary power and the power to hire and fire. By that ruling, the title isn't very impressive.

The title of executive can indeed be misleading, but many a top executive has discovered that sometimes it pays to mislead. By awarding the title, he can avoid paying overtime under the wage and hour law. For a restless subordinate, the designation can provide enough ego-satisfaction to calm his discontent and perhaps avoid an immediate pay increase as well. But titles don't make an executive, unless the man actually functions as one. Therefore, let's define the job of a genuine executive before we get thoroughly confused by titles.

My own definition of an executive is a man who does two things. First, he directs the work of others, rather than doing the work himself. Second, he makes policy decisions which his subordinates, rather than he, execute. His prime characteristic is his talent for seeing things and people as they really are, not as he'd like them to be.

Managing the work of others really means managing people themselves, because the work, whatever it may be, will be done only through the efforts of other people. Managing people is a difficult art to practice, both because our emotions are difficult to control, or even understand, and because people react in individualistic ways. The successful executive soon learns that he cannot always predict accurately the reactions of his subordinates for they frequently respond to direction in a seemingly irrational way.

The executive oftentimes finds himself utterly baffled and frustrated by his inability to produce results through the efforts of others. Why doesn't his vice-president understand exactly what he wants done? Why do the sales records differ so widely for each of the divisions? What can he do about it? Where has *he* failed as a manager? Should he fire the offenders and replace them? Will he and the company be any better off with their replacements? Or will he be saddled with a new set of problems?

Every executive will recognize this state of mind. Some will feel a sharp pain in their ulcer at the reminder of it. Indeed, problems like these produce tension, high blood pressure, and ulcers in executives who lack the ability to cope with them.

It isn't profit problems, or sales problems, or production

problems that cause executive ulcers. It's people problems. You can solve profit problems by better cost control. You can solve sales problems by better sales training, better promotion, or any one of a hundred things. You can solve production problems by modernizing your capital equipment, or adding another shift, or expanding your facilities.

But when you start to solve these other problems, you find yourself right in the middle of "people problems." People will be needed to plan your sales training, or your advertising, or your financing. If you try to do everything yourself, you become what ex-president Harry Truman called "a four-ulcer man in a five-ulcer job."

If you are the hapless executive who won his present position by outstanding sales performance, or by making astute financial or legal decisions that benefited the company, perhaps nothing in your past training has prepared you to cope with "people problems."

Yet your success in your executive position now depends on your ability to solve them. By very definition of your job, you can't implement your decisions personally; others must do so. Your success, therefore, depends on others. Now you realize that the power and prestige of your executive position is offset by the power of your subordinates to frustrate you, make your life generally difficult, and put knots in your stomach.

How frustrating it is to the new executive who wants simply to get the job done! How much easier it would be if only he could "do it himself" instead of delegating it to a subordinate.

But when you are an executive, you can no longer attempt to do everything yourself, because you're too busy. Your job is too big. Whatever the immediate crisis at hand, if you attempt to solve it yourself, a dozen other crises will arise while you try to solve the first one. It's much better to train your staff to do the job correctly and well. The successful executive does just that, but he does it by his awareness of the psychological factors that motivate his subordinates. The unsuccessful executive, in contrast, ignores, overrides, or minimizes psychological considerations. Either he makes the error of trying to do the job himself, or he concentrates on "the job," "getting the work out," and so on, instead of on the people who will do the work.

Such a "work-oriented" approach provides the inept executive with momentary escape from frustration, but it just doesn't succeed. Researchers have confirmed that the executive who concentrates on production instead of on the people doing the production will fail. Dr. Rensis Likert, director of the Institute for Social Research of the University of Michigan, cites a typical study which measured the performance of managers.* The researchers compared those who focused their primary attention on the human aspects of their subordinates' problems with those who were primarily concerned with "getting the job done." In the test, performance could easily be measured; the yardstick was the number of units turned out on the production line. The test showed conclusively that the managers who were "people-oriented" did better than managers who were "work-oriented." In other words, the manager who worries about production won't get as much production as the manager who worries about the people who work for him.

Worrying about your subordinates, however, is not the same as running a popularity contest. A popular supervisor will not necessarily produce better performance, if he forgets that high morale is only a means to the end, not the end itself —which is a specific corporate objective.

I recall a young automotive engineer who had just received a promotion to a supervisory post in a design department. He had been a designing engineer for four years, and now found himself in a position of authority over his former

* *New Patterns of Management*, McGraw-Hill, 1961, p. 7 *et seq.*

colleagues. Inwardly unsure of himself as a manager, he concentrated on winning the approval of his staff. Top management had given him considerable autonomy, and he used it freely. "Take the day off," he'd tell a man who reported his wife wasn't feeling quite well that morning. Another man who repeatedly came late for work was excused with a gentle remark. Soon, lateness was widespread in the department, and output was declining instead of rising.

The manager had confused popularity with high morale. They are not the same. He had also failed to understand that his basic responsibility to management was to increase production. Any steps he might take toward improving staff morale had to be evaluated by management in terms of whether they increased production.

To himself, the young manager rationalized that he had honestly attempted to improve morale. The real reason for his actions, however, was to be found deeper within him. His unsureness brought to the fore his strong psychological need to be liked by his subordinates. Their approval would mean that he was indeed "still one of the boys," and that he had not forsaken them for the ranks of management.

The design staff, his former colleagues, soon had sensed that he overlooked their shortcomings in order to keep their good will. Some took advantage of him, calculating that they could get away with it.

When he suddenly discovered that he had "been taken," he swung to the other extreme. "The important thing is to be respected," he then declared. "I don't give a damn what they think of me." The staff soon discovered that by the word "respected," he meant "feared." He imposed a reign of terror on the department. Last week's cockiness and casualness turned to this week's anxiety and fear, but production continued down, not up.

As the designer learned the hard way, neither loving nor loathing is an effective management tool. The skilled executive pays careful attention to the morale of his staff, but only as a tool to help him get the work done effectively by his subordinates.

The work which must be done will vary endlessly, of course, depending on the industry, the company, and the department which the executive supervises. The work may be the production of metal stampings, or the operation of an office stenographic pool, or the sale of food products to supermarkets. Dozens of metal workers may turn out the stampings; half a dozen teen-age girls may type letters from morning to night; a hundred salesmen may call on chain store buyers to sell corn flakes.

But the executive's job in all these situations is the same. His job is not to operate the machine, or to type the letters, or to make the sales, but to see that others do.

Perhaps a foreman won his job because of skill in locating troubles in the drill press. But now as a foreman, he must manage other drill press operators, and his responsibility is to teach the others how to do the repair job. If he tries to do it himself, he may fix the machine more rapidly the first time, but, in the long run, he will fail as an executive.

There are many situations in which the new executive, who should know better, traps himself by his own psychological insecurities.

One was experienced by an acquaintance of mine, a sales manager in a large building-materials company, who had a long and successful career as a salesman before winning his promotion. Harold Snyder's superiors had told him the obvious: that he would be measured by the performance of his staff. But his fears told him otherwise. In his innermost thoughts, he believed that he personally must remain the star salesman of them all, better than anyone on his staff.

So he watched diligently the "call reports" of the salesmen. Week in and week out, he searched for a prospect meeting his particular set of conditions: a prestige account, fairly well presold.

He'd call the salesman into his office on a Friday afternoon after lunch. "We can't take any chances on closing that one," he would tell him. "It's too important a sale."

"But it's in good shape, Mr. Snyder. I've got it well lined up, and the customer is ready to buy," the salesman insisted.

"Maybe," said the executive, "but I don't want to miss this one. I'll go out with you on the call."

The manager got away with it, because he had the authority. He made the sale. He took the credit away from the salesman, and sometimes the commission too.

This isn't managing. It's interfering. Such behavior, the result of the executive's psychological insecurity, demoralizes the salesmen. It leaves the manager worse off than when he started. It's a violation of the first rule of management: help other people to do the job themselves.

The second rule of management is that the executive makes the basic policy decisions which his subordinates implement. It's the executive who decides whether the metal stamping department should produce base plates or radiator grilles. It's the executive who decides whether the building materials salesmen should call on commercial builders or architects. Once he has made the appropriate decisions, his staff must decide the best way to implement them. He should help them, guide them, advise them, teach them, but it's their job, not his, to carry out the policy.

The executive's level in the corporate hierarchy will determine the scope and importance of his policy decisions. A decision by the president or chairman of the board may change the entire future of the company. A presidential decision at The Martin Company (now the Martin-Marietta Corp.) some years ago transformed an airplane manufacturer into a missile manufacturer; the decision required many years, thousands of men, and millions of dollars to implement. A similar top-level decision at General Mills, Inc., after World War II, broadened a food processing company into the research field, to experiment with high-altitude weather balloons at the same time it was making Wheaties.

These were fundamental policy decisions, and they could be made only by those who had the authority to implement them, namely, the officers and directors of the company.

Once made at a top level, the decisions were passed down the line for implementation. The Martin Company required new executive policy decisions at each lower level. What engineering facilities would be needed to make missiles? What type of engineers are required? What technical specifications must be established? And so on.

When these decisions were reached at the proper level, a new series of decisions was required at a lower level of management. What type of equipment will best meet our needs? How much space will be required? What power facilities will be needed to operate the machinery? What technical skills will the engineers require?

And when these questions had been answered, still another set of decisions had to be made down the line. Who makes the machinery we need? How much will it cost? Which is the best for us? How soon can we get delivery? Who will install it? Hundreds, indeed, thousands of similar policy decisions had to be made, and executives were required to make them.

The second essential task of an executive, therefore, is to make policy decisions for implementation by subordinate staffs. In the large corporation, each executive will be told, preferably in writing, the extent of his responsibility for making decisions; in smaller companies, custom and intuition will guide him as to the scope of his responsibility.

You can usually spot the creative executive, the man who's a "comer," by his use of authority to make policy decisions that contribute to the company's major objectives. I'll cite an actual comparison.

Each of two insurance companies had established a department to handle policyholder inquiries. The two departments each were staffed with large numbers of clerical employees.

One department head concentrated on the preparation of courteous, effective replies. He staffed his organization to provide speedy service. The other, analyzing the nature of the inquiries, discovered that several basic questions constituted the largest single segment of the thousands received. These questions related to reinstatement of lapsed policies, and payment of overdue premiums. He recommended to his superiors that basic information on these subjects be printed on the premium notice itself. His recommendation was accepted, with the result that the inquiries to his department, and the costs of handling them, were sharply reduced. He received a bonus, amply refuting those executives who believe their job security rests in "empire building."

Then this same department head went on to separate routine inquiries from those complaining of some aspect of company service. He made a policy decision to answer routine inquiries by check marks on a printed form. This reduced sharply the number of secretaries required to answer them. He decided to improve the handling of complaints, in the interest of the company's public relations. The manager upgraded the qualifications of the women assigned to answer these letters, established a training course to improve their replies, and provided them with additional supervisory assistance for difficult cases. The result was improved policyholder good will, and yet, as a result of his policy decisions, the total cost of his department was somewhat reduced.

Truly, this represents effective management, for the executive used his policy-making authority to provide better service at lower cost. If the executive had spent his time trying to write better letters (which was the job of the people in his department) instead of studying the overall operation of his department, he couldn't have succeeded.

Most managers have earned their jobs by success in a

specialized area, such as sales, accounting, advertising, or manufacturing. Few, by the time they become executives, have learned the two basic characteristics that make an executive successful: managing others, and making policy decisions. These things are usually learned after, not before, the executive is in the job.

But learned they must be, for every executive will be judged accordingly. Even in the armed forces, the standard is the same. Colonel Alan Haemer, controller of the United States Air Force's First Strategic Aerospace Division, said: "Executives have the same qualifications everywhere—getting along with people, monitoring them, and managing them. The same principles of management hold true whether it's a controller's section or a paper bag company."

Of these three, getting along with people is the most important.

3

To Start –
Stop, Look,
and Listen!

IF YOU'VE JUST BECOME an executive for the first time, you're probably feeling quite satisfied with yourself about your new authority. It will take you at least a few months to discover that your actual power is considerably less than it appears to be on the organization chart. The limitation comes not from your own supervisor, but from the employees under you.

"Your staff knows," a General Electric official commented, "that you can destroy them instantly by firing them from the payroll. But you know that they can destroy you by refusing to cooperate, and by sabotaging you in subtle ways. So you must behave in a manner that will make your staff want to cooperate with you. You can't make them cooperate, unless they wish to voluntarily."

If you have the fortunate opportunity of building a new department from the ground up, you can select employees whose cooperation and loyalty are reasonably assured. But, more likely, you will take over an already existing staff in an already functioning department. The vacancy you fill was probably created by the transfer, promotion, retirement, or dismissal of your predecessor. You can't start from scratch with total freedom to select your subordinates, and you can't dismiss substantial numbers of your staff without disrupting morale and production. In effect, your hands are tied by the past, even though your boss may have given you explicitly a free hand to do whatever you consider necessary to get the department in shape.

Think back for a moment to the days and years when you were an employee instead of a boss. How many times did a change in management produce uncertainty and fear among the staff?

Try to recall your reactions. Everyone in the department was curious about the new executive. What was he like? How would he operate? Whose job was in danger? How could you get him to notice you? Would he recognize your own contributions? Would he play favorites? If so, how could you become one of his favorites?

Because your first moves will begin shaping the staff's impression of you, it's important to start out on the right foot. You already have some definite ideas on where you'd like to begin. Perhaps you've briefly met several members of your new staff and formed some quick impressions about them. Your predecessor, before he left, may have talked with you about his problems. You're bursting with energy, and ready to go.

But my advice is to hold back. Resist the temptation to make dramatic announcements, call staff meetings, make new appointments, or whatever. Instead, emblazon on your personal coat of arms the slogan, "Don't talk, listen."

The ability to listen must be one of God's rarest gifts. Put any two people together in a room, and each will vie with the other for an opportunity to speak. Neither will quite listen to what the other is saying. Analyze the conversation as a detached bystander, and you'll discover that one person's comments seldom are responsive to what the other has just said. Instead, Mr. A continues the thought he was expressing before Mr. B interrupted him.

The habit of listening may not come easily to you. You'll constantly feel the urge to talk, possibly because you want to impress your subordinates with your own experience, ability, and wisdom. However, resist the temptation, and stand your ground bravely. If you really learn to listen, you've earned the "Medal for Executive Merit."

You may begin your new executive career of listening by inviting your key subordinates into your office for a chat, one at a time. Tell them, when you arrange the appointment, that you'd like to get acquainted, and would appreciate any suggestions they might have as to how "we" can do a better job. You may invite them in immediately, but an appointment for the following day will give them an opportunity to think about things overnight, and decide what they want to tell you.

Over the years, I've asked many executives how they started off in their current positions. Practically all told me that they studied the existing manuals and procedures, and then went to work. None said he began by listening and observing, the most effective method of all.

You can conduct your first interview in many different ways. Any of them is satisfactory provided you listen, and allow your staff member to do most of the talking. Over the years, I have developed a certain pattern to encourage employees to speak freely.

I begin by trying to put the employee at ease, often offering him a cigarette. (Usually he'll light it or let me do it, but he will never quite get around to smoking it; his mind is elsewhere.) I tell him that I have a difficult new responsibility, and that I will need his help in meeting it successfully. I explain that although I already know much about the department, my knowledge is that of an outsider, and I need to learn at first hand about its problems and its people. I need to understand its successes and its failures. With his background, he can help me to know all these things.

I make a special point of emphasizing that I am not interested in hearing criticisms of any individual person. I'll make my own judgments later on as I meet each staff member personally. But I am anxious to learn anything about present systems and procedures which he considers wrong or ineffective. If he'd care to speak frankly to me on any of these points, I'd appreciate it very much.

By this time, the employee is usually wound up and ready to begin. Perhaps nobody has ever asked him before for his ideas. But I cut him short.

"One more thing," I say. "Maybe you'd want to start by telling me something about yourself. I've read your personnel file, but I really don't know you. I don't know where you came from, where you worked before coming here, how long you've been here. I don't know whether you're married or single, where you live, or anything else about you. Why don't you begin with that?"

Then I sit back, fill my pipe, and light up. I don't have to wait more than a second for his torrent of words. He'll tell me briefly of his past work history and his experience. By his emphasis on various parts of his career, I quickly learn why he emphasizes certain things and minimizes others. Sometimes his reasons are apparent. For example, a man who didn't complete his college education may be deeply scarred by feelings of inadequacy, and will dwell at great length on the reasons why he left college, instead of emphasizing his subsequent work career, which has been outstanding.

Sometimes, he will discuss an operational procedure in detail, explain where he believes it's faulty, and comment that, a year ago, he submitted suggestions to improve it, "but you've probably never seen those papers. They must be in the files somewhere." I ask him to explain his recommendations, and he readily expands. I listen carefully, and then reply.

"Those sound like good suggestions," I say. "They make a lot of sense. But at this point, I just don't know enough about the procedure to evaluate them fairly. What I will do is look into it further. Why don't you give me a copy of your suggestions tomorrow so that I can save a long hunt in the files?"

I make a brief note on the substance of his proposals for follow-up. Later, when I interview other members of the department in similar fashion, I'll ask about his ideas to discover if they're practical. More often than not, they turn out to be sensible and workable, because their author was closer to the problem than the department head. The employee could see at first hand what ought to have been done to solve a problem. But nobody listened to him. When I confirm in my own mind that the suggestions are sound, I implement them quickly, giving specific credit to their initiator.

During these first introductory interviews, I make a special point to watch for salary complaints. Few employees ask directly for more money. More frequently, they complain that a former supervisor "told me I was doing good work, and if I kept it up, I could expect a substantial pay raise in January. I never got it."

Maybe the departed executive had said precisely that, or maybe he hadn't, but I soon discover that the employee has harbored bitterness ever since the day when he opened his pay envelope and discovered no increase in the amount of his check.

This situation is difficult for management, because the executive who allegedly made the promise (if it was indeed made) might have had no authority to do so. Equally possibly, he was trying to be a good fellow, irresponsibly building the employee's hopes. Now I come along and I'm stuck, if not with responsibility for the executive commitment, then at least with an embittered staff member.

"This is the first I've heard about it," I reply truthfully. "Tell me more about it."

I listen carefully, because I want to judge whether the commitment was ever made, or whether it was imagined by the employee. Sometimes, people hear what they want to hear. I must consider the possibility that the employee may have "heard" more than my predecessor intended to say.

If the description of the original conversation has the ring of authenticity, I'll tell him so.

"That certainly sounds as if he said it," I comment. "Obviously, I can't do anything about it right away, but I do promise you that when your salary is next up for review, I'll keep this very much in mind. If your work continues to be outstanding, I'll do everything I can to help you get what you deserve. I'll do this for you, but, in turn, I have a right to expect that you'll do everything you can to become more valuable to the company. It's a two-way street."

This is indeed an implied promise that if his performance continues to be satisfactory he'll get the raise. On the other hand, if I decide on the basis of the employee's own description that the implied promise was never made, different handling is called for.

"That's very interesting," I tell him in such a case, "but on the basis of what you say, I'm not sure Mr. Johnson actually promised you a raise. So let me suggest this. Between now and next January, do everything you can to make yourself more valuable to the company, so that we can afford to give you an increase. When we review salaries, I promise to give special attention to your case. Please understand I'm not promising you a raise. I can't right now. But I am promising that if you earn it by outstanding work, you'll get it without having to ask again."

Most of the time, the employee will be satisfied by such assurance of fair consideration. It then becomes the executive's responsibility to follow through on his commitment; if he fails to do so, the damage to employee morale will be severe.

In the days when you were an employee in the ranks, no one may have treated you quite this way. Instead, your boss may have said, "Joe, I'd like to help you, but the fact is, you're not working as well as Jack Kennett, and he's making less money than you are right now."

That may have been true, and the boss got his point across, namely, that you weren't very good. But I'm certain his words didn't stimulate you to do a better job. Instead, he hurt your pride and self-respect. You left his office sullen with hostility, angrier even than when you entered.

All of us, your new staff included, have a great need to be respected. You can and should criticize poor performance whenever you find it, but without destroying the self-respect of the employee you're criticizing. When you criticize a member of your staff, your purpose is not to build up your own feelings of power and importance, but to stimulate him to better performance for the benefit of the company. Destructive criticism hurts the company, because it destroys the morale of the employee.

The corporate executive who can't find a kind word for his staff destroys their confidence in themselves. They know he lacks confidence in them. They act accordingly.

Constructive criticism, on the other hand, frankly points out an employee's shortcomings, shows what he can do to correct them, and solicits his cooperation to improve. Constructive criticism convinces the employee that you really care about him and the quality of his work.

Many executives find it difficult to dispense criticism when it's called for, because it might hurt the feelings of their employees. So they tolerate mediocrity and inadequacy to the detriment of the company.

How should you handle this problem with your new staff? It won't be difficult if you remember that your objective is not to frighten them, not to praise them, but to motivate them.

For this, you need the ability to put yourself into their

shoes, and to imagine what would motivate you. For example, you'd want to feel that your boss understood your problems, and that he respected you. You'd want to feel that you were part of a winning team. This is hardly unreasonable.

Now climb back into your new executive shoes, and plan to communicate this understanding to your new staff. Since you have already met them individually, the time has come to bring them together for your first staff meeting.

Your interoffice memo calls them together in the conference room. For a morning or late afternoon meeting, you may thoughtfully arrange for coffee service. If you hold the meeting at lunchtime, you may arrange for sandwiches as well, thus indicating your consideration.

You walk into the room five minutes early, and discover it's empty. No one has yet arrived. They are all waiting for you to enter first. Within a few minutes, the room fills quickly and silently. A few eager beavers have brought pads and pencils to jot down your pearls of wisdom. No one says a word.

If you have a sense of humor, you might begin with a good-natured remark to break the tension. (I once attended a meeting where the president remarked, "Well, I haven't seen so much talent in one place since the *Titanic* went down!" No doubt you can do better than that.)

"I've been meeting each one of you individually," you start hesitantly. "Now it's good to have a chance to talk with you all together. You're certainly an impressive group of people." (An audible sigh will arise from the table.)

"I'm lucky to have the opportunity of working with you, and I hope we'll be working together for a long time." (You're with them, not against them.) "As you know, the president has given me the responsibility of coming in here to work with you to improve our performance. Our product hasn't been selling as well as our competitor's. We must find ways to step up our sales efforts, our quality control, our customer service. I can't do this job, but you can do it with me, if you want to."

Notice those words, "if you want to." You're not ordering them to do anything. You're not threatening them. You're asking their help. The implied, and understood consequence of noncooperation is possible dismissal. But this is never suggested or mentioned.

"When I talked with you individually, many of you gave me valuable suggestions. Jack Levine suggested a way to eliminate unnecessary paperwork and speed up delivery. Ann Morrissey suggested that we telephone the customer to ask for any other items we might add to his order. There were quite a number of other good ideas. I promise to look into all of them quickly to see which are practical, which we can put to work immediately."

The staff quickly sees that you welcome new ideas, and that you recognize you can learn from them.

"But I've seen some problem areas too. I've seen errors in processing orders, because of someone's carelessness." (You don't mention names; no one wants to be embarrassed in the presence of his colleagues.) "The other day, I listened to our handling of telephone orders, and I don't think we were as polite as we might have been. If we continue, we're going to lose some customers to our competitors."

"Let me emphasize to you, we can't continue that kind of service. We must do much better. I expect you to try every single minute to treat our customers more courteously and more efficiently. Your jobs are at stake, because we need their business to pay your salaries. I'll do everything I can to help you, and if you have any suggestions for doing a better job, I hope you'll tell me."

This puts it quite strongly. Right from the start, you're setting high standards for your new staff. You are making it clear you expect better work, and that you'll work with them to help produce it.

"Any questions?"

No, there are none. The staff wants to trade notes with each other before they'll open up to you. It may take three or four meetings, over a period of several months, before the braver souls will begin to speak up.

"Thank you very much. If you have any ideas you want to talk about, just come in to see me when you're ready."

Your first staff meeting is over, and you're ready to buckle down for the long pull. You're off to a good start.

4

Time Worshipers
and Clock Watchers

TIME GOES QUICKLY for the executive. So many things must be done. People to be seen. Correspondence to be answered. Phone calls to be made. Reports to be studied. Publications to be read.

And so little time to do it all—eight hours a day or less. Whether your office opens for business at 9:00 or 9:30 in the morning, or 8:00 or 8:30—a frequent pattern in the Midwest—the working hours for the office staff usually add up to less than forty. Your office is closed Saturdays. If you find it necessary to work past the usual closing hours, your secretary will probably get up and go home at her normal closing time. If you frequently require that she stay late, sooner or later she'll probably leave you for a job elsewhere where late hours are not required. Potent pressures keep your effective working week below the forty-hour mark.

American folklore tells us that successful executives work long hours, and indeed many of them do. The Horatio Alger-type biographies in the business magazines casually mention that the subject of the article regularly puts in an eleven-hour day. But I've known many of these men personally, and I haven't been impressed. (Maybe the stockholders were.) Some years ago, I happened to ride to the airport with a company president whose biography had just been featured in *Fortune* magazine, and I asked him about it.

"Eleven hours a day? That was an honest figure," he insisted. "From the time I get up in the morning, I'm thinking about business problems. Over breakfast, I read the paper to keep up with what I ought to know. Even at lunch, I never waste a minute. I always eat with business associates. At night, I take home a briefcase full of reading, and, after dinner, I like to stretch out in the living room and catch up with my paperwork."

So he added it all up, and it amounted to eleven hours daily. I'm surprised he didn't throw in the sleeping hours he spent dreaming about his business problems.

If, however, you don't include breakfast time, reading-at-home time, and dreaming time, your regular working day probably won't exceed eight hours. The total amounts to 2,080 hours annually. From that point, you begin subtracting.

Take off two weeks for your vacation. That's eighty hours. Subtract an average of six holidays, or forty-eight hours. That gives you a theoretical year of 1,952 hours. Now begin your private arithmetic (don't show it to your boss), and subtract lunch hours, days out for illness, religious holidays, and the day before Christmas when everything stops for the annual office drinking spree. You'll end with not much more than 1,600 hours of actual working time during the calendar year. Divide your annual gross salary by 1,600, and you'll discover the actual cost to the company of an hour of your working time.

Many times during the year, the pressure of business will compel you to work extra hours until a particular job is done. That's part of the executive game, and you expected it when you took the job. An occasional evening working late is a small price to pay for the privileges and emoluments of your position.

But if you work late regularly, you may indeed be doing

a disservice to your company as well as to yourself. After a full day under intense pressure on the corporate firing line, you have good reason to feel fatigue at the day's end. Regardless of your vitality, your energy will flag in the final hours. Important company decisions should not be made by weary men with tired brains. You won't receive any gold stars on your toothbrush chart, therefore, for working long hours each day. My admiration, rather, goes to the executive who uses his time effectively every single minute during regular working hours. Skillful management during the day can easily add an hour or two to your real working period, without actually lengthening the time you spend at your desk.

Planning your time is the answer. You can do it the first thing when you arrive in the morning, in five minutes' time.

To begin, take a piece of paper, and jot down at random all the things you have to accomplish that day. List the problems you want to deal with, the people you want to see, and so on. Then go back and assign a priority to each. Perhaps the first priority will go to personnel recommendations you are expected to make. Your lowest priority may be given to answering routine correspondence.

Keep this list in front of you during the day, and refer to it frequently. Tackle the problems in the order you have listed them. Don't go on to problem number two until you have completed problem number one. When telephone calls or unexpected visitors interrupt you, return immediately to the problem you were concerned with. Keep at it until you're satisfied that you have accomplished it completely, or have done as much as you can pending receipt of further information.

You don't have to give priority number one to your most important problem. It depends entirely on your personal habits and work methods. You may prefer to dispose of routine matters first, to free your mind for concentration on a complex subject. If you prefer this method, assign higher priorities to your correspondence, or meetings with members

of your staff. It really doesn't make too much difference as
long as you have some kind of a plan.

Your plan should also make allowance for the hours of the
day during which you work at your best. Psychologists' charts
show that many people work best in the late morning hours,
decline in efficiency after lunch, pick up again for a final spurt
from three o'clock until four, and then taper off.

Each of us is different. My good wife likes to classify
people as either "Larks" or "Owls." The Lark is the fellow
who cheerfully gets up at an unearthly hour of the morning
to go fishing, or to read the morning paper leisurely over his
breakfast coffee. He's alert and at his best in the morning
hours. The Owls are those who enjoy staying up at night to
watch The Late Show, or maybe The Late Late Show. At an
evening social event, they're at their wittiest. In the late afternoon, when the Larks are fading, the Owls are warming up,
and getting more effective every minute.

If you were to chart their vitality on a graph, you'd show
the Larks starting high and declining in a straight line. The
Owls would start low and climb steadily until their high point
is reached at the end of the day.

Perhaps, as with so many other habits, our work patterns
are formed in early childhood. Certainly, by the time you become a corporate executive, your hourly habits are strongly
set. Don't fight them. Make the most of your daily cycle,
whatever it is. When you plan your day's activities, take it
into consideration. If you work at your best in the morning,
you may schedule meetings, appointments, and activities for
the before-lunch hours. At the bottom of your priority list for
the late afternoon hours you may place your routine activities.
If you're an Owl, turn things around. Match your schedule
to your personal efficiency chart, and you'll find it easier to
operate at high effectiveness.

Your well-laid priority plans may be disrupted by a constantly ringing telephone. The phone rings; you answer.

(You're conditioned like Pavlov's dogs to respond instantly when it rings.) You become absorbed briefly in the phone call, then return to the original project, your thoughts interrupted.

But you don't have to answer the phone. That's what your secretary is for. During the hours when you wish to be left alone for concentrated work, she can answer your telephone, interrupting you only for those calls of an urgent nature. To other callers, she can say that you are out of the office and will call back later in the day. (But never, "Mr. Gilday is working, and doesn't want to be disturbed.") This is another way to control your time, instead of letting it control you.

Of course, you shouldn't habitually decline phone calls or play "hard to get." It's discourteous to do so, and wasteful of time as well. Only when you're working on an important matter, or at a meeting, should you not be disturbed unless it's absolutely necessary. At such times, your secretary can help you. The rest of the day, however, you may wish to answer your phone directly, without the intercession of your secretary.

One technique I use is to list each morning all the people I wish to telephone during the day. To this list, my secretary adds those whose calls I did not take, and who must be called back before the day is over. Next to each name, she adds the number.

Then, at some time during the day, I take the list and begin working it from top to bottom, one after the other. I prefer making my own phone calls, but even if your secretary places them for you, the idea is to make them uninterruptedly. This method will save you considerable time compared to the usual executive practice of making them intermittently during the day as matters arise. I keep a pen and pad handy to make notes on each call for subsequent follow-up.

You may use the same method for grouping appointments together. List all the people, whether from inside the company or from outside, you want to see during the day. Your experience will tell you how much time each will require: some, only five or ten minutes; others, perhaps an hour for adequate discussion. Schedule them one after the other. You gain extra time through this technique in several ways. First, you can utilize certain hours of the day which are otherwise lost. For example, if you're in the habit of lunching from 12:30 to 1:30, you can make appointments from 12:00 until 12:30, and from 1:30 to 2:00. During those hours, it's difficult to get people on the phone. Or you can see people between 4:00 and 5:00 in the afternoon; it would not be practical to use that hour for dictation, for instance, because it would be too late to get the letters typed and into the mail that same afternoon.

Another way you can gain extra time is by putting an automatic time limit on each appointment. When someone is sitting outside waiting to see you, you will be less inclined to prolong a discussion, or to allow your guest to do so. You have a ready-made excuse for terminating the conversation.

Cutting short a conversation without discourtesy or offense to your guest is an art in itself. I've seen it practiced by masters. I remember the first time it was practiced on me.

I had been discussing a business matter with an aging vice-president of a manufacturing company. He was polished and courtly. He had listened to me attentively and given his reaction. But I had talked on, beginning to repeat myself.

Almost immediately, he brought his hand down on his knee firmly and decisively. "Well," he said, "you certainly were kind to come in and tell me about this. I appreciate the time you gave me." As he said it, he arose and walked around to the front of his desk to shake hands with me. Before I knew it, I was standing outside his office door, and his secretary was handing me my hat.

A dozen variations may be developed on this theme, but the combination of words plus physical action works best.

Getting up from the desk was his signal that my time was up. Another method, less subtle but equally effective, is to look conspicuously at your wrist watch, and apologize for keeping your guest so long; unfortunately, you have someone else waiting. For variety, you can use the secretarial technique. Your secretary phones, or enters the room wordlessly and hands you a note. You must excuse yourself; Mr. Hoffman is outside.

Whatever the method you use, the important thing is to terminate the conversation courteously as soon as it has accomplished its purpose. The subject under discussion will determine a proper length of time. Your skill in terminating the meeting will affect your caller's impression of you and your company. It's not necessary to be brusque with an over-talkative guest when you may accomplish the same time-saving results politely.

A business lunch provides more opportunity to find extra hours in the day, if you really use it for business purposes. The Internal Revenue agents want to be sure that our tax-deductible business lunches really are business lunches. The corporate executive wants the same. Business lunches should be productive for your company, whether you are on the selling or buying end of the proposed deal. Not all of them are.

I wish, for the purposes of research, that it were possible for us to eavesdrop on individual luncheon conversations in a New York midtown restaurant. Perhaps we could use one of those "rifle microphones" employed at the presidential news conferences; a highly directional microphone is hand-held like a rifle and pointed at one person across the large room. It picks up his voice clearly, but no other.

If we were to do this, we would hear, as we pointed the mike from one table to the next, an endless succession of aimless social conversations. Salesmen will be engaging customers in social conversation about sports, hobbies, women, or what-not until the dessert course is served. Only then will the seller gently bring up for discussion the business purpose of the luncheon. Presumably, the customer has mellowed after a good steak and bourbon, and will be more receptive to the salesman's presentation.

I don't know who's fooling whom. In my own business experience, I've always known, when I accepted the invitation, what the seller wanted to accomplish during his luncheon conversation. Subtlety and coyness in introducing the business matter deceives no one, nor is it necessary. Few executives these days will be corrupted into accepting an unwise business deal by the price of an expensive lunch.

This isn't to suggest that there's no place for the business luncheon, and even if I did feel that way, I wouldn't make any progress in abolishing a pleasant custom which supports hundreds of restaurateurs and thousands of workers.

You can, however, use the business lunch as a tool to make more of your limited executive time. You can use it to meet with someone unavailable to you during the remainder of the day. You can use it to meet with someone of equal status, who would prefer not to go to your office, or have you go to his. You can use it to discuss a problem without the telephones and distractions of the office. The business lunch provides a relaxed setting away from an environment where tension and argument might develop.

In other words, transact business over the luncheon table when you can't do it as well in your own office. Otherwise, unless you want to mooch a free lunch from a supplier or salesman, you'll do as well or better by using your lunch hour to take a break from pressure, or even to think through the problems ahead of you. At your executive salary, you can't justify the need for a free lunch anyway.

If you took an early lunch hour, you will be back at your desk while others are still out. It's a quiet time; the phones are not ringing, and you can't telephone others until perhaps two o'clock when they've returned to their offices. This may be a good time to catch up with your dictation.

I arrange to dictate correspondence twice a day. The first time is early in the morning, as I read the morning mail. The second is immediately after lunch. The morning mail is mostly from outside the company; the afternoon mail is mostly inter-office. The pattern may differ in your own company, depending on the nature of your business and the frequency of inter-office mail collections and deliveries. Unless the volume of correspondence is unusually heavy, this will allow my secretary time to prepare all the work for signature and mailing by the end of the business day. Anything that develops later, unless it is urgent, is held for the next morning.

Four or five years ago, my practice was first to read the morning mail, then set it aside for other things, and finally to return to it when time permitted. Then I reread the mail, and answered it if a reply was required. This pattern was wasteful of time, so I changed my work pattern to read the morning mail only once. As soon as I have read a letter, I immediately reply to it before going on to the second letter. If more information is needed to prepare a proper reply, I indicate to my secretary exactly what information I want, and then set the letter aside until she produces it. Using this method, replies to most letters will be ready for signature and mailing by the end of the same day in which they were received. Time is saved, and the recipient appreciates the prompt attention he has received.

You can also slash the time required to answer interoffice memoranda. If a staff member has written you regarding a proposed action, you may write your decision with pen and ink right on the margins of his own memo and return it to him. This simple technique, if applied in some companies, would slash their paperwork and secretarial costs by 30 percent.

Another method some executives use successfully is the untranscribed memo. Instead of writing a note which must be transcribed and typed, you talk into a dictating machine, and send the actual tape or belt to your associate for playback on his own machine. The dictation is never reduced to paper. You don't save your own time this way, but secretarial time is eliminated, and costs reduced sharply.

The major battles of your war against unnecessary paperwork will take place on your own desk. Your desk is a place to arrange necessary papers while you work on them. It should be only that, and not a filing cabinet.

Arrange it any way you will; the way you do will tell much about your efficiency. For best work, you should keep available on it (or in its drawers) only the material you actually need to do your job. A cluttered desk indicates something's wrong.

I saw this confirmed when I called on an electronics executive in his Phoenix, Arizona, office. His desk was piled high with papers of all kinds: correspondence, blueprints, specifications, data sheets, catalogs, technical magazines. It created the impression of an overwhelmingly busy man.

As I sat at his desk, he was interrupted by a number of lengthy telephone calls. While he talked, the opportunity presented itself to take a closer look at the papers. To my surprise, much of the material appeared to be quite old; the assorted magazines dated back six months or more, and a copy of *The Diners' Club Magazine* was sandwiched between two editions of *Electronic Design*.

When he hung up the telephone, he resumed his conversation at a leisurely pace despite the seeming pressures. He spent more than two hours with me, when, in truth, he could have heard me out fully within a half hour. In my inexperience, I was puzzled by the apparent conflict between his heavy work load and his generous gift of time. The visit remained vivid in my memory. Only in later years did I become acquainted with his boss, and learn that his seeming disorder was merely a stage setting to impress higher executives with his heavy work load. He used his desk as a filing cabinet to look busy. It was the mark of an inefficient executive and a frightened man. But his supervisor had not been deceived.

Avoiding his error, I constantly reduced my paperwork so that I could spend more time meeting people face to face. Correspondence would arrive; it would be answered, and out it would go. A few folders would hold matters immediately pending; others would remain with my secretary, available when and if needed.

Finally, when I became a president for the first time, I had the opportunity of designing my own office. I decided to put paperwork in its place, and concentrate on what I considered my main executive job: meeting people to supervise their activities and to make decisions.

"Please remove the desk," I asked the office manager.

"What kind would you like instead?" she inquired pleasantly. "Just let me know and we'll order it."

"I don't want any desk," I replied. "The papers I handle will come in and out quickly. I can keep them in folders on the cabinet. There won't be many."

And there weren't. Since that day, I've never had a desk in my office. The only furnishings are a few chairs, a low coffee table, a small cabinet, and a setee.

Elimination of the desk cut paper-shuffling to the bone, but another benefit resulted too. I had long felt that a desk served as an invisible wall behind which executives entrenched themselves for their own protection. It was a barrier against colleagues and subordinates alike. With the desk gone, I could now meet with my associates in an informal atmosphere. Tension was relaxed, and it seemed to me that people spoke more freely and directly.

Since an executive's time is spent largely talking with other people, I felt that the experiment was successful. Perhaps your work requires a desk, but come out from behind it for personal meetings. Your most important activity is dealing with people. Paperwork and office routine shouldn't be allowed to take precedence.

5

The Organization Ties
That Bind

ORGANIZING your own time efficiently will give you more time to organize the work of your staff. This will constitute your major executive activity. C. L. Ferguson, writing in the *Atlanta Economic Review*, described good organization as one of four key factors in a well-managed company.

Four basic elements are always present in an exceptionally well-run company. First, it has direction. It knows where it is going. Second, it has a well-designed structure that can perform effectively and withstand the battering of competition. Third, it has a fine set of controls so that it handles well. And finally, it has the power or energy to move itself.

You need an organization to run your department well. It need not be formal, nor must it be elaborate. But you'll find it essential to assign specific responsibilities to each member of your staff, and to delegate to each the corresponding authority he'll need to exercise his responsibilities. Everyone in your department should know to whom he reports, and who reports to him. This, nothing more, is the essence of organization. That darling of the corporate bureaucrats, the organization chart, is merely a graphic presentation of such an organization.

The organization chart isn't a meaningless diagram of lines and boxes, but an arrangement of people and functions which enables them to work together at best efficiency. It specifies who is your boss, and who is his. The channels of authority are firmly laid down.

From your position on the chart, one line goes upward, and a number go downward. They are two-way channels. Your superior will give you direction, and you will report to him on your activities. The same relationship applies to your subordinates. These lines are your principal channels of communication. Because many a promising young executive has wrecked a promising career on the rocks of these channels, they are worth further consideration.

Your vertical lines of communication are your most important. You must always communicate (and listen) both upward and downward. In addition, you will usually have need to communicate "sideways," for example, to other departments which may be jointly involved with your own in a particular project. Or you may need to communicate diagonally with staff executives at a higher level such as the personnel, legal, or accounting departments. The chart indicates the path to follow in an orderly way.

The opposite of organization is disorganization. If you fail to plan, disorganization will result. Only in a small business, where the proprietor makes all the decisions, and everyone does a little of everything, does the enterprise manage to survive disorganization. If your department is part of a large corporation, however, chaos will result from the absence of planned effort.

For one thing, the assignment of specific responsibilities provides a yardstick by which to measure employees. You'll be unable to know objectively how well any employee is doing unless you've previously established such a yardstick.

Furthermore, you conserve time by establishing channels of authority, and defining who reports to whom. You don't want to spend your time solving each minor problem that develops within your department; delegating minor matters to lower levels frees you to face major problems. You also free yourself for the future day when six department heads instead of six employees may report to you. At that point, even more than now, an organizational chart will reserve your valuable time for major problems which reach you through channels you have established. The organizational chart maps the corporate landscape for all to see.

You can have a lot of fun drawing up organizational charts. They're a great corporate plaything. Georg Olden, a distinguished New York art director and veteran observer of the corporate scene, developed them into a hobby. He created fanciful organization charts suitable for framing. They hung proudly in many an executive office. His line of horizontal boxes sprawled across a long sheet of paper, finally doubling back on itself with a profusion of wiggles. Boxes were inserted in boxes, and occasionally a line wandered across the chart in disorderly fashion.

One giant company whose management was constantly engaged in acquisitions and mergers, took the subject more seriously. It maintained an entire department to prepare its organizational charts. A little man sat in front of a big desk and sketched out the position of each new acquisition in the vast structure of the parent corporation. The corporate structure actually was unwieldy and hardly workable, but the little man followed his self-written book of rules and always managed to tidy things up by working a new box somewhere into his diagrams. As rapidly as he completed his sketches, they were rushed across the hall to another office where a corps of trained draftsmen translated them into the very picture of corporate orderliness. They looked fine.

The flaw was that the president paid no attention to them. He was a strong personality, who had the habit of moving in and out, up and down all levels of the organization, making on-the-spot decisions at every level without regard to the pretty charts.

The president can ignore channels and get away with it. Not so the lower ranks. If you skip over your immediate superior and communicate with his boss directly, you're headed for difficulty, and probably quickly. Your superior will conclude that you are undercutting his position by failing to go to him first. He's right. You may have good reason for so doing, but the fact is that you are threatening his position. Unless you're engaged in a last-ditch struggle to save your own job (in which case, no holds are barred), going outside of channels to reach over your boss's head will lead to trouble for you. A pink slip may be waiting for you before you ever know what happened.

Many times, you may find yourself frustrated and angry because your immediate superior does not pass your own recommendations up the line. Outside of resigning your job, there is relatively little you can do about this. It's equally annoying when your superior passes along your recommendations, but removes you from the discussion.

In Grand Rapids, Michigan, a furniture executive once told me that when he discussed with his superior a proposal that originally emanated from a member of his staff, he always brought the staff member into the meeting. The staff member was invited to speak for himself to be certain the matter was properly presented. It provided the senior executive with a chance to observe the staff member; and the latter received proper recognition for his proposal.

This was good management in action. Open channels made it unnecessary for the staff member even to think of ignoring them. Teamwork like this is essential to corporate success.

An organization chart will become meaningless if it's ignored. Whatever form your own organization takes, follow it and enforce it to derive the full benefits from your planning.

The form of your organization chart is no more important than its systematic implementation.

Besides establishing lines of authority, the organization chart provides a quick picture of the number of persons who report to each executive. From this, you can quickly deduce whether your department is efficiently managed.

If the chart shows, for example, a long row of boxes in a horizontal file, each neatly tied by a firm black line to a single vice-president, you may suspect that the vice-president is not providing genuine supervision to his staff, because he necessarily will lack the time to do so. There is a reasonable limit to the number of persons whom any executive can really supervise. In this case, the chart reveals that too many people report to him. But he likes it that way, because all those boxes on the chart underneath his own inflate his ego with delusions of importance. In many large corporations, executives rate each other's importance by the number of persons reporting to them; the greater the number of subordinates, the more important they are. In practice, however, a long line of boxes on the organization chart frequently results in a long line outside the vice-president's office as his subordinates wait impatiently to seek his counsel. A management executive said: "When I see this situation, I know there's something wrong with the setup. The executive who builds an oversized staff to feel important deserves to be made an ex-executive."

At the opposite pole is the executive whose organization chart shows only one single box under his own. If he is the executive vice-president, perhaps only the senior vice-president reports to him. This too is a sign of bad organization, for it certainly isn't a full time job for one man to supervise the work of one man. If the senior has properly delegated authority to his subordinate, he doesn't have much to do. If he was the one who organized his executive staff this way, you might conclude that he's a man who doesn't like to work very hard. Sooner or later, the Board of Directors inevitably will ask whether he's earning his $30,000 salary, or whether the company wouldn't be better off eliminating his position and giving the title and authority to the senior vice-president who's actually doing the work.

Somewhere between these two extremes is the right number of persons to supervise. Too many means inadequate supervision; too few means not enough work for the supervisor. My own rule of thumb is that six to ten is about the right number, depending on your level of supervision. It could, of course, be twelve, but not many more if supervision is to be meaningful. You may think that you can easily supervise a greater number, but caution is in order. You'll have a hard enough job to keep posted on activities of the six, but each of them in turn must keep posted on the activities of the other five as well as those of their own staffs.

The six you supervise can each supervise six more, making thirty-six employees at the next level. At that rate, a company with 8,471 employees could operate well with four levels of management below the president. This is indeed only a theoretical construction, and corporate reality is never quite so simple and orderly. But many smaller companies, which now operate with more than four levels of management, could easily prune the corporate rosebush.

If the men you supervise are themselves junior executives, six is a good maximum number. The senior executive who supervises a half dozen heads of large departments will have his hands full.

Much less supervision is needed for semiskilled or unskilled jobs, and a junior executive can satisfactorily supervise a dozen or more clerical employees.

The right degree of supervision will enable management to respond quickly and effectively to changing conditions. If management becomes excessive, hardening of the corporate arteries is induced, and the company's "nervous system" breaks down. Symptoms are most likely to develop in large companies as they expand into huge enterprises.

In one of the largest and best-run corporations in the United States, executives joke that if you kick it hard in the tail, something will happen at the other end, perhaps two years later. If your company is in a fast-moving, unstable industry, two years isn't quick enough to change things. Your organization should be able to shift gears with the speed made necessary by competitive business conditions. Slashing unnecessary layers off the corporate structure is one way to accomplish this.

Last year, I saw a company organization chart that piled no less than seventeen layers of executives atop one another in a paper pyramid. Pity the fellow at the top when he wants to determine the actual state of affairs at the bottom level. If anything goes wrong in the factory, or with the activities of salesmen in the field, it would take a long, long time before word reached the decision-makers at the top.

When the need for reorganization becomes apparent, management consultants and professional managers are frequently called in. Some try to create a management mystique which requires following "the rules of organization." The consultants know the rules, they say, and, as a new executive, you don't.

But it isn't true. There are no rules at all that you must follow, except for the one that assigns each person a definite responsibility, tells him what it is, and holds him accountable for the results. The rest of the so-called rules are nothing more than the formalized experience of other companies. They may or may not be suitable for your company or your department. You may profit from the experience of successful companies, but, in the end, you'll have to decide what's best for the needs of your own particular organization.

Once in a while, a company boldly breaks the rules and organizes its functions in an original way. Genesco, Inc., maintains an organization chart with no lines and boxes, but instead, only circles, four of them, to be exact. The innermost circle consists of the chairman and the president. The second circle includes the executive committee of nine, the chairman, the president, a director, and six others. The third circle is made up of the executive staff, accounting and administration, systems and procedures, product development, research, and personnel. Finally, the fourth and outermost circle consists of the operating companies and divisions.

Why such an unorthodox organization? Because Genesco feels that "this form of organization best suits our particular types of business. We are dealing with consumers in a fashion industry, where changes occur very rapidly. It is important to have delegated authority to make decisions quickly without reference to some central headquarters."

So don't worry about established rules when you prepare your department organization charts. Analyze the functions for which you are responsible, decide who'll perform each, and you've solved your problem. Only when vagueness or divided responsibility exists are you in for trouble.

For instance, someone in your organization may happen to possess two skills which functionally are not directly related to each other. In a small company, one man may serve as sales manager, but, because of his background and experience, may also double as personnel manager. In the latter capacity, he functions as an assistant to all departments, helping them select qualified job applicants. The two posts have no relationship, except that, for the moment, the same man happens to be filling both.

Double duty is frequently necessary when neither position is sufficiently time-consuming to justify a full-time jobholder. However, beware of the situation that splits a man into two, especially if, as a result of the split functions, he reports to two different superiors.

One man I knew in the leather industry held responsibility for both advertising and labor relations. In his advertising capacity, he reported to the vice-president in charge of marketing. In his labor relations capacity, he reported to the president. In neither area was his work going well. When the president called him in to inquire about a threatened strike, he rationalized the situation. But the president persisted; why had the difficulty been allowed to develop to this point?

"I've been under great pressure, Mr. Jeffrey," he told the president. "We have a deadline coming up on our advertising for the fall selling season, and I had to meet it."

And when the marketing vice-president complained about the poor quality of the forthcoming advertising, he had a different story.

"I'm sorry, Mr. Todd," he declared. "As you know, we're threatened with a strike, and I've had to spend a lot of time negotiating with the union. There's no point in advertising if our production is going to be interrupted by a strike."

Whether or not either or both of the stories were truthful, the split responsibility made such conflicts inevitable. You can prevent such problems from developing in the first place by giving each person in your department a firm and fixed responsibility, for which you hold him accountable.

One or two people in your department may not, however, fit into a proper niche when you sketch out your organization chart. Their duties are undefined, and their jobs have evolved over the years to fit their particular combinations of talents. They report to more than one person. If a need did not exist for their functions, they have gradually created a need, just as the administrative staff of the British Admiralty grew while the Royal Navy which it managed shrank in size. (This observation by Professor Parkinson led to the formulation of his now-famous Parkinson's Law.)

When cost-cutting time comes, these undefined people are the first ones to scrutinize. Are their functions necessary? What would happen if the jobs were abolished? You might discover that the department would continue to function, only more profitably.

That doesn't mean that you should dismiss able employees

with long and loyal service. There's a difference between abolishing a job and firing an employee. Instead of firing him, you may be able to transfer the employee into a spot where he's needed, and where your present staff needs strengthening. Often only brief retraining is needed. In this way, you can apply maximum manpower to the important work your department is doing.

But such a transfer won't be easy, particularly if it involves a veteran employee. You can expect resistance from him. He has built a home for himself in the company, and now you, as a newcomer, propose to demolish it. He will give you fifty-seven varieties of reasons why his work is vital to the company. I've heard the arguments so often I can repeat them almost verbatim. He'll tell you that the effects of his work can't be measured, but that he is building good will for the company; he has improved customer relations, and so on.

Listen thoughtfully, because he may be correct. But if you decide that he isn't, start chopping away at the tree until it falls to the ground, and your man is safely transferred to a post where his abilities can be put to more productive use for the corporation. Then move ahead to place everyone in positions where their responsibilities are well defined.

Some experienced executives emphasize the importance of the military concept of "staff and line." In a corporation, a line executive is one to whom authority and responsibility for one segment of the firm's operations have been delegated. The manager of a plant is a line executive, if he has been given authority to run the operation freely in accordance with company policy. The sales manager is another line executive. The key words in their job description are "authority and responsibility."

A staff executive, on the other hand, is an assistant to someone who has been assigned authority. He has none of his own. He may be a personnel officer, who assists the plant manager in hiring and firing. Or he may be a public relations man, serving on the president's staff and assisting the president and divisional managers with public relations and publicity services. The "house lawyers," members of the company's legal department, are also staff members. The president may have given them authority to approve all legal agreements of the various divisions, but their function is essentially to advise various corporate executives on legal matters. Characteristically, the staff executive is concerned with a particular problem, while the line executive has full responsibility for one segment of the business.

On paper, this distinction between staff and line seems clear enough. In actual practice, however, the waters are often muddied. The president's staff members sometimes behave not as if they were mere advisers to the president, but as if they were themselves vice-presidents, actually exercising authority. They usually get away with it, because lower echelons assume the president approves their doing so. In some corporations, the president surrounds himself with a large and amorphous staff, each member with undefined functions, each prepared to act anywhere problems arise. Sometimes this arrangement solves problems, but sometimes it creates them, as I have seen at first hand.

In a large tobacco company the president had decided to market an additional brand of cigarettes with the aim of capturing a larger share of the total market. He had assigned a task force to the project. But the controller, a staff executive, halted marketing plans because the company's cash position (funds on hand or available) could not meet the needs for additional capital required to launch the initial advertising campaign.

The president exploded violently when he heard what had happened. "Dammit!" he pounded the desk, "the accountants aren't going to run this business." He made an immediate decision to go ahead. "Now tell Van Horne [the controller] to figure out how to finance it. I'll make the marketing decisions around here, not he." The controller was in trouble because he had assumed authority the president hadn't given him. He had conveniently "forgotten" his advisory position, and had acted as if he had line authority.

In Boston, I once visited an administrative vice-president, whose duties were sharply limited by the table of organization to finance, personnel, and purchasing. When his secretary ushered me into the room, he was in the middle of instructing the advertising manager on the design of a new product package. To my surprise, he got away with it, even though he had no qualification to recommend anything, and no authority from the president to interfere in such a matter. The humiliated advertising manager later explained why he had succumbed without a fight. The offending vice-president had the office directly adjacent to the president. The entire organization, including the browbeaten advertising manager, assumed that he acted in the name of the president. The president had never said this was the case, and the vice-president had not dared to imply it. But junior executives feared to ask the president directly whether this was what he wanted. If the presidential answer turned out to be yes, the questioner would be in hot water with the vice-president. So the abuse of power flourished to the detriment of the company, and the organization chart was flouted. A staff officer exercised the authority of a line executive without authorization.

To prevent the abuse of executive power, and to keep yourself well informed on the actual state of affairs in your department, you will need some kind of reporting system. Once again, there are no rigid rules which the ideal executive must follow. The reporting system of one company, or even of another department within your own company, doesn't necessarily provide a working guide for you.

One friend of mine has a standing rule on reporting which his staff knows by heart: "Put it in writing." He told me that, years earlier, when he relied on informal personal reports, he one day suddenly discovered an acute crisis had developed in his department. He summoned his staff into his office, and angrily asked why he hadn't been warned before the situation reached serious proportions.

"But I did warn you," the accounts receivable clerk told him. "I mentioned it to you a week ago Friday when we were discussing the April figures."

And then he recalled. Yes, he had been told. But the warning was so obscurely worded, and so carefully buried amid other information, that he had understandably missed its significance. Once burned, twice wary. From that moment on, he insisted on receiving all reports in written form so that he could study them properly.

If you supervise a department of sixteen or twenty-six or thirty-six people, you may, of course, find it necessary to receive reports in written form because of their number. But if your department is closer to the ideal size, it's entirely possible and practical for your staff to report to you orally in face-to-face meetings. With a department of proper size, you should find it possible to meet with each person almost daily, and to spend at least a few minutes with each. Sometimes, you may set aside one day a week to discuss with your staff the longer-range trends and problems rather than the immediate activities.

This "once-a-week longer look" may prove extremely valuable. A sales executive who once reported to me was accustomed to telling of his daily calls and sales results. But on Fridays, we consciously avoided this discussion and talked in broader terms. It was in such a conversation one Friday morning that he commented on what seemed to him to signify a new trend in the market. If it continued, as he thought it might, the new trend would reduce the demand for one of our services. As a result of this conversation, we delved deeply into the problem. His intuition later proved correct, and our market strategy changed as a result. He had not intended originally even to mention this point to me, for he was much too uncertain of his observation. I'm sure that had he reported to me in writing, he would not have mentioned it.

So a good case can be built for informal reporting. When your staff member must refer to statistics, or to detailed analysis, he should prepare such information in writing, and bring it with him into your office, for your later review. But such written documents are a supplement to, not a substitute for, the face-to-face impressions you form in a personal meeting.

Whichever type you prefer will depend on the nature of your operations, as well as on your own personality. The choice isn't between oral or written reports alone; there are innumerable variations and combinations. For example, some executives ask for one-page written summaries to accompany an oral presentation. One office equipment company asked that junior executives report monthly in person. Once a year they were requested to complete a written questionnaire no less than eighty-six pages in length, which probed into every aspect of their departments. I saw several of the bulk replies, and will testify that they were less revealing of the actual state of affairs in the departments than the report an errant husband gives his wife on returning home late at night.

Get the information in whatever way you prefer, but always know exactly what's going on in your department. The trick is to learn the truth, and avoid being hornswoggled by masses of meaningless verbiage. Without an efficient reporting system, the best organization may fail because you won't learn of the difficulties in time to help solve them.

The head of a New York retailing organization told me that the pressures of his position were so overwhelming that the only time he had to read written reports from his executives was while taking a morning shower. Sixteen executives reported to him. No wonder his own performance record became increasingly soggy!

6

The "Let-'Em-Fight-It-Out" School

THE BEST ORGANIZATION CHART in America will not transform your department into a smoothly functioning organism unless you want it to. More necessary than any plan is your active effort to weld the individuals on your staff into a team, pooling their efforts so that the net result is greater than the sum of its parts.

Ever since the Industrial Revolution, and compounding in complexity until today's automation, industry has required the coordinated efforts of many people. The handicraft era of one-man workshops is no more. Today, one individual may provide the leadership, but an entire organization is needed to execute his decisions, and to keep the company functioning soundly.

If you really want everyone to pull together for common benefit, you won't find it too difficult to accomplish. In fact, it's easier to get people working together than to get them fighting each other. Excepting only the occasional individual who's angry at the whole world (and he doesn't belong on your payroll anyway), most people enjoy their work more when their relationships with one another are pleasant and harmonious.

The ideal situation exists when the energies of all your employees are directed against the "enemy," the competitors in the marketplace. The wise executive will frequently remind his staff what the competition is doing. He will emphasize that the security of their jobs depends on defeating the "enemy" by outproducing him and outselling him.

He can do this in many ways. An executive in one appliance manufacturing company arranged a showing of competitive products, complete with price tags. The display was prominently placed in various plant locations to remind employees of their target. It had a salutary effect.

His effort to get employees to pull together contrasts with the actual state of affairs in other companies. A management consultant, whose work takes him inside a half-dozen corporations in a single month, told me that internal harmony is the exception, not the rule, in the companies he visits.

"Everything looks fine on the surface," he said. "But when you start talking with each member of a department in the privacy of his own office, the curtain drops away. In our work, we guarantee absolute anonymity to each person who talks with us, if he wants it. As soon as he's convinced that we won't divulge what he tells us, he begins to open up freely. Then we discover that half the executives are dueling with the other half. Colleagues who should be working together share mutual distrust. Some are gunning for the jobs of others. Subtle sabotage—you can call it that, for that's what it is—exists between executives and departments."

He and I discussed over a luncheon the reasons for this state of affairs.

"Almost always," the consultant told me, "it begins at the top. The boss encourages it." I nodded agreement and he continued.

"The boss wants it that way. He figures that he'll get the best work out of people if he can throw them into competition with each other. The idea is supposed to be that each man will knock himself out to do a better job if he knows he's being measured against someone else."

"There's nothing wrong with competition," I observed cautiously.

"No, there isn't," the consultant nodded. "But the competitive instinct has to be turned against the competitor, not against fellow executives. When executives start fighting with each other, the company is the one that gets hurt, not the competitors."

He described the symptoms to watch for. They may exist in your own company right now. One executive may regard another as his special rival. Each of the two seeks the approval of the boss. Each creates opportunities to criticize the work of the other. Each seizes on the shortcomings or failures of the other to bolster his own position. By interoffice memo or offhand remark, each casts aspersions on the other's ability.

Neither of the executives enjoys his role. Probably both are living under anxiety and tension. When they get home at night, their wives are waiting with the first Martini already mixed and chilled (at a 5-to-1 ratio). The key in the front door is the sign for the wife to begin preparing the second drink.

While they gulp their Martinis, each is thinking of tomorrow. What memos can he write to knife his rival? What important information can he withhold from his "colleague" without hurting himself in the process? It's a terrible way to live.

Neither of them likes to operate in this way, but they have no choice. They seldom have time any more to think of accomplishing better results on their job. Now they are fighting for the job itself, and this requires every bit of energy and skill they can command.

Such rivalry brings severe damage to the company. Yet executives encourage it by deliberately creating situations that breed damaging competitiveness.

I recall a situation that existed in a New England shoe

factory. It was neither better nor worse than other companies in this respect. Mr. Weiner, the production manager, had responsibility for increasing output despite the handicap of an obsolete plant. His superior was the plant manager, Mr. Thea.

Mr. Weiner had long experience in the industry, and was skillful at handling the foremen. Systematically, he tackled one bottleneck after another, and most of them he solved. Broken machinery was repaired; absenteeism was reduced; quality control was tightened. By any reasonable standard, Mr. Weiner was producing good results. His job was, or should have been, increasingly secure.

But he reckoned without the anxieties of his boss, the plant manager. And there the trouble started. For supervision of Mr. Weiner constituted probably 90 percent of Mr. Thea's job. Mr. Thea had little else to do. His other responsibilities were minor, thrown into his jurisdiction for lack of a better place to put them.

As plant manager, Mr. Thea could have helped Mr. Weiner considerably. He had come up "the hard way," holding successively every job in the plant, including the one Mr. Weiner now held. But his energy and drive had petered out years ago. He was coasting toward retirement. He had little desire to help Mr. Weiner or anyone else. He wished only to hold onto his position for a few remaining years.

While, however, he never assisted Mr. Weiner, he had convinced the company president that he was needed to assist him. "Problems are always coming up where he needs help," Mr. Thea confided to the chief executive.

But problems didn't come up, because Mr. Weiner solved them before they became troublesome. So Mr. Thea soon found himself inventing troubles, or compounding minor ones until they appeared to threaten major corporate disaster. Every problem that arose in the plant became, for Mr. Thea, a new argument why he was needed, and why Mr. Weiner was inadequate. Each of the executives knew what the other was plotting, and the situation rapidly deteriorated. It was just about this time that I entered the picture. Neither of the two men discussed the problem with me, but it was not difficult to discern the obvious.

Since I was not pledged to any confidences, I decided to raise the subject with the company president at his corporate headquarters in another city. Innocent as a lamb, I thought he would be surprised to learn of the animosity that had developed, and would thank me for calling it to his attention.

But instead, the chief executive only chuckled. "So Thea thinks he's got me buffaloed, does he?" The presidential chuckle turned to a roar of laughter.

"Let me tell you this. I know exactly what's going on in that plant. Thea's trying to save his job by shooting down Weiner, and Weiner doesn't see why on earth I keep Thea in there when he never gets off his backside.

"Well, neither of them have fooled me for a minute. We don't need two men in there anyway. There's only one job of managing to be done. Thea's got two years to go until retirement, and I don't want to fire him now without a good reason. Weiner is a good man, but I decided it wouldn't hurt if I threw him into the pit with Thea and let the two of them fight it out. If Weiner isn't tough enough to handle himself, he doesn't deserve the top job.

"Either way," said the cynical and ruthless president, "the company will come out ahead. I'll have a good excuse to force out Thea two years early, and get rid of dead wood. Or I'll discover that Weiner is too weak to head up the New England plant, and I'd rather discover that before I give him the job, instead of afterwards."

Two men were fighting for what was really one job, and the president sat on the sidelines egging them on. Two formerly healthy executives had become anxiety-ridden men, so preoccupied with defending their positions that they no longer could execute their corporate responsibilities effectively.

The "play-one-against-the-other" school of management has many disciples. I encountered another case in North Carolina, where a national corporation had established three sales and service offices in adjacent cities.

In every other state, the executives told me, one man had been appointed regional manager, with responsibility for all branches within the state. But in North Carolina, no one had been appointed as manager. (Later, I found out why; management in New York had been unable to agree on which of the three managers should be given the supervisory post).

The result was exactly what one might have expected. The three managers were frantically competing with each other to achieve the best performance record. Their competition included occasional guerrilla skirmishes into each other's sales territory, and abandonment of the company's price-protection policies for the sake of additional marginal sales. Few common policies existed, and an observer would conclude, if he removed the company name from the office doors, that he was looking at three different companies instead of one.

You might say that this couldn't happen in your company because the headquarters management wouldn't permit it to happen. But it happened in this case. When a national corporation is managing operations in fifty states, a lot of things can happen before they become apparent to the men at the top.

What happened in North Carolina was, in fact, not to the benefit of the corporation. When a headquarters executive finally came down to check for himself, he was shocked to discover his company had acquired a tarnished reputation in the area. He promptly took corrective action. One of the three was named regional manager, and the wounds healed slowly over a long period of time.

Here too, management received exactly what it asked for. Three men were pitted against one another under circumstances where their competitive urges could be turned only against one another instead of against other companies, which meantime were prospering.

The "let-'em-fight-it-out" technique doesn't always originate with management, but it needs management's approval to survive. Sometimes, it originates with an ambitious employee. It happened that way in a small Brooklyn industrial paint company, which had a two-man sales department. One was Mr. Bell, head of the department; the other was his junior, Mr. Jordan.

The two worked well together. They divided their efforts amicably. Mr. Bell often accompanied Mr. Jordan on visits to a difficult customer, but only when Mr. Jordan asked him to. The head of the company respected them both. As long as together they maintained a good sales record, he was well pleased and not too concerned with which one made which sale.

But eventually, Mr. Jordan became restless with this arrangement. He came to regard his superior as a roadblock to his own progress. After all, he reasoned to himself, he was fully as good a salesman as Mr. Bell.

His strategy was simple and it worked. He went to the president early one morning.

"I've been with you for quite a few years now," he told the president blandly. "You know our sales record is pretty good, but you don't know how much of it is due to me. You've been paying me a good salary, and it seems to me, you ought to know what you're getting for it. I've reached the point where I'm willing to stand on my own two feet and have you measure my performance.

"So, if it's all right with you, I'd like to start working on my own, beginning Monday. I think I can do a better job for the company, and I'll report to you directly so that you'll always know exactly how I'm doing and can measure me accordingly." Mr. Jordan rested his case and awaited the reply.

It came immediately, as Mr. Jordan thought it might. He had played his cards correctly; if the boss had hesitated, or asked for a few days to think it over, the answer might have been different. But as soon as the president began to respond, Mr. Jordan knew he had won.

"I admire your initiative, young man," said the president. "That's the kind of thinking we need to grow. My hat's off to anyone who's willing to stand on his record and prove himself. So you go right ahead, and I'll be watching closely." He rose from his chair, patted Mr. Jordan paternally on the shoulder, and walked with him to the door. Mr. Jordan walked quickly to his office down the hall without saying a word to Mr. Bell. He was through with Mr. Bell from this moment on.

At one stroke, he had eliminated Mr. Bell's post of sales manager. Now Mr. Bell would have no one to manage but himself. Mr. Jordan had put himself on an equal plane with his supervisor. Up to now, Mr. Bell had mapped each sales campaign, selected targets, and divided the calls between himself and Mr. Jordan. Now, sales planning would be a thing of the past; each man would be on his own.

Mr. Bell, the sales manager, never got the word directly from the president. He was left to learn it painfully and abruptly from his erstwhile junior, when Mr. Jordan suddenly stopped conferring with him.

The company's sales efforts changed direction immediately. Mail contact with customers, formerly another responsibility of Mr. Bell, disappeared, for Mr. Bell was in mortal combat with Mr. Jordan, and had to spend every minute in direct selling, to produce orders *today*. Good will building toward tomorrow's orders had become a dispensable luxury. Both men stopped long-range cultivation of major prospects. Small initial orders from contractors were discouraged as not worth the effort, even though they might lead to substantial and profitable sales later on.

Both men scrambled like bugs on a frying pan. (The revealing simile was used later by the president when he told me the story, after the damage had been done). Each fought to grab the morning mail first in the hope it might contain inquiries for immediate followup. Today's sale was the only one that counted. Each man sought bulk orders, obtained in competitive bidding on a lowest-price basis. This was a type of business the company had previously avoided.

I can't even report to you that sales rose immediately before they eventually declined. I saw the actual figures for both men, and they showed a marked drop right from the beginning of the new arrangement.

Within three months, Mr. Bell quit the company for a comparable position with a competitor. His years of experience and valuable customer contacts were put to work elsewhere.

He never said a word when he left. He told the president only that he was resigning for personal reasons, picked up his check from the cashier, and walked out the front door.

Mr. Jordan, however, had a ready-made excuse for the sales decline. "Business conditions are bad," he declared. "Even Mr. Bell, who's been in this business much longer than I, couldn't seem to close any sales these last few months." Jordan kept his job; in fact, he had gained a stronger position than before, for now he was, in effect, the sales manager.

The loss of one good man, and the decreased effectiveness of the other! This is the price the company paid for allowing one man to pit himself against another.

I don't want to suggest that competition isn't a desirable thing, or that management shouldn't measure the performance of each salesman separately. Of course, sales measurement is necessary. Good sales management encourages all members of the department to increase sales, so that there will be more "in the pot" for all to divide in proportion to their efforts.

But when competition becomes destructive, when one

man's gains become another's losses, then the company will be hurt instead of benefited. It's as if management eliminated incentive payments based on sales, and instead set a total salary maximum for the entire sales force, with one man's increase to be paid by a pay cut from the other. Under such an arrangement, violent rivalries would develop, and good men would soon leave.

While the Bell-Jordan battle developed from the ruthless and destructive ambition of one man, I've seen other companies where an executive's plan to "let-'em-fight-it-out" backfired because the men wouldn't fight.

One was a large bank in Los Angeles which had just opened a new suburban branch. Key personnel had been transferred from other branches to staff the new office, and an acting manager had been loaned temporarily by the home office, pending a permanent selection. Meanwhile, at the home office, the bank's senior vice-president cannily worked out a private plan to egg on the junior executives in the new branch. Separately, he had called in the three vice-presidents, in charge of operations, administration, and trust functions, respectively, and informed each of them, in great confidence, that he would later be appointed Branch Manager.

It's difficult to keep a secret when more than one man knows it, and, soon enough, one of the three dropped a casual remark, "When I become manager . . ."

"You become manager?" said the second in a startled voice. "You haven't a chance. I've already been earmarked for the job." They talked in heated tones, and—you guessed it—the third man heard them. The senior vice-president's jig was up. The three compared notes, and discovered the bitter truth. But this time the ending was unexpected. One of them had strong ambitions, but no stomach for a knock-down, drag-out fight.

"Look," he told the other two. "I can fight as well as you, and if you want to start a fight, I'll finish it, and I'll win. But there'll be some bloody noses first. I think we'd be better off if we work together to do the best job we can. That way, we'll all look good, and we'll all have better chances for promotion. One of us will get the promotion here, and the others will have a better chance somewhere else in the company. But if we start fighting each other, all of us will get hurt."

His persuasive argument carried the day. The three men decided to cooperate instead of struggling with each other. The branch did well indeed, and what's more, the three men enjoyed their work instead of facing each new morning with fear and hypertension.

I never heard what finally happened to the trio, but when I left the picture, it appeared that the good sense of the three had prevented the crafty senior vice-president from disrupting the new operation.

You may be, like the senior bank official, a heartless and ruthless individual who doesn't care whether the human beings who work for you develop high blood pressure from your tactics. Nevertheless, you must build a harmonious team of executives, to avoid damage to the "bottom line," the net profit figure on your financial statement. In-fighting always damages a company.

When junior executives become engaged in a corporate Donnybrook, they're concerned only with saving their jobs. The effect on the company's operations becomes a minor consideration to them. It's your responsibility to make clear that their jobs will be saved only by their contributions to the company, not by their destruction of each other.

Unquestionably, encouragement of in-fighting is the mark of a bad executive. It's perhaps also the sign of a sick human being. We should not become so overwhelmed with business considerations that we neglect simple considerations of decency and morality.

A Chicago management consultant described his experience while serving a photographic products company. The company's vice-president had told him that management decisions were being openly flouted by a key executive. Only

the man's long and loyal prior service with the company had
kept him on the payroll despite his defiance of instructions.

What was the flouting, the defiance?

The vice-president quickly told what happened. Senior
management previously had decided to fire the personnel
manager as incompetent. But they did not want to release him
until they had found someone to take his place.

John Greene, the office manager, was his logical successor.
He had worked for the company for sixteen years. His conscientious devotion to the company and its officers was beyond
question. So the vice-president called him and confided the
decision. Frank Hauck, the personnel manager, would have
to go. Mr. Greene should study Mr. Hauck's operation, learn
as much as possible about it, and let the vice-president know
when he was ready to take over. At that time, Mr. Hauck
would be terminated and Mr. Greene would receive a pay
increase in his new post.

But Mr. Greene wouldn't play ball. He said so immediately. He respected Mr. Hauck and would not be a party to the
plot.

"If you want to fire Hauck, that's up to you," he insisted.
"I'm sorry, but I can't bring myself to help you. Hauck never
did anything to hurt me, and he's tried to do the very best he
can for the company. I know this may cost me my job, but
this is the way I feel, and I can't do something against my
conscience."

When the management consultant moved in, the troubled
vice-president threw the problem into his lap. Both men were
still on the payroll.

Playing the role of a corporate psychiatrist, the consultant sat down to talk things over frankly with Mr. Greene.

"I've heard the whole story," he told Mr. Greene. "Can't
say that I blame you. I might have done the same thing myself.
It took a lot of courage for you."

"You're right," Mr. Greene replied. "I know the boss is

angry at me. But he's making a mistake. Hauck is a good man. Sure, he's my friend. But the boss doesn't even know what Hauck has accomplished for the company." With nodding encouragement, he proceeded to specify.

The consultant listened at length, and then told Mr. Greene his plan of action. The whole matter would be reappraised. Management would take a fresh look at Mr. Hauck and would work with him to eliminate the cause of criticisms.

Then he went to Mr. Hauck and laid it on the line. Yes, he discovered, Mr. Hauck knew all about the plot. He, too, was frightened for his position.

To Mr. Hauck, the consultant told exactly the same story. They were going to take a fresh look at him and his work. They felt he had serious shortcomings, and would work closely with him to help him overcome the deficiencies. If he showed improvement, the slate would be wiped clean.

The results were slow in coming, but they came. Mr. Hauck gradually improved his performance, and four months later, when the management consultant met with the vice-president to evaluate him, they agreed he had surpassed their expectations. Hauck stayed, and so did Greene. The company benefited.

The moral of these stories is that you can't run a successful department by pitting one man against the other. Deliberate creation of staff insecurity destroys the effectiveness of any man, and pushes good men out of the organization. The executive who welds a good working team will be better prepared for the long pull ahead than the man who turns his organization into a weed-growing jungle.

7

Push for
the Long Pull

THE LOWER YOUR POSITION in the executive hierarchy, the longer you'll probably hold your job. At a junior level, the competition isn't quite so keen; the stakes aren't so high; the possibility that you'll make a disastrous error isn't so great.

So you should plan your activity on the assumption that you'll remain in your present job for at least a few years. It's reasonable to think that way, plan that way, and organize your staff accordingly. During your first few months, you'll establish working practices that will set your pattern for the following years.

Beginning with first things first, you'll need to decide how much authority you'll delegate to your subordinates. Will you "sit on" your staff, like the lid on a pressure cooker, or will you encourage their initiative? Will you make all the decisions yourself, or will you encourage them to grow and to assume larger responsibilities? Will you play the part of a one-man hero, who must personally surmount all obstacles, or will you encourage your staff to step forward and be recognized?

These are difficult decisions to make. Your intentions will be good, but perhaps you don't know how to implement them. Or perhaps your own leadership drives are so strong that you

simply cannot delegate important responsibility to your staff.
You may prefer to do everything yourself, meanwhile manipu-
lating your subordinates like puppets on a string.

This characteristic may ideally qualify you as a corporate
autocrat, but it will disqualify you for effective leadership at
a junior executive level, which is where you are now, and
where you must succeed before you'll receive serious consideration for promotion.

Even if your department is small, a strong staff will make
you more effective. And you'll be most effective if you develop
at least one of your staff members to the point where he's
qualified to take over your job.

This thought may frighten you. Why should you train
someone to take over your position? Won't you become superfluous? Will the company then dispense with your services
and promote your lower-paid assistant? Every executive has
shared such fears. Many have succumbed to them, and have
deliberately prevented any one of their subordinates from
becoming too strong. This happens not only in business, but in
every sphere of life. Konrad Adenauer, the West German
chancellor, at the age of eighty-seven, and after fourteen
years as head of the West German government, systematically
followed a practice of denigrating his cabinet members to
prevent them from endangering his position. He insisted that
none of them was qualified to assume the chancellorship because of their inexperience and poor judgment. When his party
finally designated a successor, Adenauer managed to defer the
actual turnover of power for six months, during which time,
according to press reports, he sought to destroy the reputation of his close associate.

"Sitting on" your subordinates is a policy so commonly
followed that if you try it, you'll have plenty of company,
with the rest of the executive pack. But the rare and truly
secure executive who instead strengthens his staff, encourages

its initiative, and proceeds to make himself nearly superfluous will stand out from the crowd.

When "management review time" comes around, as it does semiannually in most corporations, your seniors will evaluate your performance. If they're satisfied, their next question will be, "Has he trained a replacement to take over if we promote him?" A negative answer will probably bar your advancement for another year or more.

You're not practicing altruism, therefore, when you train a successor. You advance your own self-interest, and multiply the chances of your own promotion to the next higher level in the executive pyramid.

I wouldn't fear the possibility that your superiors may decide you've now become unnecessary and can be dispensed with. Never once have I seen this happen, and I don't think it ever will. Good management talent is so rare in most organizations that it isn't often cast aside.

At the moment, you may be convinced that no one in your department has sufficient ability to be groomed for advancement. Your judgment may be correct, but you won't know with certainty until you have given your staff several months to prove themselves. Some people will surpass your expectations, while others will surely disappoint you. Only after you've watched them in action can you decide what to do about each one.

The way to begin is by assigning definite responsibilities and goals to each member of your staff. If you manage a department in a retail establishment, your objective will be increased sales by each individual sales clerk. If you manage an accounting department, your objective may be speedier and more accurate processing of financial records.

Whatever goal is appropriate, the employee must be told clearly what you expect of him. A personal conversation will produce better results than a memo. When you talk with each person, your tone should be friendly but firm. Most important, you should be specific.

You and I have often attended department meetings where the boss asked everybody to work harder. Invariably, such an approach fails, because employees react by asking themselves, "We're already working as hard as we can. What more does he want from us?" The "work harder" appeal feeds antagonism and conflict between executive and employees.

Specific guidance coupled with helpful assistance, however, works effectively. Instead of asking a sales clerk to work harder, you may ask her to try to increase sales of sports coats by 15 percent next month, and give her concrete suggestions how to achieve her goal. Review her sales talk and suggest improvements; point out new features in the product line which she may emphasize to customers. Such suggestions will make it realistically practical for her to meet your objectives, and your guidance will be accepted as friendly assistance instead of executive harassment and pressure.

The office manager may set goals for an unsatisfactory telephone operator. After chiding her for lateness and discourtesy, he may insist quietly but firmly that she be in the office, and on duty at the switchboard, promptly at nine o'clock each morning. To eliminate her discourtesy, he may suggest exactly what she should say to callers in particular circumstances.

When you give such leadership to your staff, you establish a basis for subsequent evaluation of their performance. A month later, it will be a simple matter for you to check the sales clerk's performance. Her sales may not have increased, but seasonal or other factors could have been responsible. Nevertheless, you may observe her in action, and listen to her sales talk to see if she has improved. With the telephone operator, you can check her attendance record and listen to her telephone conversations. Is she following the directions you gave her a month earlier?

Once in a while, some member of your staff will follow your guidance to the letter, and then keep right on going beyond it on his own initiative. He may begin using a new operational method of his own, or find a way to reduce paperwork, with resultant economies to your department. Such an individual holds promise of personal growth and future promotion. He deserves your generous praise. Even more, he deserves public praise in front of his colleagues. It is the rare individual who will show initiative and assume additional work, additional responsibility, beyond the call of duty.

"Mr. Taurino suggested a way to combine three order forms we're now using," you might tell the staff. "We're adopting his suggestion, and he deserves credit for coming up with such a useful idea."

The initiator will feel stimulated to search for further ideas, and the others will quickly learn that you welcome new ideas, giving generous credit for them. Since they (like you and me) seek praise and approval, it will encourage them to do likewise.

But your praise for outstanding performance (a positive act) must not be negated by your public criticism (a negative act) of those whose performance was mediocre or even unsatisfactory. If you add, "Why don't the rest of you come up with good ideas like that?" you'll irritate your staff to the point of hostility.

Only your positive efforts to encourage initiative have a chance for success. Initiative blossoms forth only when the climate is right. If you make it apparent to your staff that you welcome their initiative, they will gradually begin to use it.

If, for example, your sales manager asks for your suggestions on how to handle a difficult customer, your own experience may quickly provide an answer. Your temptation will be strong to give it to your junior. How impressed he will be with your skill and experience!

But even when you know the correct answer to the problem, answer his question with one of your own: "What do *you* think we ought to do?" The problem is right back in his lap.

If your own judgment tells you his answer is the best solution, you may reply, "That sounds fine to me. Why don't you go ahead and do it that way?" He'll leave your office pleased that he, not you, solved the problem.

Perhaps you may regard his recommended solution as unsatisfactory. Then ask if any other courses of action are open. Press for a detailed explanation of the alternatives, and keep pressing until he suggests, among others, the one you believe correct.

But try at all costs to avoid making the decision. Ask him to evaluate the pros and cons of each possible course. Suggest other factors he should consider. Always encourage him to think the problem through and to reach his own conclusion. Needless to say, if, despite your discussion, he reaches incorrect conclusions, you should certainly overrule him to prevent damage to the company, but rarely will such action be necessary. Usually, the executive will grow in ability from the experience of having learned to reach his own conclusions.

Sometimes, one of your staff members will suggest to you an idea worth further consideration. You can encourage his initiative by suggesting that he develop his idea further. You may request that he prepare a detailed expense budget, and a timetable for its implementation. The employee will gain broader experience in pursuing all the information that management customarily requires for an intelligent decision.

Probably his proposal will be marred by omissions or serious errors. This provides you with an opportunity to point them out, and to help him learn from the experience. You may be certain that, as a result, his next proposal will be more carefully developed, more thoroughly worked out, and perhaps more practical as well.

Errors may be minimized, but they can never be eliminated entirely, even by the most careful supervision. Sometimes, the errors of a subordinate may seem inexcusably stupid. Why did Mr. Livingston quote the wrong price to a customer? Why did Mr. Azleng fail to have the machinery repaired promptly? Why did Miss Goldblatt, the receptionist, turn away a visitor you were anxious to see?

Of course, you must analyze and criticize their mistakes, and insist that there be no repetition. Because you're the boss, they'll listen to you and take your criticism to heart. But don't overdo it. Make the criticism fit the crime, but no more. Excessive criticism will produce the "turtle reaction"; subordinates will pull in their heads and tails under a shell for their own protection. A chastised employee will hesitate long and hard before taking the initiative again. He'll do exactly what he has been ordered to do, and nothing more. This isn't the spirit which makes a company grow and prosper.

The only place where errors seldom occur is in civil service. Anyone who has dealt with the vast bureaucracy of government, at any level, knows why. The work of civil servants is rigidly specified by law. None will make any decision or take any action without prior reference to the appropriate legislation. Those who work for the government "play it" by the book. They take no chances. They show little initiative because little is permitted. Either something is legally required, is legally permitted, or it is legally prohibited.

This policy has considerable justification, because ours is a government of laws, not men. Government employees can't be permitted to change laws at will. Strict adherence to the law by the government itself protects citizens from abuse of power. Nevertheless, such rigid, conformist thinking would be disastrous if transferred to the sphere of private industry. Yet bureaucratic rigidity will nevertheless develop gradually in any company, if management creates, consciously or otherwise, an atmosphere where initiative is discouraged. If the penalty for making a mistake is loss of one's job, or loss of promotion opportunities, employees will avoid mistakes by avoiding making any decisions at all.

Your subordinates require, therefore, a certain margin for error. You can provide it without at the same time encouraging carelessness toward their work. When you assign responsibility for a new project to your subordinates, you may tell them frankly that they will probably make some errors. But you hope these errors will be minimized by careful analysis before they act. When errors do occur, you expect them to make prompt corrections.

Let me emphasize that by tolerating some errors, I don't suggest a lowering of performance standards. Rather, your realistic acceptance of errors will raise performance standards. You encourage people to attempt things they would not do if they were immobilized by fear of failure. And when the inevitable boggles occur, you'll be better prepared to cope with them.

You may be told one day by your credit manager that Miss Zelner allowed a new customer to carry away merchandise for later billing. Now the invoice is past due, and the customer can't be located. Miss Zelner's action violated a company rule that customers without established credit must pay cash on the spot.

You call her in and put her on the carpet. You're angry at this direct violation of a standing company policy. You want to tell her so explosively. But wait a moment. There's a right way and a wrong way to do it.

The wrong way is to bawl her out directly, and insist that henceforth she adhere strictly to the rules. It will work; she'll do just that, but it will be a long time before she again displays any initiative.

The right way is to tell her that the company has just suffered a loss because of credit she granted in violation of the company rules. Since she was familiar with the rule, you wonder how this could have happened.

"It was my mistake, Mr. Kerrigan," she might tell you. "The customer looked honest and respectable. He gave me his business card and it looked all right to me. I didn't want to lose the sale."

"I appreciate your honesty," you may reply to her. "I know you were trying to do what you felt was best for the company. But we adopted that rule originally because we have been stuck with uncollectable bills several times before. So next time, Miss Zelner, we must insist that you don't extend unauthorized credit. It's for our own protection."

This way too, she'll follow the rule book, but she'll understand why. What's more, she's less likely to be angry with you or with the company. Your response won't stifle her initiative in some other situation. The next time, she'll probably come to you first if she's in doubt what to do.

If the violation was not hers, you may find the interview running off in an entirely different direction, with unexpected revelations and consequences.

"I don't think this was my fault at all," she may begin.

"Yes, I know the rule forbade me to give credit in this way, and I went ahead and did it," she continues heatedly. "But you would never have known about it if the man had paid his bill. All of us have been doing this for years, because the sales manager told us not to lose any possible sale. He knew we were doing it. In fact, he encouraged us, and told us to wink at the rule book. As long as these customers eventutally paid up, everything was fine. Now you have trouble, and you blame me, but all I did was what I was told to do."

Now you have an entirely different set of problems to deal with. Your first step is to ascertain the actual facts, and then to pass judgment on what happened, as well as what ought to be done about it.

"Miss Zelner, when did the sales manager tell you to do this?" you inquire quietly.

"I don't remember. It was years ago, when I first joined the company, Mr. Kerrigan."

"I'll look into it right away, Miss Zelner, and I'll talk with you again after I've talked to your manager."

You call him in, and probe quickly to find out what happened. Yes, she was correct, the manager admits. "We picked up quite a number of additional sales this way, and this is the first time in eighteen months that we've had an uncollectable bill. I've encouraged the sales girls to use their initiative, and it happened that this time Miss Zelner made a bad judgment."

You can, if you wish, blame the manager for violating the company rule. But before you do, decide what company policy ought to be. Was the rule too restrictive? Should it be dropped? Or was it a sound management decision which should be retained to protect the company against credit losses?

Whatever you decide, you should make your decision unmistakably clear to the sales manger. Without condemning his initiative, explain why you have reached your conclusion. Insist that he follow the company regulations, but emphasize that you'll welcome his suggestions or recommendations for change. To conclude the matter, you might invite Miss Zelner into your office at the same time, and in the manager's presence, repeat the company policy. You properly thank her for informing you accurately, and explain the new policy carefully.

Perhaps there's a lesson in this little incident. You would not have discovered the truth of the matter if you hadn't asked her in the first place how it happened. You listened, instead of talking, and once again, the company came out ahead.

All sorts of wrong practices like this can grow up in a company during the passage of time. Someone breaks a rule to cut corners. The explanation is plausible, and he gets away with it. The next time, he repeats it without being disciplined. After two or three times, the violation becomes standard practice, and the original company rule lies dead and buried.

Without continuing enforcement, management's wishes may be ignored.

In many industrial plants, safety inspectors check constantly to ensure rigid conformance to safety regulations. The inspectors know that failure to obey safety rules can result in serious accidents. But in the office, the executive must serve, in effect, as the safety inspector to ensure enforcement of company policies.

Unless you stand over an employee's desk and stare at his papers, it's difficult to know whether your policies are being followed. Since you won't want to spy on your employees (I don't believe in the use of office informants), a more direct method may give you the answers you need. Develop and maintain close personal contacts with your staff so that they'll tell you forthrightly what's going on.

Of course, you'll be too busy to spend much time at the water cooler in social conversation with members of your staff. But you can talk with them frequently, always taking the initiative. You'll frequently learn something of value.

The open door to your office will help, but it isn't enough. The typical employee will hesitate before coming in to see you. You are usually busy, and he fears his own problems are too minor for your consideration. Or he thinks you'll regard him as a nuisance for bringing his problem to you. You can't depend on the open door to keep informed of office developments.

Instead of waiting for employees to come to you with their problems, you may take the initiative and ask them. How you do it depends on your own personality. I prefer to talk right at the employee's desk, rather than in my office, to keep things more relaxed and informal. I may walk over to Miss Casey's desk and ask her how a particular project is working out. Or I might encounter Miss Morrill at the water cooler and inquire casually, "Well, how are things going?"

"Fine," she'll invariably reply.

"No problems at all?" I ask.

"Oh yes, we're having some troubles in the warehouse. We're trying to match up our inventory records, and there are some problems."

You invite her into your office to hear the details and find her only too glad to tell you. It just happens that an hour ago, the warehouse clerk called her to report that certain inventory couldn't be found on the shelves. Immediately, you explore it with her in detail and learn what steps she plans to take.

I once had a boss who didn't work this way. He spent all his time in a well-carpeted office. He permitted me to see him only by appointment. How well—and painfully—I remember my encounters with him! Whenever I brought a problem to his attention, I received wall-to-wall carping, and no assistance at all in solving it. My colleagues had the same experience. We needed guidance, and could not obtain it. Gradually, we began going to each other for help and counsel, and thus avoided his severe and unjustified criticism. If the problem was minor, we'd take a chance and try to solve it ourselves. It certainly developed our initiative, and that was all to the good, but it wasn't what The Great Man wanted. Over a period of months, his slender contact with his staff evaporated entirely, and he came to know little of what was actually happening within his department. He sensed that something of the sort was going on, and he reacted by criticizing us still more severely for not keeping him informed. Yet he had no one to blame but himself. We wanted to keep him posted, and we needed his counsel. Only when we found we couldn't get it did we turn away from him.

Executives must know what's going on in their own areas of responsibility. The only ones who can tell you are the people on your staff, and they will tell you only if you ask them. It's as simple as that. Let them know you're interested in their problems; give them a chance to talk, and you'll learn more than you expect. Come out of your office once in a while. You can make decisions in solitude, but you can't be a leader in solitude.

Cultivate a friendly relationship with your staff to keep informed. More than that, creation of an informal atmosphere often assures favorable conditions for good work. People will work harder, more effectively, and take more initiative, when they don't work in fear and trembling of the boss.

But don't carry it too far. An informal relationship isn't the same as a social relationship. Lunching with a staff member to discuss a problem is all right, but not a social evening playing bridge with him and his wife. The executive will wisely avoid social relationships with his subordinates. In the office, be as friendly as you wish; outside of business hours, keep your personal life entirely apart from your staff.

I don't suggest this because of social snobbery. Just because you happen to be the boss doesn't place you one whit higher on the social scale. My reason is very practical: when you've entertained a man in your home, and have been entertained in his home, it's extremely difficult to reprimand him the next morning or to fire him later if that becomes necessary. Social relationships will interfere with your responsibility to the company, and interfere with objective judgment of your staff.

Once, while a consultant to a service corporation, I encountered a department which had more of the atmosphere of a social club than a business organization. A maze of social relationships flourished among the staff members. Couples entertained one another on Saturday nights. Single men courted the single women. Engagement parties, marriages, even vacations, were virtually interdepartmental affairs. The boss attended most of the social affairs. He was extremely popular. On the surface, the department worked harmoniously and effectively.

I had never before encountered a situation quite like this and was fascinated. Over a period of a month, I spent considerable time with the group, and they even invited me to attend one of their parties.

The relationships puzzled me, because they violated what I considered were the rules of good management, and yet everything seemed to be working well. At the party I attended, something happened which gave me a clue to the mystery.

It was well after midnight. Saturday night had turned to Sunday morning. There was no drunkenness, but most of the guests were well lubricated. All of a sudden, they broke into song, a musical tribute to their department head. "For he's a jolly good fellow" rang thickly through the smoke-filled living room.

Suddenly I saw the picture clearly. The young executive was more concerned with being liked by his staff than with anything else. He had treated them warmly and kindly, far beyond the call of duty. He had received just what he wanted, their approval and adulation. I thanked the host for his hospitality and said good night.

Monday morning, I looked at the department through newly opened eyes. I discovered that time sheets were not being kept. Employees habitually reported late for work. The executive never criticized them, for that would cost him his popularity. The department's work was such that no statistical measurements of its performance could be made, but my closer scrutiny soon indicated that it worked at a minimal "get-by" level. The executive had tried so hard to be liked that he failed to direct and lead his staff.

It's nice to be popular and well liked by the people who work for you. But carry it too far into social relationships and you will fail as an executive.

After all, why should your staff really like you? They're dependent on you for their livelihood, and dependence engenders hostility.

People don't like it when they're dependent on someone else. No man likes to be at the mercy of another. You won't change human nature, so all you can do is to recognize the realities of the situation. Beneath the surface, your staff will inevitably resent your position of power. The best you can do is to stimulate them to good performance in their own interest, not because they love you.

8

Cutting Away
the Underbrush

THE EXECUTIVE manages to keep many balls in the air constantly, with the skill of a trained juggler. While he deals with one problem, a dozen others await his action. The outstanding executive decides which is the most important, and this is the one that gets his immediate attention. But too many executives pay equal attention to all, catching each ball as it lands, and disposing of it before reaching for the next. They treat equally with the significant and the insignificant. Lacking perspective, they don't know the forest from the trees.

I encountered a typical member of this tribe in one of the nation's largest steel companies. He had equipped his secretary with a rubber stamp to imprint the date and time of receipt of every piece of paper that reached his desk. She piled them neatly in chronological order, and he tackled them in that sequence. This orderly system suited his rigid mentality; it eliminated the necessity for him to judge what was important and what wasn't.

Administering your paperwork efficiently isn't enough. It's possible to spend your time working efficiently on unimportant problems which, even if solved, will bring no glory to you and no profit to the company.

91

Not every problem that comes to your desk has equal significance to the company. If sales are lagging, a promotional campaign will be more urgently needed than a review of internal administrative procedures. If your major competitor has begun to underprice your products, a thorough cost analysis with your accountants should take priority over problems of quality control. What you undertake first should be determined by your company's immediate problems, rather than by your personal interests or casual whim.

When you seek a solution to a difficult problem, you'll often find that the answer does not lie in doing something better, but rather in doing something entirely different. Such a creative solution was found in a company which had sought to develop a better opener for wine bottles. For several hundred years, wine bottles have been opened by pulling out the cork with various devices ranging from the traditional corkscrew to levers. But an Englishman mused that such gadgets often leave small pieces of cork floating in the wine. How much better, he thought, if he could push the cork out from the bottom! It would surpass any pulling device. But how could he get inside the bottle to push out the cork?

From this formulation of the problem, he found his answer. A hollow needle would be inserted through the cork. At the press of a trigger, compressed air would shoot through the needle into the bottle and pop out the cork from below. It worked, and his company has developed a thriving business in the sale of $5.95 bottle openers instead of thirty-nine cent corkscrews. This is truly creative thinking.

Eastern Air Lines similarly used creative thinking to solve a difficult problem. The line serves, among others, two of the heaviest traveled air routes in the country, between New York and Washington, and New York and Boston. Eastern's fares, set by the Civil Aeronautics Board, are identical with the charges of their competitors. Several other airlines serve the same routes and offer the same services. Each line sought a solution in more creative advertising to attract customers away from their competitors.

One day, someone in the labyrinth of this vast organization, I know not who, mulled over a vast study of customer opinions about the line's service. He noted that passengers expressed irritation at long waits in ticket lines and airport check-ins. He decided that this fact held the key to the company's growth. His proposed solution represented a radical departure from standard industry practice. Before the plan had been finally worked out, several dozen executives participated in the discussion.

Out of this analysis came the now-famous Air Shuttle, an hourly service between Boston, New York, and Washington where no reservations or tickets are required. The passenger simply goes to the airport, removes a ticket stub from an automatic machine, and boards the plane.

The Shuttle was not easy to develop. It required standby planes to guarantee a seat to every passenger presenting himself prior to takeoff time. In the early months, this caused substantial expenses for standby crews and equipment until Eastern could estimate its actual requirements with reasonable accuracy. It meant new arrangements for collecting fares while in flight, and dozens of other details as well.

The results showed themselves quickly; Eastern soon became the largest carrier on these routes, and operated them profitably while other routes were running at a loss. Its share of the total business between these cities rose from 20 to 70 percent.

The plan worked and the company profited because its executives found the key problem, and then solved it in unorthodox fashion.

Boldness is required to implement extreme solutions. Lynn Townsend, the president of Chrysler Corporation, wielded a meat-ax when management specialists told him his company was top-heavy with office personnel. He promptly fired seven thousand white-collar workers. Empires had been built in the company's offices; Townsend rang the bell on the whole system. It was a decision with painful consequences to thousands of people, but, in retrospect, there seems little doubt that the drastic cost-cutting saved the company and thus the jobs of the thousands of people who remained. In the competitive automobile industry, Townsend had little choice if the company were to survive.

When you sift the many problems which face your department, you'll need to decide which affect the progress of the enterprise over the short term, and which over the longer run. Naturally, your primary concern will be to maintain present profitability. But even if you're not in a position to act on longer-range problems, you can be sure that top management will notice the junior executive who shows awareness of them, and who encourages innovation in his staff to help solve them.

Sometimes you may find that solving the long-range problems creates new difficulties in the immediate present. This happened recently in my own company, which supplies temporary office personnel to business firms to meet their peak work loads and vacation replacement needs. We fill thousands of orders each month for secretaries, stenographers, clerks, and other office workers. Our immediate need for persons with these skills is so great that our sales volume would mount rapidly if we could somehow find additional workers to fill our orders. This is our immediate problem.

We had considered recruitment as our major long-term problem. Management consultants and market researchers had shown us that most customers thought poorly of the quality of the personnel they received from all temporary help services, including our own. Customers understood that the poor quality was the result of the current scarcity of skilled personnel. They expected poor service, and they received it. So they developed no "brand-name" loyalty to any particular temporary employment service.

If we could provide better-qualified people to our customers, we reasoned, their increased satisfaction would ensure their continuing business. They would also give us a larger share of their present business now going to competitors. So we retained an outstanding organization in the secretarial field to develop new screening tests for our applicants. Higher quality standards were set.

The results were a shock. Of the next 11,000 job applicants who came to us, more than 8,500 failed to qualify under the new standards, and were rejected. The immediate negative effects on our company were severe. We were unable to fill many orders because we lacked sufficient qualified workers.

But a few months later, the benefits began to become evident. Because our employees were of uniformly higher qualification, we satisfied a larger percentage of our customers. Repeat business increased. Complimentary letters praising our personnel began reaching us.

The solution had been radical; instead of lowering standards to attract more applicants, we had raised them. Clearly, the move had been sound, even though its immediate effect accentuated our already-difficult problem of recruitment. We have yet to solve the problem fully. But we must, for an unfilled order means a customer who will turn elsewhere.

This experience demonstrates the necessity to consider long-term problems at the same time you struggle to solve daily difficulties. Such thinking becomes more necessary as you climb higher in the executive hierarchy, but if you demonstrate it in your present position, you will reveal yourself as a "comer" to the company management which looks toward its future.

You can measure the importance of various problems by another yardstick: if you solve them, will the company as a whole benefit, or only your own department?

Most executives, for example, involve themselves deeply in their immediate responsibilities, and no more. They tend to think of their departments as autonomous empires, while the other parts of the company become, in their minds, less important. The production executive tells himself that his department, after all, turns out the products on which the company is built. The sales manager convinces himself that without his sales efforts, the company would quickly be forced to shut down. The employment manager knows that he supplies the manpower that keeps all other departments functioning. Each thinks narrowly, worrying about his own problems alone. Rarely does one of them ask himself how he can help his fellow executives solve their problems.

Most corporate managements regretfully have conditioned themselves to expect this narrowness in their junior executives. It doesn't have to be that way. The alert sales manager could, if he wished, suggest to the production manager ideas for improving the product to make it easier to sell. The production manager could suggest methods for closer coordination of production and sales. If they wanted to! But they seldom do. They fail to separate the important from the unimportant. They waste their time with corporate trivialities.

Before you boldly strike forth to think broadly and act decisively toward the solution of problems, you would be wise to reconnoiter carefully. What do your superiors consider is the major problem? Their ideas of major problems may differ from yours. Just be sure that you're directing your best efforts where your management considers it significant. And stop immediately if an executive says, "Just pay attention to what's on your desk today. Let *us* worry about everything else." If that's his attitude, your company may not be the right place for you.

Corporate tyrants do not welcome the initiative of junior executives. Before you concentrate on solving your major problems, be reasonably sure that management wants you to do so. They may not. If you happen to work in the carpeted chambers of that not-so-rare institution, the one-man corporation, your broad vision may lead you to a fatal corporate end. Corporate autocrats have been known to play at the game of booby-trapping unwary executives by expanding or curtailing their authority from day to day, and sometimes from hour to hour, until they develop a panic reaction like rats trapped in a maze. They are encouraged to make decisions, only to discover that their authority to follow through has been removed. When the incompleted project ends in fiasco, the company tyrant dispatches them gleefully and without mercy.

Other top executives have good intentions, but little more. Their personal insecurities, pet prejudices, and narrowness of outlook can wreck your promising executive career.

I saw it happen to Tom Hammerslough, vice-president of an Eastern instrument company. He was intensely profit-conscious, a valuable asset to his employer. He constantly studied the financial records of his operation, searching for ways to increase profits by cutting costs. By careful trimming at every stage of production and sales, Hammerslough increased profits sharply. His performance excelled, and he had good reason for pride.

Despite this, however, he was forced to resign his post within a year. Belatedly, Mr. Hammerslough had discovered that the president of his company was committed to a different method of increasing profits: increasing sales. And Mr. Hammerslough's sales record was stable. It did not show growth.

It would have been futile to attempt to convince the president that there was more than one way to increase profits. The president had climbed to his position up the ladder of the sales department, and was entirely sales-oriented. In his standard of values, more sales meant more profits. Cost-cutting was incidental. The vice-president had not increased sales, so he was forced to leave. This illustrates why you should understand clearly what your superior considers his main objectives before you go to work. Rational considerations aren't the only ones you must consider, as Mr. Hammerslough learned the hard way.

The really important problems often aren't immediately visible. You may have to study your department for weeks or months before you are able to isolate the "Achilles' heel" which is creating the difficulties. You may have to pore over production records and sales statistics; you will certainly need to talk at length with members of your staff before the heart of the problem becomes sharply evident.

Just as a military commander needs good intelligence before planning his tactical moves, so the business executive requires extensive information before deciding on a course of action. It is probably no easier for an executive to obtain accurate information for business combat planning than for a general to learn the strength and location of the enemy forces.

The basic information management needs is, of course, accurate advance estimates of its future sales. Large corporations retain staffs of trained researchers to uncover this information.

One group, for instance, released a detailed economic study which purported to project the nation's economic growth, industry by industry, and year by year for the ten-year period ending in 1970. Deep study preceded the document. Everything went according to prediction in 1960 and the first part of 1961. But when the stock market broke sharply in the middle of 1961, and was followed by an economic decline, the predictions went awry.

At that time I located the pamphlet, and reread the introduction. The soothsayers had protected themselves well. They had cautioned, two years earlier, that their predictions assumed the absence of war or economic depression. Therefore, since an economic depression (or recession, if you prefer) had occurred, they presumably could be excused for their errors. Neither they nor anyone else has found a way to predict economic cycles, although ups and downs have been with us since the earliest days of our nation. Businessmen may be forgiven for seasoning economic forecasts with several pourings of salt.

After the United States Steel Corporation had made a series of incorrect analyses of forthcoming business conditions, chairman Roger M. Blough gave up. Asked by the press for his prediction, he replied, "I'm sorry. I can't say. I prefer you go to the seers, who have a much better outlook."

The chairman of Whirlpool Corporation was even more forthright. He described economic forecasting as "a black art," and declared: "In 1960, we forecast an estimated increase of 10 to 15 percent. Sales went down 5.2 percent that year. I don't think we can forecast a year, much less ten years. Hence, our organization must be flexible. Our formula is to plan very well, but to be quick to adjust when necessary."

The candor of these industry leaders, based on their own bitter experiences, indicates that you can't make executive judgments entirely on the basis of what the researchers tell you. Some of it will be wrong; some will be correct but incomplete; much will be irrelevant. When you're facing a difficult problem, therefore, listen first to your staff and advisers, but then make your own best considered judgment of what ought to be done.

I remember a large baking corporation whose research showed that customers regarded its bread favorably, but considered it essentially the same as other brands. An advertising executive read the opinion study, and underlined that one fact alone out of a thick volume of interview reports. He regarded it as the most significant fact. He concluded that the solution was not to develop more colorful or more exciting advertising, but to create a product difference which would stand out from competitive brands. His dilemma, however, was that the bread recipe could not be changed because it had been carefully developed to satisfy known customer preferences. Because a difference could not be created in the product itself, he created a device which would surround the product with an imaginary difference. He arranged to introduce piped music into the baking plant, and then to advertise his client's product as "the bread baked to music." The campaign was outstandingly successful. But its success must be attributed not so much to its cleverness as to the basic analysis of the problem which preceded the solution. The ad man had studied every aspect of the marketing problem, and said, "our most important problem is to establish a product difference. We can't change the bread, so let's invent some other difference that we can advertise." In another part of the country, some time later, executives faced a similar problem and found their solution in a round loaf of bread. Changing the shape created a product difference. Research can narrow the area of your decisions and help you make intelligent judgments.

If you happen to work for a large corporation which uses data processing systems complete with high-speed electronic computers, your difficulties may be greater instead of less. These machines spew out statistics and information at the rate of 600 lines per minute, printing it faster than your eye can read. The head of your data processing department will be glad to give you just about any information you could possibly want.

"We've already got the raw material on tape," he'll tell you, "and we have idle time on the machine, so I'll be glad to run it through for you." This is offered, of course, not in a pure spirit of helpfulness, but to advance his corporate empire. Originally his department was supposed to reduce the size of the company's clerical staff, but he has found so many ways to be "helpful" that new charts of statistics are being produced constantly—by an increased staff.

You can drown in statistics. If the electronic brain and the empire builder are turned loose, you will find yourself with more statistics than you can possibly absorb, understand, or use. At the end of the month, you'll likely find your department has been debited with an intercompany charge for three hours and forty-five minutes of operation of the electronic computer at a high hourly cost.

To avoid the problem in the first place, you should understand that not all statistics are equally valuable. You can't do anything with many of them. If the computer tells you sales are lagging in Lancaster County, Nebraska, what can you do about it when your advertising and sales organizations operate on a national scale and simply aren't geared to move in at a county level?

A good starting point, therefore, is to list for yourself all the key questions for which you want answers. Select only those which are crucial to the success of your operation. After you've decided what's important, then is the proper time to ask the data specialists whether they can produce that information, and no more.

Even when you receive the data, you'll encounter difficulties in interpreting the figures. Unless you're unusually skilled at interpreting a mass of statistics, you'll be hard pressed to spot the figures that are meaningful. You may ask your friends in the accounting department to present the statistics to you graphically, in simple visual terms that are easily understandable. A line wriggling more or less evenly across a chart may suddenly turn sharply downward. It might be significant, but not necessarily. Perhaps you'll want to chart last year's comparable statistics on the same piece of paper. If a similar drop did not occur last year, you may decide to follow one course of action. But if last year produced a comparable decline at the same time, seasonal factors may be responsible, and you'll plan differently. It will take careful study and thoughtful effort to locate the really important problem and separate it from the secondary factors. The data-processing boys will give you the raw information, but it may provide no more help than to tell you where to look further.

Some top executives try to make their department heads

more profit-conscious by giving them monthly budgets. These budgets forecast sales, expenses, or whatever. If you find them cumbersome and difficult to work with, you may wish to ask the accountants also for a statement of variances. This lists only those budget items where you spent substantially more or less than was budgeted. Nothing is included about those categories where you met, or closely approached, your budgeted predictions. On request, the accountants will often prepare for you a brief analysis showing why certain items failed to meet the budget. For example, during June, you may have spent much more in staff salaries than was budgeted. You don't understand why, because you added no one to your staff. Their analysis might show that your salary budget was calculated on the basis of one-twelfth (one month) of the entire year's total salary. But during this particular month of June, there were five Fridays, which means five paydays. So you exceeded your budget, but the following month, when there were only four paydays, you were under the budget, and the total averaged out.

Thus, a report on variances will quickly tell you what's important and what isn't. When you eliminate all the unnecessary information, you'll find the main problem areas and act appropriately.

I've tried to indicate how much help you can get from other executives in the company, if you want help. When you ask the accountants for budget information, you'll get more than you asked for; psychological help will come too. They will be pleased because you asked them for help; have you not implicitly told them they were important to your department? Staff executives who exist to serve the operating executives usually feel unappreciated, but you have come to them for help. Instead of resenting your requests, they will welcome you. A corporate researcher once told me that he regarded a particular sales executive as outstanding not because of his sales record but because "he knows how to use our research."

If you're a promotion man unfamiliar with budgeting, or a financial man unfamiliar with promotion, you'll make friends for yourself, and do a better job for the company, by calling on others to help. The most successful executives are those who enlist the willing cooperation of others to help them solve their problems. Your search for solutions can be turned into a method of making friends throughout the organization. There will be times when you make a wrong decision, and every friend will be needed. When you come up for performance review, they'll be counted in your corner.

9

Decisions—Terror
of the Jungle

SOME DECISIONS an executive must make are no more important than whether to hire a new junior sales trainee. Others involve thousands of men and millions of dollars, like the Bell System's decision to lay an underwater trans-Atlantic telephone cable. The importance of the decision is in relation to the position of the man making it, with the scale of values decreasing rapidly as the executive's position descends on the organization chart.

An executive's ability to make decisions depends, of course, on the authority his superiors have granted to him. In large corporations, this authority is carefully specified in the organization manual. The vice-president in charge of manufacturing may have authority to spend up to $25,000 for capital investment without specific approval of the president. The sales manager may have authority to expand his sales force with no permission needed other than the approval of his annual budget. The department head may have freedom to hire and fire at will when the reason is reduced work volume, but he may be required to clear with the personnel department before firing an employee for poor performance.

In most organizations, however, lines of authority are not so sharply defined. The executive's power to make a decision is often defined by custom and the practices of his colleagues. Limitations on his authority may be undefined and nebulous, but limitations there are, nevertheless.

Some top executives have Napoleonic complexes, and won't yield the smallest measure of authority to their subordinates. Even chief executives experience frustration. The president of a $200-million Midwestern industrial corporation pathetically confessed to me that he had no authority to make decisions without approval of the chairman of the board. His problem was, he confided, that the chairman spent his time 1,500 miles away in the night clubs of New York, and sometimes couldn't be located for days at a time.

The late William Randolph Hearst wouldn't delegate authority either. In the publishing field, his management techniques are legendary. Few decisions were made throughout his vast empire without prior inquiry to his San Simeon command post. By day and night, teletype directives went out to his executive minions, beginning, "Chief says . . ."

That was thirty years ago, but even today there are many like him. The president of a 160-million-dollar consumer goods company insists on personally selecting the type faces and illustrations for his company's advertisements. How can his advertising manager operate as an executive?

I've concluded that many executives have less decision-making authority than they care to admit. What authority they do have is at a considerably lower (and narrower) level than their titles indicate. If you are frustrated by lack of decision-making authority in your present position, you have plenty of company, indeed.

The late John F. Kennedy, with the vast power of the Presidency of the United States, billions of dollars of the Federal Treasury and millions of Federal employees under his control, had at least as many frustrations as you have. James Reston, Washington correspondent of *The New York Times*, described the Presidential frustration in a report of one of Mr. Kennedy's 1962 news conferences:

During the campaign, his major theme was that he was going to "get this country going again." It was, he argued in 1960, a time for innovation in a rapidly changing world and required bold leadership that could put over controversial legislation adequate to the radical new problems of the day.

Today, however, he developed another theme, almost sadly. This was that, even with a one-third majority in both houses of Congress, he was not able to command the support of his own party, and therefore, faced with an increasingly united Republican opposition, he did not have a "working majority" capable of putting over the controversial legislation he felt necessary.

This, then, is the heart of the President's problem: as he sees it, the situation at home and abroad requires legislation that is increasingly controversial, yet the balance of political power between the White House and the Congress (and within the Congress) is so even that he cannot get legislative consent for the program he wants. . . .

Throughout today's news conference, he was constantly dealing with this conflict between what he thought was right and what he thought was politically possible.*

Frustration, as President Johnson has now also learned, is an inherent and inescapable part of the job of being an executive. Many times, you'll know with certainty what ought to be done, but for one reason or another you won't be able to do it.

When that happens, don't react by getting angry at your boss, or by getting angry inside and concealing your fury. Openly expressed anger will endanger your job; repressed anger will endanger your health. It is much better to recognize realistically that frustration is an inherent part of corporate life; that it exists everywhere; and that you must learn to live with it. Your executive decisions must be made within the limits of your authority as it exists, for better or worse. You'll learn to use your existing authority to the limit, probing gently to determine how far you can go without overstepping your boundaries.

* Copyright © 1962 by *The New York Times*. Reprinted from the issue of June 28, 1962, by permission.

I once knew a sales executive who was acutely sensitive to the unspoken limits on his authority. He was skilled at stretching his decision-making power. He had already proved his effectiveness in developing sales for the company's basic product line, but he had always been intrigued by the possibilities of another product, neglected by his management, which had never been assigned to him.

But neither was it clearly assigned to anyone else. Responsibility for this product was divided among a number of executives, and, for many years, it had more or less "sold itself." No one in management considered the product worth important sales effort or financial support, and no one paid more than routine attention to it.

The sales executive believed that, with proper effort, he could develop substantial markets and profits for the product. But he had not received authority to act in this area. Further, he sensed correctly the "climate" of his management: if he openly sought such authority, it would probably not be granted.

So he developed a more subtle strategy. As he described it, he would make a small, unimportant decision regarding the product. It would be a decision that involved a minimum of expense, and it could be easily rationalized to his superiors if they questioned it. He was prepared to drop the matter quickly if eyebrows were raised; if not, he would go on from there.

He took $125 from an unexpended budget item and spent it for a small advertisement in a trade journal. His purchase order form was duly countersigned by his superiors without comment, because of the small size of the expenditure. The ad ran, and it was moderately profitable.

Soon, he found $500 of uncommitted funds, and spent them for the same purpose. This too was approved, and it too produced a modest return on the investment.

Up the ladder he went, still with no questions asked as

the expenditures climbed. When they reached several thousand dollars, his superior, by now accustomed to seeing the item on his purchase orders, asked him casually about it. His reply was to cite the return on the investment already made, and that was all there was to it. The superior was easily satisfied, so his spending continued.

By the end of the first year, the executive had spent more than $100,000, most of which was not budgeted, and which he had never received permission to spend. But the returns were satisfactory, and management now decided to formalize the arrangement with proper budget allocations.

The executive had won his authority the hard way. A misstep probably would have been fatal to his job, but by taking a small step at a time, and proving himself as he went, he was able to get away with it to the benefit of the company and his own position as well. He emerged with expanded power.

The aspiring executive invariably thirsts for power. I've never known an executive who was motivated primarily by the desire for money. But, surprisingly, when the executive gets the power he wanted, he's often reluctant to use it. His reluctance shows itself in hesitation to make decisions. He hems; he haws; he appoints a committee; he awaits "further facts"—anything to avoid making a decision. The executive suites of many of the nation's corporations are full of gray-flanneled fellows with gray-flanneled hearts who fear making decisions about anything more important than the time of the afternoon coffee break.

The reason for the executive's hesitancy isn't hard to guess. Even his secretary discovered the reason the first week she worked for him: he's frightened. His decision may be a wrong one, and then his job would be endangered. So he plays it safe by making no decision at all. And his department drifts along without leadership.

I used to wonder how these fellows could get away with

it, and survive in their jobs year after year, but I finally discovered the all-too-simple answer. They got away with it because that's what their superiors really wanted. A weak superior hadn't wanted a strong subordinate to endanger his position.

While a good executive should make decisions, you had first better take a careful temperature reading to determine the executive climate, and try to estimate what your boss really wants from you. The penalty for a wrong guess can be serious trouble on your job.

Some years ago, an acquaintance of mine worked in a junior executive capacity in a large New York advertising agency. He was capable, creative, and reliable. But he was also a Caspar Milquetoast. He leaned heavily on his superior, never made a decision without clearing it first, and, in general, looked to his boss as to a friendly uncle, or at least a big brother. The boss loved it, and felt very superior.

But one day, a chain of events began independently which disrupted this harmonious relationship. The junior executive quietly mentioned to his superior that he had just divorced his wife.

His boss reacted in the socially approved manner for such occasions. "I don't know whether to console you or to congratulate you," he said, "but whatever it is, I wish you the very best for the future."

And a bright future it was. The second marriage was a good one. For whatever reason, the executive began to feel more sure of himself. When he walked, his shoulders were back, and when he talked, his chin had an imperceptible outward tilt. When he acted, it was more firmly, more decisively.

The boss saw clearly what was happening to his young assistant. And he didn't like what he saw. One day, he struck without warning. "Let's have lunch today," he suggested pleasantly. "Then if we have time, we can go for a little walk."

The luncheon conversation was innocuous, and after dessert and coffee, the two men strolled down the avenue. Without so much as a clearing of the throat, the boss moved in to make his point.

"I've been watching you closely, Pete," the boss murmured. "I don't know if you realize it, but you've been getting awfully cocky lately. You have a fine future with this company—if you can calm down and take it easy. Do you understand what I'm saying?"

Yes, Pete did. He understood what the boss was saying. He also understood what the boss meant, but did not say: "I make the decisions around here, nobody else." Pete learned, fortunately in time, that the boss didn't want a decision-maker in a subordinate capacity. The price for keeping his job was to "act weak," even if he didn't feel weak. He acted weakly for a while, and then one day he quietly picked up and left. Being untrue to himself was a higher price than he was willing to pay to keep the job.

If you don't have that kind of a boss, if you have a boss who really wants you to act, you'd better prepare your ground thoroughly to ensure that your decisions will be good ones.

Some executives follow the military staff custom of preparing decisions. They ask their subordinates to assemble all of the arguments pro and con, which they then evaluate and make a judgment upon. This system works well, but I think it's more effective to ask your subordinates to make their own recommendations to you. They gain valuable experience, and learn to appraise more carefully the consequences of their recommendations, since they know you'll hold them responsible.

Before you can reach effective decisions, you must know clearly the alternatives open to you. What will be the consequences if you transfer a man from one job to the other? What will result from changing the standard procedure for order taking? In facing problems like these, you must also appraise the consequences of doing nothing. What will happen if you leave the man where he is? What will happen if the present

order-taking procedure remains unchanged? You can minimize errors by insisting on such a negative analysis, as well
as a list of possible alternative actions. Standing pat is sometimes the best way to move forward.

Your best decisions will be those which are most objective, that is, made without personal or emotional considerations. Since all of us are filled with personal feelings of every
kind, this is easier said than done. But you can try. You can
consider coldly every argument in favor of a proposed line
of action, eliminating those arguments unsupported by facts,
even though they correspond to your own prejudices. I've
found it a good rule to look for those considerations that
instinctively appealed to me most. Those are the ones I scrutinize most closely, discounting my own prejudices, before I act.

You may have the authority to act, but will your superiors
hold you correspondingly responsible, up to but not exceeding
the limits of your power?

For example, as sales manager of your company, you'll
need, and almost certainly will receive, authority to hire and
fire your sales force. You'll need, and will probably receive,
authority to set salary and compensation plans for your staff.

Under these circumstances, having received necessary
authority, you can and should be held accountable for the
performance of your salesmen. Management is quite within its
rights in judging you by the effectiveness of your sales force.
They may properly evaluate you by the thoroughness with
which your men cover their territories, or by their concentration on the most profitable items in the line, because you had
authority to make policy decisions on these points.

But they should not evaluate your performance as sales
manager on the basis of your sales results alone, if you lacked
authority for key basic policy decisions. Let me illustrate.

Suppose you were a sales manager of a buggy manufacturer back around the turn of the century. You might have
had a fine sales organization, with well-trained and highly

effective salesmen. You might have made all the right decisions about people, promotions, and territories. Your company's sales would nevertheless have declined because of rising
competition from the infant automobile manufacturers. Even
correct decisions would have resulted in declining sales. You
could properly have been measured against the sales performance of other buggy manufacturers, but unless you had authority to switch production to those new-fangled horseless
carriages, the product of the future, you couldn't be blamed
for the drop in sales.

So one rule for survival in the executive jungle is to take
credit for good results only where you made the decisions
that produced those results. If you go beyond this, your claims
will certainly backfire against you. The sales manager in an
automobile company can take proper credit for a good performance of his staff when sales are up, but he had better not
forget that someone else designed this year's model which
caught the public fancy. The controller who recommended
against a new public offering of the company's equities
(because he thought that delay would secure a better price)
should not claim credit for good judgment because stock market prices fell just when the offering would have been made.
He was waiting for a higher price, but instead prices col-
lapsed. It was luck, not his wisdom, that prevented a debacle
to the struggling new company.

Some of your decisions are bound to be wrong. The government has made them (the Bay of Pigs); corporations have
made them (the Edsel); and so have you and I. I remember the
cynical comment of a World War II infantry rifleman whose
perspective of the Grand Strategy was limited to three hundred yards of battlefront in front of him. "The only reason
we're winning this war," he said, "is that the Nazi lieutenants
make more damn fool mistakes than ours do."

Like most other executives, I've been burned several times
by my own bad decisions. My analyses accurately presented

the consequences of alternate actions, but the premises on which they were based proved incorrect. In one case, a company's sales were slipping badly in the face of the much greater advertising and promotional budgets of its competitors. The alternative recommendations suggested various ways by which this company could expand its advertising with maximum impact. One proposal suggested more trade paper advertising. Another urged greater use of direct mail promotion. A third recommended an increase in the sales force itself.

All three recommendations assumed that the competitors' larger advertising budgets had caused their growing sales. In fact, this was not correct. Further investigation showed that the company had followed harsh credit practices which compared unfavorably with its competitors', and which wreaked hardship on its customers. None of the alternative proposals would have resulted in a correct decision, because the original premise on which they were based was incorrect. You can avoid errors like this by challenging constantly the premises on which the recommendations have been based.

Your boss knows, even more surely than you, that you will make mistakes. When errors occur, my advice is to admit them freely. Your heart will be in your throat the first time, but tell your boss quietly why you made the mistake, what you've learned from it, and what steps you've taken to prevent a repetition.

Curiously, your superior will probably react sympathetically to your candid honesty. He won't expect your forthrightness, because few people are strong enough to admit their errors. Since your superior may consider himself infallible, he can take assurance that your error proves he's wiser than you. Let it be so, if that's the way he wants it. Further, by establishing your integrity now, at a later date when you report good news, he'll be more inclined to accept it and give you generous credit. I've never heard of an executive fired for an error honestly made and forthrightly admitted.

But if your boss reacts harshly to your confession of guilt, get out of his office, and get out of his company just as quickly as you can find another job. It isn't the place for an honest man.

Ironically, if your decisions were right ones, which brought favorable consequences for the company, you may unexpectedly face a more difficult problem. You expect your superior to rejoice with you, and perhaps he will. On the other hand, some top executives react quite differently. One gentleman I knew winced involuntarily every time he heard favorable news from a subordinate; he feared the junior's successes would make him superfluous and endanger his job.

If you can anticipate this reaction, be prepared to minimize your part in the original decision. Give generous credit to others who participated. Or you may do still better by recalling a casual conversation of months before. At that time, your superior suggested an idea that eventually led to your decision. Give him credit for the correct decision, and he'll feel proud that he selected a subordinate like you with the good sense to capitalize on his ideas. If it's really the truth (and I don't suggest falsehood), you'll emerge in a much stronger position than if you had claimed all the credit for the correct move.

Decision-making, your key function as an executive, can be an exciting game. There are sometimes penalties for making right decisions as well as for making wrong ones. Penalties may be imposed for doing nothing, or too much. The winner is the man who faces the problems objectively, choosing his course calmly from the variety of alternatives open to him.

IO

Followers Make
the Leader

You can't dodge responsibility for your own staff. If they do a good job, you'll receive credit for their performance. If one of them botches things up, you're the one who will be called on the carpet by your superior. At the beginning, after you've just taken over your new position, the boss will be somewhat indulgent, because your department had already been staffed before you entered the picture. He will understand that it requires time before you know your subordinates well enough to evaluate them. But after several months, the honeymoon will be over. From then on, the company will hold you accountable for their performance. So you must look objectively at each person on your staff to decide whether his work justifies his continuance in the department.

If you conclude that one employee is not satisfactory, you may be able to transfer him to another post or another department within the company. His departure will create a vacancy. Or perhaps your first vacancy will be created by expansion of your department's activities. However it happens, for the first time you find yourself with the task of hiring. It is an exciting opportunity to select the first person of your choice for the new organization you have begun building.

Building your own staff is certainly one of the most

satisfying parts of an executive's job. You don't often have the opportunity to hire, because if your choice is a good one, the new employee will remain with you for a long time. If he performs so well that he subsequently wins internal promotion (even though outside of your department), it is a tribute to your judgment and objectivity. In some large United States corporations, there are veteran executives who themselves first won top management attention by consistently choosing outstanding candidates who moved up the ranks quickly. If your man moves out of your realm and up the corporate ladder, you should count it as a victory, and not as a loss.

The man you select from the available candidates will reveal a good deal about you to your superiors. The ubiquitous management consultants say that they can assess a department head accurately by talking with the subordinates he hired. The timid, uncertain executive will always, without exception, hire timid and uncertain subordinates, men who will not threaten his position by any unwanted boldness of action. If a strong-minded individual managed to squirm through the hiring sieve and enter the ranks of the department, the newcomer would be a most unhappy person. His qualities would be neither welcomed nor appreciated by his frightened boss.

Your prejudices of all kinds may also show in your selection. If your own experience is narrow, and your viewpoint provincial rather than broad, you may—perhaps without knowing it—tend to prefer, for instance, job applicants from small towns, rather than from New York or Chicago. If you are a WASP (white, Anglo-Saxon, Protestant), you may feel more comfortable with others of similar ancestry, ruling out those of Latin or other backgrounds. If you attended an Ivy League college, you may find it difficult to believe that a state or municipal university could produce men and women of ability and promise.

If you search your soul and find such prejudices, please

don't feel too terrible about it. You're not the only one. All of us are laden with such prejudices from the time of our childhood. Nobody expects you to dump them overboard suddenly now that you've become an executive. If you recognize honestly that you harbor such prejudices (or preferences, if you feel more comfortable with that word), it will be much easier for you to deal with them. Self-honesty will usually prevent them from getting in your way.

Right in New York, entire companies reflect the prejudices of a few men in their senior managements. One company is dominated by Southerners; another is largely staffed by Jews; another by Irish Catholics. One company prefers graduates of small-town colleges. Still another employs only Midwesterners. Most, of course, will hire only whites for executive posts, state law to the contrary. It isn't a question of formal policies alone. Once the pattern is established, friends tell friends, and eventually the friends apply to the company where they may work with "folks just like those back home."

The result is corporate inbreeding, a process that deprives the company of the most able men it can get, in favor of the most able WASPS, or Jews, or Catholics, or whites, or Southerners, or whatever. It's the company's loss most of all.

Now that you're in the driver's seat and need to find the best help you can get, you might well begin by making every effort to overcome your ingrained prejudice. Good men are so scarce that it just doesn't make sense to handicap yourself needlessly in your search. If you find the right man, no one will even notice six months later, if he's done a bang-up job for the company, that he doesn't have the "correct" ancestry or race.

We all tend to select employees who are like ourselves, because unconsciously we feel more comfortable with them. Our natural tendency should be resisted. Sometimes, however, this tendency is reinforced by the psychological consultants who wait in the wings, and who press their services on managements with exaggerated claims unworthy of the scientific fraternity. I'm thinking here of one psychologist who assured management that he had a sure-fire way of improving their selection of candidates for executive posts. The method was simple, he said. Just find out what qualities it takes to ensure success, and measure executive applicants against that yardstick.

How would he determine what qualities would ensure success? Ah, that was the heart of his method! He would study those in the company who had already achieved success, and determine their qualities. That would be the yardstick. Candidates would be measured for those qualities.

The psychologist lost no time in explaining whom he considered "had achieved success." They were the heads of the firm and the six or eight top executives. It was a none too subtle appeal to the egos of his prospective clients. They responded properly, and he won the assignment.

Such a method provided a pseudoscientific justification for continuing to hire executives who fitted the existing pattern. It also established incorrect criteria for the positions to be filled. The heads of the firm were successful entrepreneurs. They were bold men, accustomed to taking risks and to providing leadership. But the posts to be filled did not need similar qualities, for at the junior level where the openings existed, it was important that the new executives be able to take direction from above, as well as to provide it to the ranks below. The top executives, had they been employees, would probably have failed in the junior positions because they enjoyed giving orders; psychologically they were unsuited to receiving them. As entrepreneurs, they did not need this quality.

Beneath the principals, however, the next level of "successful" executives in the company presented a different pattern. They were second-rate men, all submissive in personality, and accustomed to accepting firm direction from the senior management. Not one among them had displayed the character-istics of a leader, because the firm's principals had discouraged them from displaying leadership. They were unaccustomed to making decisions, because top management had made all the decisions. They were inexperienced in hiring and firing, be-cause top management had done it for them. These were the "successful" executives on whom the psychologist proposed to construct an ideal profile of the desired executive!

To begin with, it was like adding oranges and apples in the same column. The psychologist could hardly construct a meaningful composite of desirable characteristics from the combination of the company's heads and its executive group, because they had little in common. That he tried to do so only testifies to the professional limitations of this particular consultant.

Other consultants to this same company (but not psychol-ogists) reported that the firm needed a different type of exec-utive to enable it to grow. They suggested men who wanted to exercise authority and responsibility, men who could make decisions and execute them. Such men, they felt, would stimu-late a revitalization of the entire enterprise.

Such men were not to be found in the company. Such men are attracted to executive opportunities only where they have freedom to operate aggressively. Throughout the business community in Kansas City (where this incident occurred), the company was known in executive circles as a company with weak management. So the best men stayed away.

The psychologist's formula ensured that they would re-main away. His tests and interviews were designed with pro-fessional skill to select men who would conform to the existing pattern. Altogether, it was a sorry experience, and, to this day, the company in question has failed to break out of its rut. It's difficult enough for any of us to break out of our patterns of conformity; we hardly need the help of this kind of "psychology" to reinforce them when we hire our staff.

Before you begin searching for a new employee, you should know what you want. What job do you need to fill? What qualities should the successful candidate possess? Exactly what will the new man do? What skills or experience should he bring to the job? All these questions must be answered before you search to find him.

They aren't always answered in advance, however. Herbert Newman, a financial executive who found himself a solid position after several months of unemployment, reported that executives of several different companies had said to him, in almost identical words, "We'd like to have you here. Would you please think over the situation and tell us what you think the job ought to be?" He did just that, and won his executive post by providing an intelligent answer.

That isn't job-filling. It isn't matching candidate to requirements. It is, rather, a transfer of confusion from the executive to the applicant. You can avoid such ineptness only by pinning down the job definition before you talk with any applicant. You don't have to write it in formal, bureaucratic English. You may provide the personnel department with nothing more than an itemized listing of the specific activities the person will be expected to perform during a single week.

Too often, the department head asks the personnel office only for a sales executive with experience in a similar field. Or he wants a man with experience in dealing with advertising agencies. The personnel department then begins searching for appropriate candidates, only to be told by the executive that none has quite the right qualifications. Four weeks later, after forty candidates and four hundred résumés have been found and sent to him, the department head decides none of the applicants has had sufficient experience. He tells the personnel department he now will require five to ten years' experience as a qualification. They duly screen out applicants of lesser experience.

But one day on the golf course, the executive meets a

friend who tells him of an unusual man with an outstanding sales record in an entirely different industry. In only three years of selling, this man has proved himself a "hard driver" and thoroughly successful. The golf partner makes a date for the employer and candidate to meet, and the candidate proves so impressive that he's soon hired. When the papers are sent to the personnel department for processing, the personnel man throws up his hands in disgust. The successful candidate meets none of the specifications previously agreed on.

The good will and assistance of the personnel department can be valuable to you. You should avoid dissipating it by such shennanigans. Personnel will help you find the best qualified candidate if you tell them as much as you possibly can about the job. The more precisely you describe the duties of the position, the easier it will be for them to search. You may also describe the kind of a man you envision filling it, but this is secondary to the duties of the job. You may expect a young man for the post, but perhaps Personnel will produce an outstanding older applicant available only because his company has just gone out of business. Or you may assume that your post requires previous experience in the same industry; yet the best qualified candidate may turn out to be a man who has dealt with similar problems in an entirely different field.

How important is functional experience? To most companies, it is the weightiest single factor. Each management insists that its set of problems is unique, and requires that the applicant be thoroughly familiar with them. I think this factor is highly overrated. When I was a public relations consultant, the chief executives of many corporations told me independently that their problems were especially difficult of solution because their businesses were so unusual. None would ever accept the suggestion that their problems resembled those of another industry with which I had previously worked. But my experience convinced me that most management problems have a counterpart in other companies and other industries. Since that time, I have minimized the importance of identical experience in hiring. Of course, I seek someone who has demonstrated the ability to solve problems similar to those he will face in the new position. But this is a broad interpretation of experience. It isn't the same as requiring that your winning candidate have performed similar or identical work in a comparable post. Such a qualification may eliminate an able man who could contribute much toward the success of your department.

Before you begin interviewing candidates, you should have not only a precise description of the job, but also a definite job to fill. I am not stating the obvious. Certain companies, and executives within them, seem to be constantly interviewing candidates for jobs that don't exist and probably never will. It is a waste of their time, and a discourtesy and inconsideration to the candidate. Just last week, Frank McGroarty, a dynamic sales executive, told me what had happened to him.

Many months ago, he received a phone call asking if he would be interested in discussing a top executive post. The annual salary was in the range of what Dun & Bradstreet would call "middle five-figures."* He expressed serious but cautious interest. As a result, a dinner meeting was arranged with the president of a leading advertising agency. The president described the position as that of an assistant to the president, to call on leading national advertisers and acquaint them with the merits of the particular agency. Selection of an advertising agency is usually a long-term consideration. It is not decided on impulse. So, said the president, "you wouldn't be expected to get any new clients immediately. We want someone who'll be able to acquaint the top management of major companies with our work, and get them to think of us some time in the future when they're considering a change." It looked like a dream position, and the president whetted

* Between $40,000 and $60,000.

Mr. McGroarty's appetite by casually mentioning an unlimited expense account.

They talked long and hard that night, so absorbed in their conversation that they failed to savor a magnificently prepared steak Chauteaubriand. As they left the restaurant, and Mr. McGroarty hailed a passing taxi, the president promised he'd call him soon. "We're anxious to make a decision," he added.

In the weeks that followed, Mr. McGroarty encountered occasional evidence that he was indeed under serious consideration for the post. The president had begun to check his references, and several friends duly reported his call to Mr. McGroarty. One day, a banker friend encountered him on the commuter train, and mentioned that the president had called to check his financial rating. His hopes grew.

But nothing happened. Mr. McGroarty did not wish to jeopardize his chances by appearing too anxious for the job. At the same time, he thought he ought to show evidence that he really wanted it. So one day he telephoned the president.

"I don't like to bother you," he said, "but I thought you could tell me where things stand. I'm trying to make my own plans, and that's difficult to do when there's the possibility I may be coming over to join you in a couple of weeks."

The president sounded a trifle embarrassed. "That's all right," he replied. "I'm glad you called, Mr. McGroarty. The job is still unfilled, and you're very much in the running. In fact, I'd say that you're our number one candidate as of now. But we're not quite sure exactly what we want. Why don't you talk with Howard Belson [the executive vice-president] and get his thoughts?"

The candidate promptly phoned Mr. Belson, who confirmed the president's description and added further details.

"I'm going to be frank with you, because we really want you. We've just lost a couple of big accounts. The pressure is on us to add some new business. I don't think we can afford the luxury of adding an expensive man to our payroll just to cultivate long-term good will for the agency. It may be a couple of years before it pays off, and we can't afford to wait." Mr. Belson continued, "Our thinking right now is that we need a high-powered man who can call on major prospects, give them a great presentation, and sign them on the dotted line. We think you're the right man for that, but we are interviewing other candidates."

Nine weeks of silence passed, and finally Mr. McGroarty again called Mr. Belson to find out what had happened.

"Oh, sorry I didn't get back to you," Mr. Belson cheerily replied. "We finally decided to do nothing on that spot. Business is off, and we figured we couldn't afford the extra payroll expense right now. Thanks anyway."

Mr. McGroarty barely restrained himself from slamming down the receiver. His hopes had been built up and then dashed, in anticipation of a position that never existed. The agency executives had wasted their time and his, and they had not made a friend.

A real change in circumstances may have necessitated this company change of plans, but perhaps the entire episode could have been avoided. When the president began talking with Mr. McGroarty, a definite opening did not exist. That's not too unusual; it often happens that candidates for a top post will be considered informally before the position is officially opened. But by the time Mr. Belson, the executive vice-president, had got into the act, the specifications had been changed completely. The job he envisioned was a different one. In the end, there was no job at all.

I wouldn't mention this story if it were unique or even unusual. But it happens all the time. Frank McGroarty told me this was the third time he had experienced what he called the "shifting sands" treatment. I asked him to write me his comments.

"They ought to make up their minds first," he said in his letter. "It was a complete waste of my time and theirs.

Before they start talking to people, even if they're not sure they're going to fill the job, they ought to know what they're supposedly looking for. Then they can measure me, or anybody else, against it. If they change their minds, they ought to have the decency to let me know promptly, instead of leaving me hanging. As for this outfit, the hell with them. I should have taken it as a warning when they couldn't make up their minds. This gang might have hired me into the first job they talked about, and then changed their minds after I was in it. Then I would have been out of a job all over again." He signed the letter, "Yours in anger, Frank McGroarty."

The manager of a highly regarded New York executive recruiting firm confirmed that Mr. McGroarty's story was not unusual. "I'm constantly amazed by the inability of executives to know what help they need," he told me. "They change their minds, switch back and forth, and reveal their complete lack of understanding of the actual needs of their own departments. One Boston executive asked me to help fill a particular post. For six and a half months, I kept sending him candidates, but none was right. Meanwhile, he kept looking elsewhere. Other executive searchers sent him candidates too. Every other Thursday, he'd come to New York and make a weekend out of it by scheduling interviews for Friday and Monday. But he never had time to see me to discuss the candidates or tell me why they weren't right. He contradicted himself in describing the opening to the applicants; many of them reported back to me afterwards. Finally I decided he was deliberately stalling, either because he enjoyed his New York weekends on the corporate expense account, or because of just plain cotton-pickin' ignorance. Anyway, he got canned, and justly so."

If you have a definite position to fill, and authorization from your management to proceed, you should try to fill it as quickly as you can. "As quickly as you can" means as quickly as you can find a man who will, according to your best judgment, meet the needs of the position. You don't want to settle for a man who's barely adequate, but neither do you want to hold out endlessly in the hope that a better candidate will come along. If you wait another month, it is entirely possible that you'll find a few more candidates, and one of them may be better than anybody you've interviewed up to that point. But maybe not. Meanwhile, your outstanding applicant may have accepted a position elsewhere. It's a good idea, therefore, to set at least a tentative target date (you can always change it), and make your decision speedily as soon as you've found a good man.

When you yourself seek a position, the openings seem few and the other candidates overwhelming in number. You may despair because other candidates seem better qualified and more experienced than you. But now as an executive, when you try to fill a position, the candidates seem unobtainable, and the number of other employers competing for their services, overwhelming. You despair because your company can't afford to offer the high pay or the job security with which larger corporations entice the best candidates.

To find a well-qualified man for your opening, you need several candidates from whom to choose. If only one or two present themselves, you don't have much of a choice. If you complain to the company's personnel department, and ask them to produce more applicants, they'll tell you they're trying, "but please be patient because the labor market is so tight." You'll get this answer whether the job pays $5,000 or $25,000.

After you've waited another week, it's time to holler. You need help now, not next year. Ask the personnel department what they are doing to attract suitable candidates. In what newspapers have they advertised? To what employment agencies and executive search firms have they talked? Have they contacted the professional organizations? How many candidates have already visited the personnel office? Why were they rejected?

Sometimes, the orthodoxy of corporate personnel departments casts aside the off-beat applicant or individualist who may be the very person you want. The résumés of such people don't conform to the traditional pattern, and they are discarded instead of being sent on to you.

The most striking approach of this type I've ever seen was made by a young public relations executive in New York. She broke through the personnel barriers by sending her unusual application directly to 225 company presidents. It was before the craze for "executive coloring books." She prepared a twelve-page brightly illustrated booklet, titled, "The 'How to succeed in business by really trying' Coloring Book."

It started off like this:

"My name is Betty Vaughn. I am an executive. I am looking for an executive position. Color me gray."

It went on to describe her employment history.

"I worked for the Steubenville *Herald-Star*. That's a newspaper in Ohio. I wrote stories. All kinds. Found small-town life not to my liking. So I came to New York. Color me Ambitious.

Four pages later, a cartoon showed Miss Vaughn sitting on a curb dejectedly. "Big chance came with new public relations firm. Firm going places—and me with them. Firm folded. Not my fault. Color me blue."

Finally came the closing. "Now I'm with a big industrial design firm. I'm in charge of promotion. I attend meetings, write memos, handle the budget, write direct mail, brochures, and presentations. Big budget for department. Too little budget for me.

"Don't color me. Call me."

Apparently the presidents did, because Miss Vaughn received sixty-eight replies, which led to thirty interviews, and finally ended with four firm job offers. I don't know what would have happened had she applied to agency personnel departments, and I doubt whether her technique would have been successful outside of the promotional field. You ought to be certain that such fresh approaches aren't discarded by corporate bureaucrats before you yourself get the opportunity to meet the candidates personally.

If the personnel department produces few candidates, you'll accomplish nothing by merely needling them, but you may be able to help them with specific suggestions. For instance, one company involved in the Project Apollo program sought to recruit electronics engineers. An engineer who was in the habit of listening to concert music late at night suggested to the personnel department that they advertise for applicants on an FM radio symphonic music program instead of using the usual newspaper and magazine advertising. The personnel department had never previously used such unorthodox methods, but they tried it, and successfully.

When they locate several candidates worth your serious consideration, you're ready for the next stage, a personal interview. Of course, you'll want to see the applicants promptly (Why next Monday? Why not tomorrow?) to eliminate delays that might lose the best man to a competitor. Try to see them as close together as conveniently possible, for you can make better comparisons while the memory of each is fresh in your mind. It would be preferable to interview one applicant in the morning, and another in the afternoon, rather than one each on successive days.

Finally, after the appointments have been set, you wait for the first candidate to show up. Maybe you'll be lucky and will find the man you want in the very first interview. Hope springs eternal in the executive breast. But don't jump to a quick conclusion, and make a mistake.

By acting too quickly, I've made some dillies. Once I hired a man I had known in business for many years. My entire contact with him had been in business situations; I had never socialized with him. My high opinion of him developed from his skillful handling of several business matters.

After he had been in a top executive job for only one week, I realized I had made a serious error of judgment. My perspective on his abilities had been incomplete, and I had compounded the error by failing to check with his previous employers. I had assumed I knew him well enough to make reference checks unnecessary. But five days at his desk was enough to make it apparent, beyond any reasonable doubt, that he was totally inadequate for his new responsibilities. I waited two weeks more to be overwhelmingly certain, and then had the painful task of telling him so.

When you once make a bad judgment of this kind, you naturally are reluctant to hazard a repeat performance. The second time, you may find yourself strapped by indecision. This time you think you've found the right man, but you're not sure. So you set the matter aside for a while, leaving the applicant to perspire with anxiety.

But there's no foolproof way of ensuring 100 percent successful selection. You may screen and interview, check and recheck, but nevertheless you're certain to err occasionally. No one has yet figured out a way to predict with unfailing accuracy the performance of the human animal in a particular situation. His behavior on the job may only be estimated in advance, and the job itself may differ from advance descriptions. The personnel specialists can make tentative predictions; a computer might estimate the odds for success, but there is still a strong element of gambling involved.

All you can hope is that you make more good appointments than bad ones. If you've defined the job requirements accurately, and tried honestly to eliminate your prejudices, you'll score better than 51 percent to begin with, and, as time goes on, your experience will raise the percentage of successful selection.

Don't Give
Your Head to
the Psychologist

THE CALM, smooth, self-assured corporate psychologist, the man who makes everybody nervous, is a familiar figure on the management scene. Surrounded by awe, and surmounted by a halo of mystical infallibility, he has by now achieved veto power over many executive appointments. To reach your present position, you probably passed his scrutiny, and won his qualified approval. He never gives anyone unqualified approval. If you had the unlikely opportunity of examining his evaluation of you, which is now locked in the personnel department safe, you'd probably discover that he approved you only "with reservations."

While he has reservations about you, however, he has none about himself. He is utterly confident that he can help management avoid costly mistakes in hiring, and thus save tens or hundreds of thousands of dollars a year. He presents his case to management, well armed with a doctor's bag filled with impressive psychological tests, and supplemented by horror stories describing what happened to other companies when they picked the wrong man. Such mistakes are unnecessary, he declares quietly. Science knows how to evaluate a

133

man, to learn his inner strains and weakness, to determine whether he'll be successful on the job. Science has developed techniques to study job candidates, and to learn more about them than the most skilled interviewer. For a modest fee, ranging from 15 dollars a candidate to a "retainer fee" of thousands of dollars a year, he'll "be able" to make this scientific knowledge available to the employer. Since most senior executives lack the "benefit" of scientific training in psychology, and since they won't have to take the tests themselves, they usually prove an easy mark for the low-pressure, high-intensity salesmanship of the commercial psychologists. Soon, the psychologist has established himself in a visiting office in the personnel department with his tests, ink blots, disassembled cartoon strips, children's drawing paper, and sets of play blocks ready for use.

How much weight should you give to his counsel? That depends on his own qualifications. If he is a promoter-turned-psychologist, or a movie-film-salesman-turned-psychologist, with no professional training in psychology, his words of wisdom merit no special consideration.

Such "psychologists" have purchased standard tests from publishers, together with instructions on the right questions to ask. They are not handicapped by lack of training. There are many such, and they have found good livelihoods in the psychological industry.

They lose no opportunity to let management know when their predictions prove correct. Typical was the man who tested the industrial sales force of a New Jersey pump manufacturer. After his "research," the psychologist predicted to management, among other things, that Robert Crissan, a salesman, would soon quit the company. The forecast came as a surprise to the executives, for the man in question was a high producer, the company's most effective salesman—and one of the best paid. Less than a year later, Crissan made the prediction come true by announcing his resignation to take a better job elsewhere. The company tried to induce him to change his mind, but to no avail.

"You see, I was right," the psychologist reminded the executives. "I could tell that he was discontented. It was no surprise to *me*." His reminder won renewal of his consulting contract for another year.

I happened to know both the psychologist and the salesman personally, although neither knew I was acquainted with the other. So I asked the salesman, Bob Crissan, to give me his version.

"I had been dissatisfied for a long time," Bob told me as we sat in his new office. "The company had been falling behind the competition, and I knew it better than management because I was out on the firing line. We hadn't brought out a new product in years, while other firms were releasing newer designs, more efficient pumps, and at lower prices."

"Maybe you didn't have the whole picture," I suggested. "Perhaps there were plans you didn't know anything about."

"No," he replied firmly. "I did know their plans. They told us exactly what their plans were. At our annual sales meeting, the president said they were going to stick with their present products as long as possible. They couldn't afford to tool up for a new line right now."

I asked Bob how the psychologist, who had never met him before (and who knew nothing about the industrial pump business), discovered his state of mind.

"Hell," he declared, "I told him right out. I said I was dissatisfied and that I'd leave if some basic changes in company policies weren't made."

"Why did it take a psychologist to tell management of your dissatisfaction?"

Bob snorted. "I told them," he said, "many times. But they never listened. It wasn't what they wanted to hear. They told me to stick to selling and let them worry about the product. They took the psychologist's warning as a sign to watch me closely instead of watching themselves. Well, it's too late now. I've switched to a company that's on the move, and I'll have no trouble beating my last year's sales figures."

It's unreasonable to criticize the psychologist in this case. He heard the warning and passed it on to management. A management decision was needed, not a psychological analysis. The failure was management's. Claiming credit for hitherto unseen symptoms, however, was nothing less than fraud wrapped up in a pseudoprofessional package.

There are honest psychologists too, some superbly skilled; others, well-intentioned incompetents. If your management expects you to use the services of the company psychologist in selecting your staff members, it's quite proper to inquire for evidence of his professional qualifications and success. He may be able to tell you how many successful candidates he selected for another company, but somehow he does not know how many candidates he rejected who subsequently succeeded in comparable posts elsewhere—"there's no way I could find that out." In the absence of scientific documentation, you should regard him as possessing something less than scientific infallibility.

But if his professional record is truly outstanding, and he manifests genuine integrity, there's no doubt that he may bring unique contributions to the corporation. As a result of his professional training, he'll be able to tell you quite accurately about an applicant you wish to hire. His interview report will describe the applicant's personality in detail and depth. Again and again I've pulled out musty files from the company safe and have been impressed that a skilled psychologist accurately delineated a candidate's personality at the time of employment. He spotted the man who hated his father, and who ever since has gone through life hating every boss he ever had. He detected the fellow who was dominated by his mother, and whose working career has been consistently marked by inability to work satisfactorily with women. He duly noted the man whose insecurities had developed a working pattern of "playing it safe," avoiding controversies and never initiating anything.

You can find it all there in his neatly typed report, sent to you in a plain brown sealed envelope marked "personal and confidential."

The psychologist didn't find it difficult to learn what he needed to know about your candidate, because he is trained to capitalize on the Great American Tradition of blabbering. Without the benefit of all his magical tools and professional mumbo-jumbo, you could have learned almost as much by careful listening and intelligent questioning. The psychologist has learned from experience, unlike most of us, that an applicant will talk and talk and talk if given the opportunity.

The layman finds this hard to believe, but the psychologist knows it's true. Back in the mid-fifties, interviewers from the University of Michigan Survey Research Center under a Rockefeller Foundation grant questioned more than two thousand married women in detail about their sex habits and family planning practices. In the words of the editors of *Fortune*, "the interviewers reported that virtually all the wives they spoke to were remarkably cooperative, and were willing to discuss frankly even such intimate subjects as their contraceptive practices."*

The Michigan interviewers discovered a line of privacy beyond which they could not intrude. It reflected a peculiar concept about what was too personal to discuss with a stranger. "Many wives who freely answered several dozen questions about contraception said the interviewer was getting 'too personal' when she asked questions about the family's income."

Ordinarily, the psychologist will be uninterested in money (your income, not his own). But since he is working for top management, usually the president, his standards must reflect the attitudes and prejudices of the president. If they don't, the psychologist will soon find himself without a valued client,

---

* From "The Markets of the Sixties," reprinted by courtesy of *Fortune* magazine.

and may have to return to the less profitable business of meas-
uring the reactions of rats in a maze. So he applies the president's standards. They may be what he thinks the company
needs, and they may be right, but this isn't scientific objectivity.

We can discover what the president wants by studying the
standard written tests which are widely used in many corporations. The man the president wants, the ideal executive, is the
conventional individual, the conformist, the "square." He is a
handsome, well-groomed, polished young man of slightly
better than average intelligence and slightly more than average drive.

The presidents of some of those same companies see themselves with no more realism than they visualize the ideal
executive. One of them, Morris Speizman, a North Carolina
machinery manufacturer, described "The Boss" in these
flowery words:

Really to qualify for the title, The Boss must first of all be a
dedicated man. He is usually happily married to an understanding
woman, but he has an equally strong love for his job. It is not
merely a way for making money; it is a fascinating chess game,
combined with a table stakes poker game, with a touch of pure
poetry thrown in for good measure. The poetry that I speak of is
the fitting together of the diverse pieces made up of ideas, things,
and people which The Boss daily rearranges and develops into a
finished lyric of coordination.

The Boss sees himself as a gentle poet, but detached observers know that an iron will, driving power, courage, and
a touch of ruthlessness are often essential ingredients of executive success. The Boss, however, doesn't want these same
qualities in his subordinates. The psychologists are only too
happy to eliminate them. "The worst of it is," says consultant
Richard Enion, "some of the excluders are people who reached
the top on the basis of drive and unorthodoxy which they
don't want in subordinates."

If some of your fellow executives are mediocrities, it may

not be accidental. Maybe that's the kind of man the president wants. It may be a warning signal to you. If other executives don't exercise dynamic leadership, top management may not want it, and won't look kindly on you if you attempt to provide it.

Presidential preferences aside, what qualities does a particular job require? At lower levels, it's not difficult to determine. A key punch operator, for instance, must sit hour after hour, read statistical information (in plain English, numbers), and operate a keyboard to punch holes in an IBM card. The simple, repetitive, tedious operation requires modest intelligence plus the ability to withstand boredom. Add manual dexterity, and you have all the qualities needed for satisfactory work performance.

But the executive's duties become less definable. The job specification sheet, prepared by the personnel department, often bears little resemblance to the actual work he will do. The executive's main task is to motivate the people on his staff, so that a man who can stimulate others will be the ideal choice. Suppose, however, a young man displays only moderate skill in dealing with people, but excels in the ability to organize the work efficiently. This combination may put him ahead of the man who can win enthusiastic cooperation from his staff, yet is utterly disorganized in his personal habits. Or perhaps an executive possesses the ability to stimulate his subordinates effectively, but simultaneously lacks the ability to get along with his superior. Will he succeed or not? The answer can't be foretold. Further, a given combination of abilities may prove successful at one time, and fail at another, because changing business conditions affect the position itself. No wonder the psychologists fail so frequently in trying to predict what will happen when a particular man is placed in a particular job.

And the dimensions of an executive job aren't rigidly fixed. You'll change the job to the extent that you differ from your predecessor. You'll emphasize certain aspects at the expense of others, reflecting your own strengths and weaknesses. If the definitions were compiled on the basis of the way your predecessor shaped his duties, you may fail to fulfill those demands and yet still succeed in your own way.

If the psychologists were to stop after describing the job applicant's personality, they and the business community would be a lot better off. But they don't. They proceed to evaluate their findings, and to predict whether or not the applicant will succeed in the job. This is where they cast science aside and go off the deep end. One top executive discovered this when he submitted himself, bravely and anonymously, to the standard tests given to executives in his own company. The results were a shock. W. Maxey Jarman, who as president and later board chairman built Genesco, Inc., to a 400-million-dollar company, was found by the psychologists to be too shy and self-conscious ever to deal successfully with people.*

If the "doctors" had described Mr. Jarman as shy and self-conscious, they might have been accurate. (I say "might have been" because I've never met Mr. Jarman.) But when they went on to assert that he would be unable to deal successfully with people, they were crystal-ball-gazing, rather than stating discovered facts. To rub salt in the wound, the psychologists warned that Mr. Jarman "could" be a failure in management. They were talking through their Ph.D.'s.

For to know whether a candidate will succeed in a particular job, two sets of facts are required: a knowledge of the candidate, and a knowledge of the job. The two can then be compared and a judgment reached. The psychologists "knew" Mr. Jarman, but they did not know what his job required. So they went beyond their professional competence and made a guess, not a scientific conclusion. The result was an embarrassment and a failure.

Martin L. Gross, in his carefully researched study, *The*

* As reported in *Women's Wear Daily,* April 8, 1963.

Brain Watchers, lists a whole series of failures by the psychologists.* He tells how Army "experts" during World War II eliminated one million men, the equivalent of fifty-five divisions, from military service. Veterans will remember one question in psychological screening: "Do you like boys better than girls?" After the war, when the records were restudied, the conclusion was that "the screen was not very effective and it had little predictive value."

Other branches of the armed services reached the same conclusion. The Office of Strategic Services conducted the most time-consuming and thorough psychological tests in history. More than five thousand men under consideration for undercover service were exhaustively analyzed. After V-J Day, the OSS found the tests had failed completely. "None of our statistical computations demonstrates that our system of assessment was of great value," the OSS declared after the war was over.

On Madison Avenue, the advertising agencies likewise learned the hard way that the psychologists were unable to predict success or failure on the job. After World War II, the American Association of Advertising Agencies tested seven thousand job applicants, and made careful follow-ups during the next five years. In 1956, they abandoned the program in failure, and Gross quotes a AAAA spokesman, "Sizeable numbers of men rated both good and bad ended up in the advertising business, anyway. And from what we could learn, they were apparently doing well."

The life insurance industry had a similar experience. The Life Insurance Agency Management Association, which has tested more than a million applicants in the past thirty years, says none of its personality standards have predicted anything "for some time." Despite this, however, the tests are being continued because they help the industry "to gauge person-

* *The Brain Watchers*, by Martin L. Gross, Random House, New York, 1962.

ality." Gauging personality, one might add, can indeed be done by the psychologists, but it's a lot less than their claimed ability to predict success on the job.

The OSS psychologists decided, for instance, that they needed "team players" and "men of good will"; actually, as Gross points out, they might have done better with "highly neurotic GI's anxious to fulfill their boyhood dreams of playing 'spy.' " The life insurance psychologists may have been seeking salesmen "who like people and who like to deal with them," but other psychologists observe that many professional salesmen actually dislike people. Inwardly they regard selling as an opportunity to overcome an enemy (the customer). Several years of successful sales experience might prove a more reliable indicator of future selling success than a man's score in the psychological tests. But if this idea ever caught hold, it would halt the booming growth of the psychological industry.

So work with the company psychologist to the limit of his qualifications, but no further. If properly trained, he's skilled at understanding human behavior. He can delve deeply into the motivations of your applicants. His description of the candidates' personality, combined with your own interview (and perhaps with interviews with one or two of your associates), will give you a more rounded picture on which to make a judgment. All of this, together with a thorough reference check, will present a balanced picture of the candidates.

The psychologist can indeed help you make good personnel choices. But he isn't a businessman. He doesn't bear responsibility for the growth and profitability of your company, or for the successful operation of your department. He is not an oracle, but a guide. His counsel must be weighed along with many other factors before you decide whether to hire a particular man.

12

Initiation
Rites—
and Wrongs

Now THE TIME has come to make your own judgment. Your secretary enters, and pleasantly announces that the applicant, Mr. Rhody, has arrived for his appointment and is waiting outside. She hands you the personnel file containing his application and résumé.

You haven't met him yet, but your evaluation has already begun. You look at your watch and notice the time. He's right on the minute. A good sign; the interview is important to him. He really wants the job.

It doesn't always happen this way. Candidates sometimes show up late for their job interviews. Last year, I went to Cleveland to conduct final interviews with three candidates for an executive position. The three men had been screened in preliminary interviews from a considerable number of applicants. In the morning, I interviewed the first two, but neither seemed right for the post. So I looked forward to meeting the third applicant who was due at the local company office at two o'clock. He didn't appear until a quarter past three. Then he walked in with profuse apologies for his tardi-

143

ness, explaining that his car had broken down, and caused the delay.

It was certainly a reasonable excuse; after all, automobiles do break down occasionally.

"When did it happen?" I inquired, more out of politeness than from genuine interest.

"Last night," he replied. He showed no trace of embarrassment for his lateness a full eighteen hours after the car trouble had allegedly occurred. Immediately, I suspected that he didn't really want the job, for if the interview had been important enough to him, he could easily have made other transportation arrangements in the meanwhile.

We proceeded to discuss his qualifications for the job. Despite my initial irritation, he nevertheless impressed me quite favorably. Certainly, he was the best qualified of the three men. Privately, I decided he was the man I wanted. I told him I'd let him know the decision tomorrow. But the personnel department interviewer told me after he had left that he also had come late for his preliminary appointment a week earlier. On that ocasion also, he had offered profuse apologies and another seemingly plausible excuse.

Twice was too much. He didn't get the job. I interpreted his double lateness as a warning signal that he really didn't want to be interviewed, and that if I did hire him, his negative attitude would probably show itself in other ways as well. Tardiness for an employment interview, especially when the excuse is flimsy, offers a clear sign of difficulties ahead.

Today's candidate has arrived on time, but you delay for a moment to take another brief look at his résumé. You have already studied it carefully; now you need to refresh your memory on the salient points. You mentally note a few of the important dates and places he worked, then put aside the paper.

Before inviting the applicant to enter, review in your own mind what you wish to accomplish in the interview. Otherwise, you may end with nothing more than a pleasant and inconclusive conversation. You should seek to learn three things during the interview: Does his experience qualify him for the position? Will his personality fit acceptably with other members of your staff? Is he motivated to succeed? Anything beyond these three points may have interest and supplementary value, but its importance is secondary. By concentrating on his answers to these three questions, you'll gain the maximum from the interview.

When you ask your secretary to usher him into your office, it's a considerate gesture at the same time to ask her to cut off all telephone calls during the interview, in order to give him your undivided attention.

In a moment, Mr. Rhody is standing before you. He is smiling and pleasant, although you know that, however self-assured he may appear, employment interviews inevitably stimulate nervousness and even some degree of fright. You invite him to sit down in a comfortable chair facing you. (Do some executives place themselves in front of a window deliberately to blind the applicant by the glare?)

In these opening minutes of the interview, observe closely whether the applicant is aware of his surroundings. He should be fully conscious of you and the environment around him. The man who is wrapped up in himself can't function effectively because he isn't fully alert to where he is and what he's doing.

Some years ago, I developed my own ten-second alertness test. At that time, I was fortunate enough to enjoy a particularly comfortable office. It was located high in a midtown New York skyscraper, lined solidly with windows along two entire walls. A spectacular view of the river lay far below. Brightly colored furnishings and carpets added charm to the setting, and attractive paintings hung on the wall. The appearance and decor were so striking that it would be difficult indeed not to notice.

Yet some applicants failed to see. They would walk into the office, sit down in a chair, and instantly begin talking *at* me. They rarely looked me straight in the eye. During the entire interview, they never once looked around them to notice the dramatic setting. At the end, they stood up, shook hands with me, and walked out, without even a glance. You could hardly describe them as perceptive or inquisitive.

Other applicants, however, would enter the room and their eyes would instantly sweep across the view. Even if they didn't comment, you could tell that they were aware of it. As my secretary commented, their "radar was rotating." They talked to me, not *at* me.

After a while, it got to be sort of a game, and I would make a judgment ten seconds after the applicant entered the room. I think it was a fair test, because it told much about a man's alertness and inquisitive mind.

William A. Hertan, president of the Executive Manpower Corporation, explained why these qualities are important. "The questioning, inquisitive man is the one who will lend weight to the team, who will think out a solution to a problem—or an approach to it," he wrote. When interviewing an applicant for an executive position, Mr. Hertan said, notice whether the candidate asks questions, or does he accept every policy as standard operating procedure without question? Does he have a history of suggestions and innovations to improve the standard approach to problems?

These are the things you'll look for, but first you should give the applicant the information he'll need to speak intelligently about the position.

Mr. Rhody already understands the requirements fairly well. He learned something about the job originally from reading your help-wanted ad, and he was given more details by the personnel department. To add more clarity, it's good to begin by describing the position once again, this time in considerable detail.

Right from the beginning, he should know what you want,

so that, a year later, he can't be criticized for failure to perform a function you never told him was part of the job. There should be no possibility of misunderstanding.

So I make it a point to tell the applicant all aspects of the work he'll be expected to do. I specify how many people would report to him, and their own qualifications. I tell him why the post is now vacant; if the previous occupant was promoted, it implies opportunity for him. If the previous occupant was fired, he should know how and where his predecessor failed. Always, I emphasize the difficulties of the position, seeking to paint it a few shades blacker than I actually see it. If he discourages easily, I'd prefer to discover it now rather than after he's actually begun. I warn him he'll find the going tough, and that it will call for all his energies and abilities.

Up to this point, I've done all the talking and none of the listening, but there are good reasons why. It gives the applicant a chance to catch his breath (literally). It also provides him, if he is listening intently, with clues to help him describe his own qualifications to me. If, for instance, I've placed importance on close liaison with other members of the staff, his reply should emphasize those aspects of his past work experience which included such liaison.

I ask him if he has any further questions about the job itself. He may have several, and I try to answer them.

Then I go on to discuss the job in its larger context, as part of the functioning of the entire department. I speak briefly about the department's activities, organization, and goals. It may take fifteen or twenty minutes to cover the ground, but it establishes a solid basis for the applicant to tell me about himself.

"That's the picture, Mr. Rhody," I tell him. "Now you have a pretty good idea what we're looking for. I'd like very much to hear about you and why you think you're the right person to help us. Please take all the time you want; I've set aside enough time for us to go into this thoroughly."

He leans forward. "Where do you want me to start?"

"Anywhere you'd like," I reply. I'm watching how he organizes his presentation. Now I play the role of a listener.

Experience has taught me to beware of certain opening lines. One of these is, "I'd call myself an idea man." There's nothing wrong with being an idea man, but the man who so portrays himself may lack the desire or down-to-earth ability to execute his ideas or those of others. When I hear this opening line, I probe the applicant's record of following up the detail work necessary to implement an idea.

He may begin by concisely listing his previous jobs, and then describing each in detail. Or he may begin almost at random, wandering from one subject to the other in no apparent sequence. I try not to interrupt, but keep nodding to encourage him to continue.

I try not to refer to his written résumé, which is lying covered on my desk. To reassure him that I have read it thoroughly, I may ask a question based on it.

"What about the year you spent with Jones & Laughlin right after the war, Mr. Rhody? You haven't mentioned that."

He'll answer my question, filling in details about his experience. I concentrate attention on his words, listening intently, and avoid the temptation to begin talking. Only if he becomes vague about a particular function or job do I intrude with a question. I want to be sure I understand quite precisely what he did. When he tells me he was "responsible" for a particular function, I'll ask what that means. Did he hire the people who actually did the work? Did he instruct them on their duties and guide their performance? Or was his "responsibility" simply a routine enforcement of operating policies already established by higher management?

In his résumé, has he failed to account for a particular period of his working career? I want to know why. It may conceal a job from which he was fired. The knowledge that he was unsuccessful in one post doesn't particularly disturb me, because I have yet to meet an executive who hasn't been fired at least once in his working career. I'm much more interested in his attempt to conceal it.

Or does his lapse represent a period when he didn't work? If so, why? There may have been good reasons, such as illness. Perhaps the reasons for his inactivity may offer clues to his motivations.

How badly does he want the job? How strongly does he want to succeed? How important is success according to his personal standard of values? You may ask him directly, but his words will tell you less than his manner, his voice, and his past employment history.

Of course, he'll say he wants the job. But if you must ask him a leading question to extract the answer, you already have learned a great deal. If he answers affirmatively, but without much conviction, you've learned still more.

If he pursued you aggressively to obtain the interview and follows it promptly with a thank-you letter, you have good indications that he really wants to work for you. But if he leaves your office to await your decision passively and silently, he shows a lack of initiative and desire to win the post.

As he describes his past experience, does he cite examples of his initiative and drive, or does he describe his previous work in terms of positions he occupied? His answers will provide many clues to predicting his success.

While the applicant speaks, I try to visualize him as if he were already on my staff. I seek to imagine him in a staff meeting, dealing with his new associates. Projecting him in my "mind's eye" often helps to evaluate his suitability.

I am not disturbed if the applicant is nervous during the interview. An employment interview is one of the most trying experiences any of us can have. I've been through many, and I've been nervous too. I don't think nervousness proves very much. I try to notice it when an applicant who has otherwise been calm and collected suddenly shows anxiety and disturbance at a particular point in the discussion. There are the telltale signs; the shaky voice, the clearing of the throat, the restless eyes, the jumping Adam's apple. It may be important to question him further to find the cause. Perhaps he wants to hide something important on a particular subject.

In this connection, I recall the time I was interviewing a mature and successful executive for promotion. I regarded him as an unusually stable person, whose judgments under pressure were consistently good.

During the interview, he gave lucid and crisp answers to my questions. Forcefully he described his experience and qualifications. He made an outstanding impression. But suddenly, he interrupted a sentence and stammered, "Excuse me if my answers aren't right to the point. Something is on my mind. I had a terrible tragedy yesterday, and it's upset me."

"I'm sorry," I said quietly. "May I ask what happened?"

"Our little dog died suddenly," he replied. His eyes blinked and filled with tears. It was heartrending to see this middle-aged executive overcome with emotion. I expressed sympathy, and abruptly changed the subject. His composure returned. Throughout the rest of the interview, he was calm and collected, showing no trace of emotion.

If I were an amateur psychologist, I might have attempted to analyze why he reacted so painfully to this experience. But I was not qualified to do so, nor was it relevant to his performance on the job. He would be working with people, not animals, and his tender emotions on the latter subject were entirely irrelevant to his work. When you conduct an interview, your purpose is not to psychoanalyze the candidate, but to evaluate him in terms of a particular job you are seeking to fill.

In another case, which happened almost ten years ago, I was interviewing a man named George Stevenson for an executive post. He had been recommended to me by his previous employer whom I knew well, and in whose judgment I placed considerable confidence.

The interview went well, and Mr. Stevenson convinced me he was highly qualified and highly motivated. But toward the end my eye caught a line on his résumé which I had previously missed. It stated that he had been graduated from the School of Commerce of a well-known university, with the degree of B.B.A. (Bachelor of Business Administration). I read it twice to be sure I saw correctly, and then asked him about it. He calmly confirmed the details as given.

The catch was that I happened to know that the university he named did not have a School of Commerce. It did, however, have a School of Business Administration. Had he been careless in recalling the correct name? My suspicions were aroused.

Without further reference to it, I tactfully terminated the interview, and made another appointment to see him two days later. As soon as he left my office, I telephoned the registrar of the university to check their records. Sure enough, they had no record that Mr. Stevenson had attended the university either as an undergraduate or in the School of Business Administration.

When he returned two days later, I promptly confronted him with my discovery and asked an explanation. He didn't blink an eye.

"I lied to you," said Mr. Stevenson. "It was a calculated risk, and you caught me. The fact is that I didn't attend college. I didn't even graduate from high school. My parents were hard up; it was during the Depression. I dropped out, and went to work when I was seventeen."

He exhaled deeply, as if a great weight were off his shoulders. "I've been working now for eighteen years, and I'm perfectly willing to have you judge me on what I've done for the last eighteen years. But I had to lie, because I found that nobody would even consider me without a college degree."

He spoke with calmness almost to the point of resignation.

The burden of decision now fell on my shoulders. I knew

that in other companies, deceit was ground for automatic elimination. It would be interpreted as evidence of lack of moral character, and some would say that a person who lied once would not hesitate to lie again to protect his job.

It was indeed a serious matter, and it provoked considerable introspection. Should I risk selection of Mr. Stevenson under the circumstances?

To reach my decision, I balanced his eighteen years of work against this significant falsehood. I checked his references with special thoroughness. They held up well. His former employers, right back to his earliest job, uniformly spoke well of him. They described him as a capable, hardworking, conscientious individual who had cheerfully undertaken every assignment, and executed them successfully. Several mentioned his exceptional drive and leadership. All said he had never betrayed a company confidence, and had been entrusted with financial responsibility.

Against this, I weighed the significance of his lie. Did this indicate a dishonest character? No, there was no evidence that it was part of a pattern. I checked every other statement in his résumé, and each was individually confirmed. I finally decided to hire him.

Would I have done the same, had I been in his position? Very possibly, I had to admit, I might have. In the interest of self-preservation, he had lied. He rationalized that it was not relevant to his qualifications. He wanted to be judged only by his actual working record, and nothing more. So he took a calculated risk.

As events later proved themselves, I'm glad I took a chance on Mr. Stevenson, even though I know some other executives would not have. He worked out well, and proved a desirable employee in every way. We never again mentioned the incident to each other.

My decision would undoubtedly have been different had I attempted to set myself up as a judge of his moral character.

When you are in the seat of the employer, it is terribly easy to pass moral judgment on others. But you have neither the right nor the qualification to do so. "Judge not that ye not be judged."

I had to remind myself that only one consideration was significant: how would he perform on the job? The lie was relevant only insofar as it might affect his performance. When I decided that it would not, I stopped and probed no further.

A similar problem confronted the president of a Pittsburgh laundry. He employed a large fleet of truck drivers who picked up and delivered laundry bundles, collecting payment along their routes. For many years, he refused to employ drivers who had been caught stealing in previous jobs. They were certainly bad risks to entrust with the handling of cash receipts. But when the manpower shortage became severe, and the company was unable to recruit enough route men, the president reopened the whole question. After new procedures were instituted to forestall petty thievery, the company decided to hire a small number of the drivers previously barred. In each case, a trained interviewer discussed the matter bluntly with the applicant and tried to assess the likelihood of a recurrence. In cases where the interviewer thought the offender had seen the error of his ways, he hired him.

Two years later, the president's analysis unexpectedly showed that the previous offenders had achieved a better record than did the regular drivers. I doubt if I would have taken a similar risk, but at any rate, he did, and it worked. How he managed to secure bonds for these employees, I'll never know.

Some psychological testers warn of similar risk when you hire a man who has been recently divorced. One of the largest testing organizations, the Klein Institute for Aptitude Testing, Inc., flatly describes divorce or separation within the past two years as a "knockout factor" for salesmen in *any* field, in *any* company, in *any* territory, and in *any* industry, regardless of previous record of accomplishments, and regardless of good sales aptitudes as measured through psychological tests. That's a pretty broad statement, but the Klein Institute doesn't stop there. It goes on to predict failure even though the applicant may have remarried during the two-year period.

They're talking about salesmen. I wonder if they would say the same thing about executives. Several sales executives with whom I've discussed this point insist that it's plain balderdash. If a man has been divorced, whether within the past sixty days or the past six years, you want to know about it before you hire him, but only because it may give you some clues to his job performance. I've met many married executives (and salesmen) who were leading miserably unhappy lives at the family hearth, too distraught with tension to perform effectively on the job. I've also known divorced men who, released from the strains of unsatisfactory marriage relationships, poured themselves into their jobs with renewed energies. Despite the "experts" of the Klein Institute, you can't generalize and conclude that all divorced men, or even all pipe smokers, won't succeed.

An engineering executive once told me how an interviewer had eliminated him from consideration for a good post. His name was Richard Celliers, and his qualifications were impressive. Toward the close of his second interview, it appeared that he had won the job. The interviewer absent-mindedly reached into his desk drawer and took out a pack of cigarettes. He offered one to Mr. Celliers.

"No, thank you," Mr. Celliers replied. "If you don't mind, I'd prefer my pipe." He reached into his pocket and took out a briar.

The interviewer slapped his hand forcefully on the desk. "That settles it!" he shouted. "You've just lost the job. We don't want any leisurely pipe smokers in this company. We're looking for cigarette smokers, the nervous type, men who are pushing constantly. You wouldn't have time here to sit back and meditate while you blow smoke clouds."

Since I'm a pipe smoker myself, I sympathized with Mr. Celliers. I don't know whether or not he was the right man for this particular job, but a flat rule against pipe smokers is as insane as a flat rule against divorced men, Mormons, redheads, or any other group. The interviewer held a stereotyped image of what pipe smokers were supposed to be like, and on this "profound" basis, eliminated Mr. Celliers as a probable failure!

It hardly needs be said that such arbitrary decisions are sometimes responsible for the loss of able men. When I find an outstanding individual, I always spend a few minutes selling him. If he's the best candidate, I want to stimulate his desire to join the corporation. Even if he's finally turned down, I'd like him to leave with friendly feelings for the company. So I tell him briefly something about the organization as a whole and its long-range plans, before concluding the interview.

"Mr. Rhody, thank you very much for coming in to see me. I'm very much impressed by you and your qualifications. Before we make a decision, naturally we will want to see a few more candidates, but we'll positively reach a decision by the end of next week. I know you're anxious to learn where you stand, and we'll tell you just as quickly as we can. You'll hear from me without fail by next Friday, and I hope it works out well for both of us. Thanks again."

If Mr. Rhody looks like *the* man you've been looking for, you may want to go a bit further. You may tell him that he's the best of the candidates you've seen, and in the lead for the job. If he really is, you don't want to lose him to another employer during the next few days. If subsequently you find a better qualified applicant, you can later tell him so honestly. Don't encourage false hopes when you know they're false to begin with.

You'll notice that I didn't refer to salary in my interview with Mr. Rhody. It wasn't an oversight. In a large company, the rules usually require that only the personnel department negotiate salary. In his first interview with personnel, the applicant was asked his previous salary, and this was duly entered on the records. During successive interviews with other executives, salary was not discussed. This enables the personnel department to negotiate pay and fringe benefits in accordance with overall company policy, secure in the certainty that no other executive has offered terms that might conflict.

This system prevents the hiring of new executives at salaries which are out of line with those of other persons of comparable ability and experience. If, however, you are in a smaller company, and salary determination is your responsibility, you should negotiate the terms matter-of-factly and without embarrassment to either party.

If an applicant raises the subject with you during an interview, you may tell him that you'll be glad to discuss it but only after you've made the more important decision that he's the right man for the job. I always add, "and after you've made the basic decision that you want to join us." After all, employment is a mutual decision, and he'll appreciate recognition that he, as well as you, has a decision to make.

After you've selected your man, but before you notify him of your decision, you'll want to check his references thoroughly. During your conversations with him, you've assumed that his background and experience are as he stated them. But now, before going ahead, you should challenge this assumption and attempt to confirm his statements.

"The bigger the job, the more vital reference-checking becomes," says Rawle Deland, a senior partner of Thorndike Deland Associates, a New York executive search firm. "If you are not convinced, ask someone who has been burned, like the president of a Louisiana firm who hired a new executive VP. The man was an obvious answer to the company's prayer: young, brilliant, likable. His record showed a series of triumphs with three Eastern firms. No one bothered to write or phone these firms; that would have seemed a bit distrustful.

"The punch line is probably unnecessary, but for the record, he was wanted in Canada for fraud."

So it's wise to take nothing for granted. It is proper and necessary to check references to minimize your hiring risk. Applicants expect to be checked out; they'll be surprised if you don't take the elemental protection which an investigation of their references provides.

Executives are usually extremely cautious in providing references. Under certain circumstances, they expose themselves to the possibility of damage suits if their negative evaluation deprives an applicant of a job which he otherwise might have had. Therefore, experienced executives will seldom write a damaging evaluation. There's always the possibility that the letter may inadvertently (or deliberately) fall into the hands of the applicant. If you want an accurate evaluation, the only way you'll get it is over the telephone.

To check the prospective employee, you need the right information from the right people. Neither is easy to find.

For example, you'll certainly call his former employers. But if he was associated with a large corporation, it may be difficult to locate the precise person who personally knew him best. It may not be the person whose name he gave you. If a number of years have elapsed since he left that employment, that person himself may have since departed. The personnel records of the company may politely rate him as having been satisfactory, while the actual facts, known to his superior, may have been quite different. You may have to make several phone calls to a single company before you locate the proper executive who can (and will) tell you the truth. You may have to do some amateur detective work and track down his former superior, now in another company. The only phone checks which will have value are those made with someone who actually worked personally with the applicant; second-hand data are worthless.

Your phone inquiries to references may, however, be

suspect. You may be a friend whom the applicant is using to find out what his former employer is saying about him. Some executives forestall such planted calls by asking you for your phone number and then calling you back, after they've first checked your company to confirm your own identity and position.

Just as your contact checks you, you also must check him. How much weight should you give to his words? If he launches into a diatribe against your candidate, his words deserve serious thought on your part, but how much? Perhaps the applicant deserved the severe criticism, or had this same superior conducted a vendetta against him? When you get an extremely negative report of this type, check further in the same company to learn more about the relationship of the two men. You should neither discount the report completely nor should you dismiss the candidate from further consideration on that basis alone.

Here too, the listening technique will bring forth valuable information. After you've described the job under consideration, and asked the reference to evaluate the candidate, sit back and wait. Say not another word. The executive at the other end will invariably begin with kind words about the applicant. Instead of responding, or asking further questions, watch what happens when you simply say, "Uh-huh" or "Yes" and nothing more. He'll keep talking. Many people can't tolerate a moment's silence, especially on the telephone. They feel compelled to keep talking. Your contact will add more details, and the more often you repeat "Uh-huh," the more specific his comments will become.

You may ask questions if you need still more specific information, but save them until you've worked the "Uh-huh" routine to the limit. When you do ask questions, you should describe the specific duties of the position, so that your contact may comment specifically on the candidate in relation to them. If his comments are enthusiastically laudatory, it doesn't hurt to heckle slightly. For example, you might ask,

"Well, Mr. Williams, if he was so good, why did he leave? Why didn't *you* try to hold on to him?"

Checking references in depth will require time. You may spend most of a morning, or even a full day, doing it. Better to spend your precious time now than to wait until the man has actually begun work. In this way you can avoid failures owing to factors that a thorough reference check would have uncovered in the first place.

After you've made the basic hiring decision, you should be prepared to settle the salary question rapidly. Before you meet with the successful candidate, you should have firmly in your mind the salary at which you would like to hire him, and also the maximum salary you can afford to pay for the position.

It isn't difficult to determine the proper rate, or range of rates, you should pay to get the man you want. Your minimum should approximate the "going rate," that is, the salary which other companies (or other departments in your own company) pay for comparable work. The maximum should represent additional skills or experience which a particular candidate will bring to the job. If you exceed the "going rate" without solid justification, you will increase your overhead costs without proportional return. The result will make it more difficult for your company to compete with other firms in the marketplace.

I've been involved in many salary negotiations, for myself, and for others. I think that the most successful were those where the matter was quickly settled. When the talks become prolonged, emotional considerations add to the difficulty of reaching an acceptable agreement. In our society, salary does not represent a man's economic value alone; it also signifies his status. If you decline to meet an executive's wage demand, he may be inclined to think you are demeaning his worth as a person. This is utterly unrealistic, of course, but in an emotionally charged area, people may react in emotional ways.

Immediately after you've made your decision is the best

time to discuss pay. "Now about salary," you tell the executive. "The pay for this job is ten thousand. In addition, there are certain fringe benefits, and I'll go over those with you later." If he accepts, your deal is made. But to ask him, "Is this acceptable?" only opens the door to a request for more. He'd be foolish not to try, after you've given him an opening.

Suppose, however, you know from his record that the man earned more in his last position than you are about to offer him. In such a case, you'll find it necessary to prepare the ground for your offer; otherwise, he may reject it out of hand.

"I know from your record, Mr. Rhody, that you were making twelve thousand five in your last position. I don't have any doubt that you're worth it, and I wish we could pay it to you here. But the particular position we're talking about has a starting salary limit of ten thousand, because that's what *the job* is worth to us, in relation to other jobs.

"Please understand I'm not saying you're worth only ten thousand. I'm saying the *job* is worth only ten thousand. If you work out well and win promotion, I'm sure your pay will increase to twelve five and beyond it. But that will be because you are doing more important work."

Usually this approach will do it, and the two of you smilingly shake hands.

Now the new employee is ready to begin work. You'll watch him closely and help him to adjust to his new duties. You have high hopes that he will meet your expectations. But like all new employees, he's on probation. If he doesn't work out, you'll be forced to let him go. He knows this as well as you; in fact, probably better. So you'll accomplish nothing by telling him that, for the next six months, he'll be on probation. It will only add to his anxieties; rather you should minimize them, because men can't work at their best when they're under tension.

So from the moment he joins your payroll, talk with him

and act as if he'll be with you for the remainder of his working life. In such a climate, a new executive will perform at his best.

During all this time, while a parade of applicants has been entering and leaving your office, your staff has not been asleep. They have been sizing up each candidate as he opened and closed your office door. Now the time has come to introduce them to their new colleague, just as soon as your decision is final, and negotiations completed. This is better than waiting until the Monday morning when he reports for work, for it prevents the spread of rumors in the interim.

In a small department, it may take you less than an hour to introduce the new man to everyone. As you lead him down the office corridor into one office after another, the names will blend into utter confusion in his mind. Several weeks may pass before he learns to identify each person by face and name. Nevertheless, it provides you with an opportunity to tell each person, in his presence, exactly what he'll do, and where he'll fit into the department's operations. In these first meetings, he won't say much, because he's anxious to get home to his wife, and tell her the good news. The staff members won't say much to him, because they're too busy assessing him. When the formal introductions are completed, the ice has been broken, and it will be easier for him to begin work without total strangeness.

You wish him well, and tell him when to report. For better or worse, the decision is made. Only time will tell whether your decision was a good one.

13

....

Actions
Speak Louder
with Words

THE EXECUTIVE can't ignore his communications any more than a driver can forget to oil his engine. The car will run briefly without outward signs of damage until suddenly overheated parts burn out the engine. So it is with an executive's communications. Neglect them, and damaging consequences will quickly appear.

Many companies have discovered this hard truth. In one organization, rumors arose from nowhere that a merger with a larger corporation was under consideration. Nobody in management said anything, leading key executives to believe the report had substance. In self-protection, they began scrambling for jobs elsewhere before the ax fell. By the time the false rumor was denied, the company had lost valuable men. A prompt denial would have been sufficient to prevent the damage.

A department store advertised a holiday sale. Full-page newspaper advertisements featured price reductions, and invited readers to phone in their orders. When they called, the telephone operator knew nothing about the sale, because no one had informed her. Result: customers irritated and sales lost, because one store executive failed to tell a telephone operator about his plans.

A salesman and an engineer, both employed by a manufacturing corporation, met in the reception room of a customer's factory. They had an appointment with the industrial purchasing agent. The salesman had brought along the engineer to answer certain technical questions, and to help him close the sale. But when the pair walked into the purchasing agent's office, their lack of coordination became painfully evident. The engineer had not been briefed in advance on the specific problem; the salesman had been "too busy" to sit down with him, so the engineer too was not prepared to provide answers. Still another meeting was made necessary. Meanwhile the sale was jeopardized; for the purchasing agent understandably wondered what kind of service he could expect from a company whose sales force was so poorly prepared. Had the salesman briefed the engineer in advance of their appointment, the situation could have been prevented.

In a textile office, a bookkeeper was fired for incompetence only three weeks after a clerk had been terminated for the same reason. No one told the remaining staff why, so they promptly reached the conclusion that a general staff reduction was under way as part of an economy drive. Result: anxiety, and, within a month, three voluntary resignations. A few words of explanation and reassurance could have calmed the atmosphere and prevented further staff turnover.

These are typical consequences of communications failures. They occur when executives regard communications as a luxury or a gimmick to keep employees contented. It's much more. Good communications are essential to business because many people are involved in carrying out decisions; they must know what they're expected to do, when they're expected to do it, and, often, why. During the secret wartime years virtually none of the thousands of workers at Oak Ridge, Tennessee, were aware that they were processing uranium ore for an atomic bomb, and they knew better than to ask questions. But a normal competitive business can't operate successfully in secrecy. Employees want to know. They don't want to work as automatons. They want to know why so that they can better perform their jobs, and be able to improvise solutions when prescribed procedures break down. Finally, they feel more confidence in the company if they're kept well informed about its plans. They'll share pride because they have been considered important enough to be kept posted.

It's possible to tell them too much, to divulge trade secrets carelessly, to reveal personal information about an employee indiscreetly, of course. But for most executives, this isn't nearly as real a hazard as the danger of telling too little. Many major corporations customarily keep their employees in the dark; many keep them reasonably well informed; but I've never heard of a case where a management overinformed its staffs.

Company secrets do exist, but they are relatively few. The chemical industry, for instance, guards its precious refining processes, since these often have not been patented to prevent disclosure via the public records of the Patent Office. Cosmetics companies protect the secrecy of their new marketing plans to prevent competitors from getting the jump on their product introductions. For the most part, however, routine company information can safely be divulged to employees without damage to the company.

What information falls into the "routine" category? Is it a new chemical formula or a new marketing plan? Not at all. Such information will be beyond the understanding of most employees anyway. It will neither enable them to work more efficiently nor enhance their pride in the company. But employees might appropriately be told that the company's scientists have developed a process that will create new jobs and build new markets, thus benefiting all employees through increased job security. Financial information may be treated similarly. Few employees know how to read a profit-and-loss statement, or a balance sheet of assets and liabilities. If it were presented to them, they would only be confused. But a simplified summary can be prepared which doesn't require interpretation by a Certified Public Accountant. The employees would like to know whether the company's sales increased or decreased last year, and whether the corporation operated at a profit or loss. They'd like to know whether management is planning for future growth, since this will affect their own future. The employees would like to know how well their own department performed last year, whether its operations grew or contracted. If you can develop the knack of simplifying information and presenting it understandably, you will surely enhance the confidence of your staff in your leadership.

Whenever you make a decision, whenever you are informed of some decision, immediately ask yourself, "Who *should* know about this? Who *needs* to know it? Who might benefit from knowing it?" Perhaps only a few persons must be advised of the action, but others might like to know as general background information. Unless positive harm will result, it's usually worthwhile to pass the information along as widely and quickly as possible.

Speed is important, because your report on the actual facts must anticipate the grapevine, and beat the rumors. When you plan an operational change which will affect your employees, the time to let it be known is now, before the first signs of your activity generate rumors. If you've decided to hire someone, or fire someone, your decision will initiate certain paperwork between your department and the personnel department, which will involve several people in processing the necessary papers. However pledged to confidence these employees may be, the chance of a "leak" exists. The best way to eliminate gossip is to shorten the time between your decision and its implementation, and let the facts be known as quickly as possible. One company which changed its top management group subsequently heard rumors that the change resulted from the private, unannounced sale of the company. The gossip was entirely inaccurate; there was no foundation for the report. Since it was so farfetched, the board of directors decided to ignore it. Only after the rumor had been widely repeated, reaching outside the company to customers as well, was a formal denial released. Meanwhile, it created anxiety among the staff, which could have been prevented had the correct facts immediately been made known.

If you haven't previously paid attention to your internal communications, don't be surprised if your first announcements meet with skepticism from the staff. They'll wonder what you're up to. Does some sinister purpose lurk behind your new revelations? Only after experience has demonstrated that you have told the complete truth in each case will your staff be willing to accept your words at their face value. If you deny rumors that a staff reduction is impending, and, three weeks later, top management tells you to institute such a cutback, you will have destroyed their faith in you. They simply won't believe you didn't know that a cut was coming. So be sure of your facts before you say anything.

And before you open your mouth, think carefully what impression you wish to convey. Otherwise, you may talk and talk, but after you've finished, your staff won't quite understand what you are up to. You may want to discuss a major problem with them, but if you sandwich the discussion between three or four other matters, they may miss the point completely.

When you call a department meeting, therefore, it's a good idea to open it by listing the subjects you wish to discuss, in the order you will talk about them. You may even write them down on a blackboard, or on a sheet of paper, giving a copy to each person. Then, when you arrive at each point on your agenda, you may say, "Now for point two, the new procedure for ordering supplies." After that subject has been covered adequately, you could conclude with: "We've covered point two. Let's move on to number three." No one should be in any doubt about what you're discussing, and an agenda will help pin things down.

Sometimes, it's a problem to determine the best sequence for discussion of various matters. If you wish to criticize the way a certain operation is being performed, or if you wish to request cooperation, discuss it before going on to routine matters. When you leave the unpleasant matters for the end, and the staff knows they're coming, they'll pay little attention to anything else until you reach the distasteful subject. On the other hand, if you immediately bring it up, and dispose of it, they'll be more receptive to the encouraging news.

And don't assume that because you tell something to your staff, they will hear it. If it's unpleasant to hear, they may filter it out before it reaches them.

This invisible filter is demonstrated in college elementary psychology classes. The instructor lines up the students and whispers a message to the man at the head of the line. By the time the message has been repeated in turn to each student, it emerges at the end of the line in unrecognizable form. The distortion is not caused by improper hearing, but by the interpretation which each student has unintentionally placed on the message before passing it along. Similarly, between your lips and the ears of each member of your staff is an invisible filter representing his prejudices. The filter sifts your words through the barrier of his prejudices to make them acceptable. If he is unreceptive to criticism, his filter will screen it out, and he'll never hear your words. If he doesn't like people, for instance, he won't hear your requests to deal more courteously with customers.

We unconsciously screen out anything that disturbs us. Some years ago, the American Cancer Society analyzed the readership of newspaper articles on the relationship between cancer and smoking. The researchers found that few smokers had noticed the newspaper articles, compared to the large number of nonsmokers who had noticed and read them. The explanation was that smokers did not want to know about the smoking-cancer connection, so they unconsciously avoided "seeing" the articles.

To break through the screen between you and your staff, extreme clarity of presentation will be needed. You may even find it desirable to go back to the beginning, and repeat your main points once again, before you invite questions from the group. The discussion period may prove the most valuable part of the entire meeting. No matter how busy your work schedule, no matter how difficult it is to assemble your staff for a meeting, the staff members should be encouraged to speak up and ask any questions they may have. Ample time for their discussion must be allowed if the meeting is to succeed.

Many meetings may be required before your subordinates will feel brave enough to speak up. Even then, their first questions or comments will be routine. They'll want to discover whether you really seek their questions and comments, or whether you're simply following the rules of polite courtesy in inviting them. If you pause only a moment for questions and then proceed before they can collect their thoughts to speak up, you may unwittingly discourage them from asking questions in the future.

If you truly want their comments, however, you can get them by waiting only another fifteen or twenty seconds. If no one volunteers after you've asked for questions, sit back, light a cigarette, and wait. An embarrassed silence will follow. Fifteen seconds of silence can seem endless when a half dozen people are sitting around a table. Usually, someone will speak up just to break the deadly quiet. The first comment may be inane and irrelevant, but the second will not be, and, in moments, you'll have all the discussion you could want.

How much discussion do you want? The answer depends

on the subject you've discussed. At a minimum, you want enough discussion to clarify the matter, and to ensure that everyone understands clearly what you've said. Beyond that, you'll wish to receive any information that will help you operate. When the conversation begins to repeat itself, or when individuals begin talking primarily for the purpose of hearing themselves talk, and letting you hear them talk, it's time to close the meeting.

On some occasions, instead of informing your staff directly, you may find it preferable to ask your supervisors to pass along information to their subordinates.

The advantages of this method are considerable. By "going through channels," you show respect for their position as junior executives, and provide them with a practical lesson in the importance of communication.

Even more. By allowing them to transmit the information, you engage them in support of the activity under discussion. Participation may transform their personal attitudes from neutrality to active support. A bank official who supervised a clerical section of six working bookkeepers confirmed this from his experience. One of the six bookkeepers supervised the other five, but otherwise their duties were identical. When the official wanted to tell them of a change in procedures, he had been in the habit of telling all six at once. On one occasion, he told only the supervisor of a change, and asked her to pass the information on to her associates. She did so, and he was surprised to note that they accepted the change more willingly than when he had previously dealt with them directly. This was not what he had expected would happen. He had feared that the other bookkeepers would feel offended because he had not taken the time to talk with them directly.

Exploring further, he noticed that the supervisor herself displayed enthusiasm for the changes, because she felt part of them. The bank official had taken her into management's confidence. Because of her favorable reaction, the five other women reacted positively to the changed procedures. All six felt a kinship with each other, and they were pleased at the treatment he had given one of their number.

To eliminate the hazard that, in the process of repetition, supervisors may misinterpret the information, you may give them a written memorandum which repeats the essential facts. And sometimes, when face-to-face discussion is impractical, the memorandum will do the communications job by itself.

The memo has undoubted advantages of its own. It conveys its message in precise words that can be read and reread. It provides a historical record for the file. It can be produced in sufficient copies to inform a large number of people simultaneously, more than could conveniently be reached by a meeting. It conserves the time of the staff, since they may read the memo at their convenience. And it can reach people who are away from the office, and are unable to attend a meeting.

Since the memo is such an effective communications tool, it's often abused. Executives apparently like to write memos, for they send so many of them. After a while, employees become so accustomed to receiving them that they pay little heed to the contents. When they go unread, the bureaucrats next adopt a different colored paper, such as red, for important memos. What usually follows is that the red urgent memos increase until they soon receive no more attention than did the white memos previously. As for the remaining white memos, they are now hardly looked at.

So write memos only when you can't communicate in person, or where you must have a written record for the future. The fewer the better, for those few you do write will get more attention.

The shorter the better, too. A one-paragraph memo will receive more attention than a two-paragraph memo, and a one-page memo will be more carefully read than a two-page document. A long time ago, the tabloid newspapers and *Reader's Digest* learned that people preferred to take their information short and straight. The lesson applies to office communications as well.

Other forms of communication are available to the executive besides meetings and memos. The telephone is one. It's cheaper and quicker to transact much of your business in this way. One corporation president I know rarely writes a letter; he has trained himself instead to pick up the phone, and call the person directly. Comparing the cost of a phone call, even a long-distance call, to the secretarial cost of producing a single letter, the phone call usually wins.

The employee publication is another tool of communication. By its nature, it must interest a broader group, so its subjects are selected for general interest. It provides information about the company's progress, new products, plans, and personnel, which are of interest to the entire organization, not merely a single department. The company "house organ," as it's called, also informs each department about what the others are doing.

But too many company publications fail to accomplish their purpose because they don't have a clearly defined purpose to begin with. The best internal publications tell the employees the things they want to know, those affecting the security of their jobs. News of a new factory opening, a new corporate acquisition, a new research development, a new product, a new marketing plan—all these interest employees and build confidence and pride in the company.

The publications which fail, however, are the monthly magazines that open with a benign portrait of The Founder, followed by an inspirational message from the president. They include gossip columns written by correspondents in each department, providing full details about how blonde Susie Schmaltz, who works on the evening shift in Department B-24a, is engaged to handsome Art Muckelman, a crane operator in Mill 37. They are read, because everyone likes to see his name and the names of people he knows in print from time to time.

But they fail as effective communications because they avoid dealing with the significant subjects in which employees are really interested. Even when they have something worthwhile to say, their leisurely publication schedule releases the news long after the more efficient rumor mill has informed everyone. You can't rely on such publications to keep your staff informed. If your department is a large one, and face-to-face personal conversations aren't practical, you may publish a simple one-page mimeographed newsletter from time to time. It doesn't have to be formal, and it doesn't need to appear regularly. But it must be distributed promptly when you have something to say that can't be said face to face.

Good communication presupposes listening as well as talking, opening channels of communication so that your staff may let you know what they're doing, and advise you of their day-to-day work problems. It may prove to be more difficult for you to obtain information than to dispense it. Employees are reluctant to talk candidly to their supervisor. Usually they won't take the initiative unless you encourage them to do so.

And they'll tell you exactly what they think you want to hear—no more, no less. If you show irritation the first time they tell you bad news, you can be fairly certain that it will be the last time you will hear bad news. Make it clear that you wish to be informed fully on their activities, and you'll be told the good and the bad alike.

Typically, we don't like to hear bad news. Our faces show displeasure as we listen. Sometimes we react by blaming the person who tells us, although he may have had nothing to do with the cause of the difficulty. A sales manager who fancied himself a perpetual optimist flatly told his sales staff he wanted to hear only of sales made, not of sales lost. They obliged him willingly. As a result, he failed to learn why his men were encountering difficulties, and thus cut himself off from vital information which he needed to plan corrective action.

Employees show remarkable sensitivity in learning how to please the boss. If your soft spot is procedures, they'll curry your favor by reporting on new forms and systems they've developed, and nothing more. If they sense that your current "kick" is cost reduction, they'll tell you only about that, failing to report the resulting deterioration in customer service. One employee carefully noted particular words and characteristic phrases I often used, and systematically worked them back into his own reports to me.

Learning the whole truth will require your careful effort and great patience. You'll find it necessary to repeat, over and over again, that you want to know fully what's going on, the good and the bad alike. When employees tell you of unsolved problems, thank them especially for their frankness; don't scold them for allowing the problem to exist. When employees give you a suggestion, consider it thoughtfully, instead of dismissing it out of hand. When one employee complains that another is "goofing off," tell him that you'll investigate promptly and fairly.

Finding the right balance between listening to everything, on the one hand, and encouraging informers on the other, is difficult. "I'm glad you've given me this information," you may tell a staff member. "Naturally, I can't accept it just because you've said it, but I promise to look into it promptly, and find out if your facts are accurate. If they are, we'll take prompt action, but if they're not, then I'll have to talk with *you*." It's a way of keeping open your channel of information without encouraging destructive gossip. It is important to hold the employee responsible for what he says. When you emphasize that you want to hear everything, as long as it's truthful and complete, your staff will test you in various ways, until they convince themselves you really mean exactly what you said.

Such informal methods of information-gathering won't suffice if your operations are complex. You'll require certain information on a monthly basis, other data weekly, and possibly certain facts at the end of each business day. One way to get it is to establish a written reporting schedule, specifying exactly what information you want, and when. This can be followed up by a plan which asks Mr. Merkelson in the shipping department, for example, to send to your office each Friday at 11:45 A.M. a summary of the week's shipments.

Another method, which I prefer, is to tell each staff member what information you will need from him, and how often, without establishing a definite reporting schedule. It then becomes his responsibility to keep you informed. The burden of following through falls on him. When given latitude, some employees will meet their commitments dependably, while others will lag. Some will fail completely. By allowing them to exercise initiative, you give them an additional opportunity to demonstrate their responsibility. Those who fail will be asked to correct their shortcomings, but, in the process, you will have further opportunities to evaluate their efficiency and ability.

If you regard communication as a vital part of your job, you'll use it to make your corporate life easier and better. Telling people what they need to know, when they need to know it, and in ways they can understand clearly, is one-half of your executive communications; listening is the other half, equally important. Together, they are neither a luxury nor an afterthought, but a vital element in ensuring your success as an executive.

14

Preserving
the *Status Quo*

AN EMPLOYEE I once knew had a standard cynical reply whenever his department head complimented him. "Never mind the pretty words," he would say. "Just put it into the pay check."

His blunt words may or may not be a typical employee's reaction, but they are utterly foreign to an executive. For the basic financial needs of the executive have already been met. Money means relatively little, for he "owns" a ranch home in Suburbia (his "ownership" consisting of $1,500 down payment and $23,500 mortgage); he owns a new car (the payments still have two years and three months to run); and he can easily afford to take his wife and children out to dinner once or twice a month (even though he is slow to pay his Diners' Club bill when it arrives). Money is far less important to the executive than public recognition.

In the highest corporate ranks, where more money brings little additional purchasing power, money means everything as a tangible symbol of status. How else could one explain why in 1962, General Motors Corporation paid Frederic G. Donner, chairman of the board, $791,475? It was the highest executive pay recorded in the United States since the boom of the late 1920's. The estimated Federal income tax on Mr. Donner's pay was $682,065, and State and other taxes presumably whittled the amount substantially below the $100,000 mark. But Mr. Donner must have glowed with pride as the highest paid man in the United States. As a symbol of success, $791,475 was infinitely important.

Long ago, corporations learned that money alone was insufficient to motivate executives. Dr. J. A. Brown, a British psychiatrist, explained why. "Trying to satisfy people with material gifts," he wrote, "is like filling a bottomless pit. When psychological needs are satisfied, on the other hand, they continue to give pleasure." So the modern corporation satisfies them by providing an executive with appropriate symbols of authority.

Executives aren't the only ones who crave public recognition. In the military forces, campaign and decoration ribbons are proudly displayed, row on row, across the uniforms of generals and privates alike. In World War II, it appeared that every last man was awarded the Good Conduct Medal after one year of service, provided only that he had not gone A.W.O.L. or had a venereal disease during the twelve months. Yet the red- and white-striped ribbon was conspicuously displayed on millions of khaki-clad chests. A century and a half earlier, when Napoleon awarded the coveted Legion of Honor, he philosophized, "With these bits of ribbon, a man can build an empire." And so he did.

Today, other decorations of honor are used to build vast corporate empires. A leading New York financial institution has awarded the title of vice-president to 130 of its executives; some 570 others have been made officers of the same corporation, with a variety of designations.

In one New York advertising agency, seven men have been named executive vice-president; three others are senior vice-presidents, and there are 124 ordinary run-of-the-mill vice-presidents. Another agency lags behind with "only" 90 vice-presidents, but, to top its competitor, it has divided itself, amoeba-like, into separate corporations, so that its roster includes five men bearing the rank of chairman of the board, and nine presidents. Thirty-three executive vice-presidents and senior vice-presidents help balance the reckoning. In both cases, the agencies rationalize that their clients prefer to deal with "an officer of the company." The solution is easy: award an officership to each person who regularly deals with clients. In addition, of course, the title provides powerful psychological satisfaction to the hundreds of vice-presidents. A vice-presidency is something to tell their neighbors about, and it undoubtedly contributes to their general sense of importance.

Sometimes, an executive wants the title so badly that he can't wait until he has earned it. In a Baltimore industrial company, a key executive who tired of waiting for a vice-presidential appointment actually went to a printer, and, incredible as it may seem, ordered company stationery identifying him as vice-president. He instructed his secretary to guard the letterheads carefully, and to use them only on outside correspondence. For two years, the ruse worked. His incoming mail, often addressed to him as vice-president, was delivered by the mail boys, who, after all, had no way of knowing whether or not he was a legitimate vice-president. When top management discovered his game, they were too astounded by his effrontery to fire him. Apparently they concluded that anyone with such gall ought to be working for them rather than for a competitor. The phony "vice-president" kept his job, and henceforth, they winked their eyes at his practice, although they never did legitimize it.

Corporate titles, whether vice-president, supervisor, manager, or director, suggest comparison to the knights, barons, earls, and dukes of British nobility. One company wit suggests a further comparison between the executive thermos jug and the mace, the ancient British symbol of authority. Like the traditional trumpets played to herald the approach of Her Majesty, the Queen, the little brown jug on the executive's desk silently shouts, "I'm an executive. I'm important."

For some top executives, mere titles or desk-top thermos jugs are insufficient to satisfy their thirst for recogntion and glory. Their egos require more grandiose tokens of power, and if the board of directors is willing, there is sometimes no limit to their imaginations. One company head negotiated a long-term charter for a DC-7 aircraft for his personal use. The DC-7 seats ninety-nine passengers in airline use, and even if you substitute executive reclining chairs, generously spaced, you could comfortably seat forty or fifty. But in this company, the aircraft was reserved for the use of the president exclusively, unless he chose to bring along a friend or two for the ride.

No functional reason can justify such corporate extravagance, for ordinary commercial jet aircraft are faster, safer, and more economical. But preferred status does not come to the executive who flies on an ordinary airline ticket, even first class. On the other hand, it provides a great psychological kick for a company president to say to a customer, "My DC-7 is out at the airport, so I'll fly out this afternoon and have dinner with you tonight." The customer, who is president of his own company, will be certain to be waiting on the taxi strip with his company limousine when the great DC-7 rolls to a halt. Of such stuff are executive egos built and maintained. The customer is impressed but no one is quite as impressed as the executive himself who enjoys such largesse tax free at the expense of the stockholders.

One executive who decided that, after all, every major company president already had his own corporate aircraft, topped them all by arranging round-trip helicopter transportation from his front lawn directly to the company parking lot each morning and evening. To the board of directors he provided many rationalizations: the helicopter conserved his precious time and energy; it wasn't much more expensive than a chauffeured limousine. The true reason, of course, was that it gave him a feeling of importance that no amount of money could supply.

Public relations executives report that the desire for personal recognition frequently is the real motivation behind a company publicity program. When the president tells the public relations man he doesn't want personal publicity "unless it will benefit the company," the public relations man knows exactly what he means. The president has visions of seeing his photograph and personal success story emblazoned in the pages of *Fortune* magazine or the Chicago *Tribune*. Since the president is rarely newsworthy except in his capacity as president of the corporation, the public relations man satisfies his desire for glory in a form which will likewise satisfy the corporate board of directors. He publicizes the accomplishments of the president in revitalizing the company.

Veteran public relations men have told me of presidents who deny ambitions of personal publicity for themselves, but nevertheless suggest that press attention be sought for their favorite executives. "Get Mr. Robertson's picture in the paper," one president declared, "and he'll be a new man, worth more to the company." The president could have spoken of himself in identical words. The public relations man usually gets the message.

An attractive and impressive executive office provides status recognition in more tangible form. Your office is far more than a place to transact the company's business. It defines your exact status for all men to see. A corner office, with windows on two sides, signifies that you outrank ordinary mortals with windows on only one side. A two-window man outranks a one-window man, and, in some companies, three-window offices are the mark of major department heads.

The size of your office is meaningful to the man who knows the secret code. If you happen to work in a newly constructed building, you can figure out your relative position in the hierarchy by studying the office blueprints. It is not accidental that your office is slightly smaller than that of the other department head down the hall. It was planned that way because he outranks you in importance. The interior designer and the architect received their guidance from a "status chart" prepared by your company's personnel officer. From this chart, the interior designers assigned proper footage to each executive rank.

A neatly lettered nameplate on your door provides additional recognition. Some companies reserve this distinction for executives. One carpet company saw an opportunity to cash in on the executive's desire for status, and promptly ran a series of ads under the slogan, "A name on the door rates a Bigelow on the floor." Presumably, the new executive should expect wall-to-wall carpeting to underline his new importance.

But sometimes senior management becomes so preoccupied with its own status that it fails to pay proper attention to the psychological needs of the staffs at lower levels.

When management places an executive's name on his door while leaving the staff unmarked, it may indicate that they regard the rank-and-file as nameless automatons, menials whose individual identity is unimportant because they can be replaced and interchanged like cans of tomato soup on a supermarket shelf. So if your name is on your door, you might consider preparing similar signs for everyone in your department. Each member of your staff seeks recognition as an individual, and there's enough glory to go around for everyone.

Seemingly insignificant symbols can acquire a status importance to employees. Professor Fritz Roethlisberger, of the Harvard Graduate School of Business Administration, told of an executive who had developed a severe emotional disturbance. In the corporation in which the man worked, higher executives used desks with drawers on both sides, while lower-ranking officials had desks with drawers on only one side. A two-pedestal desk was the symbol of status.

During an internal reorganization, this executive had been transferred laterally to another position of equal pay and status. But when he moved to his new office, he discovered it was equipped with a one-pedestal desk instead of a desk with two sets of drawers. He promptly and privately concluded that his transfer was an actual demotion. As Professor Roethlisberger described it, the man developed "all the symptoms of acute anxiety. He lost sleep, his appetite fell off, and he couldn't concentrate on his work."

The solution was simple and effective. The one-pedestal desk was removed; a two-pedestal desk replaced it. And the executive's symptoms disappeared. It wasn't the desk that had bothered him; it was rather what he believed the desk symbolized to his associates. Obviously the size of his desk meant something to him which had never occurred to top management.

Sometimes, management's unawareness or insensitivity to the individual drives away present or potential employees. A Southern light and power company, in its annual report, listed its many executives in a standardized format. Each executive was given two initials and a last name, "R. H. Buchanan, J. R. Glenn, R. B. Ingram, R. S. Sarasin, N. L. Weissman," and so on. It made a neat and orderly column. But an engineer noticed the list and reached his own conclusion about the company.

"They could just as well have listed their people by social security numbers," he said. "I knew I'd be only another set of initials if I went there." Initials meant no status, so he turned down their offer of an executive position. His status was as important as his salary.

If you wish the status of an executive, you must look and act like an executive. You need only study the magazine cartoons to realize that custom prescribes the executive's appearance just as rigidly as the uniform of an Army sergeant. An executive is expected to look like an executive. His dress and appearance are his personal "package." The American Institute of Men's and Boys' Wear puts it this way:

A young man looking for a good executive position is loaded with talent, but hides it in inappropriate, out-of-date clothes. How is the interviewer supposed to know at first glance that there's ability behind the unattractive camouflage?

Maybe it doesn't always follow that the dressed-right man always succeeds in business or always has more friends, but the connection between dress and success is too strong to be denied. Good appearance does attract favorable attention. Good appearance does command respect. Every employer counts on this. If he is willing to pay for a man's time and talents, he wants him handsomely packaged to create a favorable image of the man and the company.

Without proper executive dress, you unavoidably focus attention on a poor appearance instead of on your ability and experience. You're handicapped and have placed yourself at a competitive disadvantage.

Most job applicants sensibly appear for interviews in their "Sunday suit," making sure to show themselves at their very best. But after they've been hired, they sometimes relax their efforts. One fellow wears slightly soiled "second-day" shirts; another still wears a suit with wide lapels and wide trousers, years after they have gone out of style. Such signs indicate a man who is gauche. They are noticed and commented on unfavorably by his colleagues. His ability may be outstanding, but only his careless appearance stands out. He doesn't look like an executive, and management finds it difficult to think of him as one.

It's even more important to act as an executive should act. This means doing the job of managing for which you were hired. Some executives don't. They become paper shufflers, carefully initialing a procession of memos, and then moving them from the "in" basket to the "out" basket. Others become

memo writers, dictating endless streams of suggestions, comments, analyses, and evaluations to other executives in offices
only a few dozen feet away. They conclude their memoranda
with the line, "Would you please think about this and give me
your recommendations." This generates a never-ending supply
of incoming memos, none of which are ever acted upon, but
which can eventually be routed to still other executives for
their lengthy comments and analyses.

Other executives concentrate on trivia, conducting lengthy
cost studies on the cost of paper clips, or how to eliminate
usage of rubber bands. The less consequential the subject, the
busier they become.

But they're headed for trouble. While they're concerned
with paper clips and rubber bands, major problems are developing in their departments. And they aren't involved in
solving them. They usually don't even know about them. They
fail as executives because they aren't acting like executives.
Sometimes it takes a while before top management becomes
aware of their derelictions, but eventually their misdirected
efforts indeed become noticed.

Some executives, often of the paper-clip-economy type,
expend their energies on letting everyone know how important
they are.

There is the man, for example, who transforms the telephone from an instrument of communication into a symbol
of his superior status. He never makes a phone call himself.
A dozen times a day, he calls to his secretary, "Please get me
Mr. Burke." It would be quicker for him to dial the call himself, but he thinks Mr. Burke will be more impressed if his
secretary makes the call. "Mr. Burke, Mr. Stollmack is calling.
One moment please." If Mr. Burke's secretary has answered
the phone, Mr. Stollmack's secretary, acting on instructions,
won't put Mr. Stollmack on until Mr. Burke has actually
picked up the phone, and is awaiting him. If Mr. Stollmack
outranks Mr. Burke in the corporate hierarchy, he can get
away with it, but the fun develops when both men have equal

status. Then the secretaries begin arguing over whose boss should pick up the phone first. Secretarial hassles which stopped just short of hair-pulling have resulted from such childish emphasis on rank and status.

Executives also argue over where to meet each other. When you want to meet with members of your staff, it's quite proper to hold the meeting in your own office, although you'll suffer no loss of face by occasionally getting together in the offices of your subordinates. But when two executives of equal rank arrange a meeting, the status-struggler seeks to hold it in his own office, so that he can magnanimously play the role of host. He feels very superior when his colleagues come to his lair. The insecure executive struggles for status like a gorilla battling for supremacy over the other males in the troop.

Some executives demean their privileged status by fawning over their subordinates. Expected to act with executive dignity and reserve, they instead cast self-respect to the winds to court popularity.

One new executive, for instance, mustered up his courage to reprimand an employee for poor performance, and to tell him that his work would have to improve. But the executive's firmness endured only long enough for his warning to be delivered. Then he felt seized by pangs of remorse, and began to backtrack.

"You know, Mr. Koyen, I'm sorry as the devil to have to tell you all this, but I just had to do it. If I didn't, I'd catch hell from my boss. I'm sure you understand. Let's go out to lunch today, and forget the whole thing."

His desire to keep the approval of his subordinate had destroyed any effects the warning might have had. The employee was left confused. Was he being criticized, or wasn't he? Was an improvement in his work required to hold his job? It was all unclear.

And he could scarcely leave such a meeting feeling kindly toward the executive. After all, if the criticism was unjustified, why did his superior pass it along? If it was justified, he could hardly respect the executive who weaseled. Either way, he felt that his boss hadn't acted like an executive.

If you act like an executive, you must expect realistically that some of your subordinates will not love you for it. Even when you treat them fairly and honorably, they recognize their dependence upon you for their livelihood, and a fundamental law of human relationships is that dependence engenders hostility. It is almost as certain and inescapable as a mathematical equation. Employees who know that you determine their destiny cannot avoid fearing you and, frequently, resenting your power over them.

As a nation, we should have learned this lesson in the postwar years. We spent billions of dollars to buy friends with our openhanded generosity. We distributed wheat and butter, busses and trucks, bulldozers and air hammers to needy peoples around the world. To make sure that we received credit for our generosity, we painted on every flour sack, every truck door, every piece of equipment, in bold letters the words, "A gift from the people of the United States of America." Everywhere, people accepted our gifts and then reacted with denunciations of the United States. They knew that they were dependent on us for survival, and they bitterly resented their dependence.

The gifts go on, because we have not yet found a more satisfactory way of helping needy peoples. As a nation and as individuals, our lessons have yet to be learned. We still expect gratitude and appreciation from those who depend on us for assistance. It is unrealistic. The executive must reject such expectations, and instead must set his course to treat people fairly without expectation of appreciation. If they react well to his leadership, so much the better. But even if they don't, he must steer a straight course ahead, doing what he thinks is right. For the man who wants to act like an executive, there is no other way.

Another sign of a competent executive is his firmness in

handling difficult employees. Management has publicly vested him with responsibility and authority over his staff. Authority should mean providing constructive leadership, not peremptory ordering and the exercise of military leadership. But sometimes an employee will not respond to suggestions, good example, or encouragement. Hostile to his supervisor, he will resist direction and obstruct the executive. With such employees, the executive must use his authority to the limit to enforce company policy.

Perhaps there is an employee who habitually reports late for work. The executive calls him into the office for a warning. The first time, the employee has a ready excuse. It sounds at least partly plausible. The executive accepts it, but adds a warning for the future.

Soon it happens again, and this time, another excuse is presented. This one is carefully documented, and so the executive accepts it, although with reluctance. He wants to be reasonable and fair. But after the pattern repeats itself several times, the executive is entitled to ask himself whether he is being played for a sucker. The employee may be using repeated lateness to show his dislike for the boss. The executive who tolerates such defiant behavior rapidly destroys himself in the eyes of the employee.

Employee hostility manifests itself when an employee refuses to perform a particular additional function which you have assigned to him; "it's not what you hired me for." He has a point, so you yield. From the moment of his victory, his attitude worsens, and soon he begins acting like a prima donna. Of course, you may fire him, but you're reluctant to "rock the boat" because his work is satisfactory in every other respect. Almost before you know it, the employee is acting as if he, not you, were in charge. If you allow this situation to develop, your subordinate has usurped your authority. You aren't acting like an executive, for you have yielded your responsibility to do what you think best.

Just as an executive must actively direct his staff, so he

must expect to be directed by his superiors. He must be prepared to receive suggestions, guidance, and criticism, in the same manner as he dispenses it to others. But many an executive follows the ancient rule that it is better to give than to receive. He enjoys directing others but resents being directed himself. I once visited a supervisor in a Nashville printing plant who had been hauled on the carpet for alleged dereliction of duty. The supervisor was boiling mad when he talked to me.

"If they treat me like a boy," he said, "I'll act like a boy. If they treat me like a man, I'll act like a man."

What he didn't see was that it was just the other way around. His superior, the vice-president, had begun treating him "like a boy," only after he had reacted to criticism with pouting and sullen anger. The vice-president then curtailed his authority, and insisted on receiving frequent and detailed reports from him. Now he felt like a child who had to account for his weekly allowance. He had failed to act like an executive, so he lost the right to be treated as one.

When I first became a senior executive, I was continually frustrated by one employee, a junior executive who met his minimum work responsibilities, but not a whit more. Nothing seemed to stimulate him. I criticized him. I appealed to his pride. Later, when, by heroic struggle, I found something to praise, I praised him. Nothing improved his performance. Successively, I used every technique I had ever heard of. All failed.

One day, I discovered that he had spent seven years as an Air Force officer before joining the company. His military background suggested a new approach.

"Burnaford," I barked, "here is a job I want done. You will do it, and report back to me Monday at 9 A.M."

He visibly snapped to attention, and did everything but salute. "Yes, sir!" he replied. He took the papers, turned smartly on his heel, and walked out of my office.

From that moment on, I had no further difficulty with

Mr. Burnaford. He could not accept guidance, but he could take military orders. So I provided them. He became more valuable to the company, but he was not an executive, and could not act like one, his military rank notwithstanding.

There are many executives who enjoy the privileges of office but are unwilling to assume the responsibilities. They relish the symbols of power, forgetting why they've received them.

The privileges, the status, and the titles that accompany it are yours to enjoy for the duration of the office. Wear your epaulets lightly. The corporation gives them to you as a reward for accomplishment, and as tools to help you work more effectively in the future. They're not hereditary, nor do they indicate you're a better human being than anyone else.

It's perfectly proper and desirable for you to exercise your privileges to a reasonable degree, but take them too seriously and you're headed for difficulties. The man constantly preoccupied in struggling for status would do better to apply his energies to the job itself. When you act like an executive, both your subordinates and your superiors will treat you like one. Thereafter, the trappings of corporate power will become less important and less necessary to you.

15

....

Are You –
or the Unions –
Too Hot
to Handle?

IN A NATION where 18 million workers are unionized, the chances are considerable that you'll have to deal with a labor union at some time in your executive career. The occasion may be a dispute with union members in your own factory, or an organizing drive aimed at them. It may come when an unresolved union grievance provokes a work stoppage, or when one of your own suppliers is shut down by a strike. Your company plans are suddenly interrupted, and you get good and angry.

Your blood pressure rises. Union disputes can indeed frustrate you. Struggling to meet sales quotas or profit objectives, you are irked by the union's restrictive work rules, arrogant union delegates, and sometimes disruptive activities from your own employees.

If you were faced with declining sales, you would study the problem calmly, plot your counterstrategy, and move to solve the problem. But when faced with a labor union, all too often the executive loses his objectivity. He reacts with emotion. When he tells you the details, his veins stand out at the temples. If he's the president, he threatens to close down the plant before he'll negotiate with the union. If he's a junior department head, he battles the union at every turn, willingly carrying the company flag of resistance.

Why does the executive react so emotionally to the thought of dealing with his organized workers? For one reason, the executive personality differs markedly from that of his employees. He thinks and acts so differently from them that he can't understand their actions. His communication with them is limited; no bridges of understanding have been built. Although the executive may have been a worker himself when a young man, he was, so to speak, "with" the ranks rather than "of" the ranks. More typically, the average executive never was a worker, but began his executive career on college graduation, moving up through sales or administrative posts. The thoughts of an industrial worker are foreign to him. Like all things he does not understand, he fears them.

Contrast the life of an executive, even a junior executive, with that of the union member. The executive is an individualist. He knows that his career will depend on his individual performance. He believes that his security lies solely in his own ability. While he takes pride in his company, he takes even greater pride in himself. In a vigorous, dynamic economy, he knows that promotion opportunities will be his if only he performs well. He is highly competitive, gaining psychological satisfaction by surpassing others. The man with the outstanding sales record, the department head with the best profit performance, the executive with the greatest cost reduction success—these are men who exemplify the management mentality.

The executive is well educated. He holds a college degree. He has acquired the social polish necessary for success. His financial resources may be strained by the demands of a suburban home, but even here, if he needs additional cash, he can usually negotiate a bank loan on favorable terms.

His mentality is flexible. He has worked for three or four firms during his career. He expects to change jobs once or twice more before he reaches his peak. He is prepared to move himself and his family to another city if his company needs him there.

The union member is a different man indeed. His education is limited, probably to high school. The skills he offers for sale are much more limited; few require more than a year or two to learn. Any further training he receives merely refines or updates those basic skills. They have limited dollar value in an increasingly automated economy. The tool- and die-maker, considered the aristocrat of United States labor, earns an average of $3.50 hourly, while the intercity truck driver, protected by one of the nation's strongest unions, averages $3.00 an hour.

The factory worker's job is insecure, for he is paid by the hour, not by the week or the year, and when sales drop off, his job immediately disappears. His security is threatened by mysterious electronic machinery whose feedback mechanism can do his work more skillfully, speedily, and inexpensively.

He lives in a city apartment, or in a small home not too far from the factory. If he needs money, he must borrow it from personal loan companies, paying the highest legal rate of interest to obtain a few hundred dollars cash.

Inevitably, such a way of life develops a different mentality from that of the executive. The worker, threatened by insecurity at every turn, looks toward his fellows for security, since he cannot find it in himself alone. Essentially, he has only one power at his disposal, the right to stop working. This power is meaningless if exercised by an individual, but if the union member combines with other employees, he gains the power to force management to grant his demands by halting production until they do.

The employee watches many of the same television programs as the executive, and reads many of the same magazines and newspapers. He sees the same advertisements. They whet his appetite for a fine home, a new car, a modern kitchen for his wife, travel to distant places. But his earnings will not permit such luxuries; they are beyond his financial reach. He feels "left out." In a country that rewards individual initiative, he lacks the qualifications to climb the corporate ladder. In a country that admires material success, he is, so he believes, a failure. And he is sometimes bitter, sometimes resigned.

The executive and the worker are employed by the same company. But they have two different backgrounds and two different outlooks on life. Where poor communications exist, minor misunderstandings rapidly compound into major conflicts.

There are no gimmicks to produce good employee relations, nor are communications the sole answer to the problem. You may communicate effectively, but good communications can't make up for low wage rates, bad working conditions, or arbitrary treatment by management.

More money by itself isn't the answer either. All too often, managements "put it in the paycheck" but fail to win the labor harmony they seek. For labor disputes are usually caused by more than arguments over pay and hours. The employee who would never quit his job to battle for a seven cents an hour increase will willingly, even enthusiastically, walk a picket line for weeks, if he believes he is fighting for his dignity as a human being.

The foreman who insulted his pride, or the personnel man who refused to satisfy his grievance, has aroused in him a militancy thoroughly disproportionate to the seeming slight. Into his union activity, he then pours all his accumulated frustration, hatred, and resentment of his status. All these feelings had been there to begin with, but they had been submerged. Now, management's insensitivity to his human needs has brought them to the surface, and fused them into a burning determination to get even with the company. Winning that seven cents an hour really means winning revenge for the hurts he believes he has endured.

As the battle is joined, union and management take their case to the public. Statements are issued. Resolutions are passed. The dispute heats up. The union accuses the company of "callous disregard for the welfare of its employees." Management angrily replies that the union's unrealistic demands will drive it out of business. Sometimes the company suggests that perhaps its loyal workers have succumbed to subversive influences.

The union organizer calls a meeting. He knows how to capitalize on management's thoughtless statements. His voice cutting with sarcasm, he reads the company position aloud to the workers. Jeers greet the management statement. The suggestion that the employees may be abetting subversion is taken as a personal insult to their patriotism. They leave the union hall more determined than ever to fight to victory. Even when the strike is settled, they will return to their jobs filled with bitterness and resentment.

At an arbitrator's hearing on wage dispute, the union's paid organizer did not take the stand. Instead, he presented more than two dozen employees, representing all sections of the factory, and all levels of skill. The workers were asked by the union lawyer only one question, "Tell us, please, how you manage to live on your salary."

The witnesses invariably began by itemizing their payroll deductions, and describing their fixed expenses, such as rent, food, medical care for an aged mother, clothes for growing young children, and the like. The final witness, father of six children, revealed to the arbitrator that he was receiving supplementary relief from the city welfare department as an addition to his modest salary for an unskilled job.

Each employee witness gave the impression he was purging himself of the shame of poverty and hardship by public confession. Against such testimony, the company personnel executives could only protest that the employee's personal needs were irrelevant to the economic value of their jobs.

The company protests were duly noted by the employees who packed the arbitration hearings. The word was soon passed back to the men at the workbenches that the company said it was not concerned with the employees' personal needs. Their bitterness increased still more. Moral: a company position which is, or seems to be, insulting to the employees, will antagonize them still more. It may be a reasonable argument, but it won't be listened to. Employees, like executives, will fight to protect their self-respect.

The conditions of modern industrial employment tend to deprive a worker of his individuality. He often feels like a cog in a wheel, lacking in personal worth or importance. He experiences a need to belong to something larger than himself, to gain status and importance. In this need, he does not differ from the executive who likes to tell his golfing associates proudly that he's "associated with" General Electric or United States Steel or Olin Mathieson.

The worker too wants to identify with his company, and to take pride in the association. When management understands this desire, and acts with fairness and decency to deserve the employees' confidence, they receive it. Only when management actions destroy a worker's sense of identification do their employees turn to a union to find it. An AFL-CIO organizer admitted this to me.

"The workers won't listen to me until the company has pushed them around," he said. "When I first call on them in their homes at night, they don't want to listen. 'Everything's OK,' they tell me. 'It's a good company to work for.' I try for a while, and then have to give up. But I always leave my card behind and tell them where to reach me if they want me."

He refilled his glass of beer, and continued. "They often

tell me they're proud to be working for such a fine company. When they talk like that, I know I can't get anywhere.

"But when they start cursing the supervisor, I know they're ready. Only then will they listen when I tell them they've got to stick together, and take pride in the union, instead of in the company."

It's never too late to build a sense of identification with the company. Even in the midst of a strike, it can be done. One corporation in the Southwest had been shut tight by a work stoppage for higher pay. The company had decided it would compromise over the amount of a wage increase to halt the strike quickly and minimize loss of business.

The personnel man gave the president another argument in favor of a quick settlement. Every day the dispute continued, he said, the union members would become more united and more militant, making a final settlement more difficult to obtain on reasonable terms.

The plant manager, too, wanted the strike ended quickly, but only by smashing the union. He was thoroughly fed up, and wanted to break the organization once for all. Year after year, he had wrangled with the union delegate. Ever since he came to manage the plant, annual strike threats had hung over his head. The union has become increasingly difficult to deal with on day-to-day grievances. Now, he recommended fighting it out, and forcing the union to surrender, no matter how long the strike. He argued that a long strike now would produce labor peace for years to come.

But the affected plant was only one of a nationwide industrial empire, so the vice-president in charge of labor relations was called from New York to decide strategy. He arrived at the airport in early afternoon, met briefly with the plant manager, and then withdrew to his hotel room to work. Two days later, his strategy became clear, published for all to see in the local paper in the form of a half-page ad.

"We're sorry our employees are out on strike," the headline read in large letters. Underneath, in a brief text surrounded by large areas of white space, the advertisement continued:

We're proud of them, and we hope they're back with us soon. Their skills and experience have earned our company a nation-wide reputation for fine products.

They've treated us well, and we've tried to treat them well.

Our employees, through their union, have presented us with a series of wage demands. These demands are certainly reasonable, and we would like to meet them. We've always tried to pay our employees the highest wages in our industry, and we want to maintain that record.

But unfortunately, we simply can't afford to meet their current demands. If we were to do so, we'd be forced to raise the price of our products, and the result would be lower sales to the consumer. Many other companies, all over the nation, compete with us, and we must match their prices or lose our present customers to competitors. Inevitably and quickly, that would lead to fewer jobs here in our plant.

Of course, we can afford to increase wages somewhat, and we're ready to sit down with the union and reach agreement. We can cut our production costs in a number of places to compensate for a slight wage increase and we're ready to do so.

So we hope, as we know you do, that the strike will end quickly for the benefit of all.

Three days after the ad appeared, the union members voted by a large majority to negotiate a settlement and return to work. How different this approach from the customary company position during a strike! It's worth analyzing thoughtfully to understand why it worked so effectively and rapidly.

First, it was honest. It was not a clever gimmick, but a realistic statement of the company's competitive position. Had the company been the strongest and most efficient producer in its field, the approach probably would not have worked because the men would have known that the company could afford to grant a substantial wage increase.

Second, it was reasonable in tone. It was quiet and factual, not strident and argumentative. It calmed the waters, rather than agitating them. Without saying so specifically, it appealed to the reasonableness of the reader. Too often, emotion substitutes when the company lacks a reasonable position to defend.

Third, it appealed to the pride of the men, instead of insulting them by suggesting that they were not worth higher wages.

Fourth, it presented its case to the strikers, instead of against the strikers. The company recognized that its problem was to win over the strikers, rather than to defeat them in open battle.

Fifth, it avoided any attempt to split the union ranks by encouraging a back-to-work movement. The company correctly understood the unity which the strike had developed; its approach, therefore, was to win the strikers over as a group rather than as individuals.

And finally, the company did not place its employees in a take-it-or-leave-it position by specifying its terms for ending the strike. Instead, it left the terms open to negotiation, thus salving the pride and self-respect of the negotiating committee which the membership had elected.

Altogether, it was a management approach which succeeded because it was based on honesty as well as on the employees' desire to be proud of themselves, their work, and their employer.

Other managements have discovered that fair dealing is appreciated by employees. One was a Connecticut appliance manufacturing concern, which learned some time ago that it was the number one target for a new union organization drive. The president was a rugged individualist, and his initial reaction was to begin a slam-bang antiunion educational campaign among the unorganized workers. But his calmer second judgment prevailed, and he took a different tack. He began writing a series of signed letters for publication in the company monthly magazine each month. In each letter, he outlined an employment benefit which the company had already provided. In one, he discussed fringe benefits, explaining them in detail. In another letter, he described the company's efforts to provide stable, all-year-round employment. Finally, he discussed specific wage rates, giving dollars and cents figures and comparing them to comparable wage rates in nearby factories.

But he never mentioned that the other factories (where wages were lower) all operated under union contracts. He resisted the temptation to point this out, rightly concluding that his own employees would know this already.

In fact, he never even mentioned the union. He never suggested, even by implication, that the workers would be better off without a union. He simply ignored the subject completely, and let his case rest on a positive presentation of the advantages of working for his company.

Then he figuratively held his breath, and waited for developments. Nothing happened. Two months went by without any employee reaction. The president worried, and wondered whether the union was proceeding secretly to sign up the plant workers. It was almost by chance, a few weeks later, that he learned what had happened. The union organizer had quietly packed up and left town in failure. His arguments had fallen on unreceptive ears.

The reason was that the workers had confidence in the company. They believed what the president had written because he had treated them well in the past. If, however, his solicitude for their welfare had suddenly germinated a week or two after the union organizer appeared on the scene, no amount of slick communication or antiunion propaganda would have succeeded. Nor would it have deserved to.

This isn't an argument for or against unions. It is an argument for treating your employees with fairness and frankness —not just when a union enters the scene, but constantly, because such treatment will produce satisfied employees to the benefit of the company.

One corporate executive who successfully cultivated good labor-management relations is Charles H. Salesky, president of the Hat Corporation of America. He took over his company in the aftermath of a bitter strike that ran for more than six months, during which both the union members and leaders had toughened considerably. But thanks to his basic formula, the corporation has since prospered under reasonable harmony with its two thousand workers. What's Mr. Salesky's secret formula?

"I have a formula, but there's nothing secret about it," he insists. "It's fair. It's strict. It's wide open."

The Salesky formula starts with basics, the need to provide the employee with decent earnings. Careful management planning stabilizes production on an annual basis as much as possible, to eliminate peaks and valleys. This isn't easy to do, but the company makes every effort in this direction, and increased year-round earnings are the result. It constantly introduces new production efficiencies, and voluntarily shares some of the resulting savings with the employees.

Fairness in dealing with employees is another part of the Hat Corporation formula. When grievances arise, as they inevitably will in any company, "it is our definite and declared policy to meet the aggrieved party more than just halfway," Mr. Salesky declares. "If a worker is as much as 10 percent right, we try to find reason for going the other 90 percent of the way."

He estimates that this policy costs the company a very few thousand dollars a year, a sum the company can afford better than the workers. "It's no real hardship for the company, and it makes the men feel 100 percent better about the whole deal," Mr. Salesky says.

Workers at the Hat Corporation plant confirm that management deals with them fairly. "That doesn't mean they give in to us all the time, but they really try to be reasonable," one elderly man told me.

Keeping people informed is another key point in the Salesky program. "When I say 'be frank,' I mean more than exposing my salary or Hat Corporation's income. I mean keep the workers informed about the serious things that concern them."

Asked by *Business Management* magazine if this led to union interference in management functions, Mr. Salesky replied: "It is my experience that workers don't demand to know or have a finger in things that don't concern them. They don't ask for profit forecasts. They don't tell us how to set wholesale prices or what our retail price structure should be. They don't interfere with the handling of our advertising. They respect our right to invest our money where and how we please, as long as we treat individuals right in the process."

Other executives have discovered the same simple truths, stripping away the notion that mysterious techniques are necessary to maintain good labor relations. SKF Industries, Inc., in Philadelphia, had a stormy labor history of conflicts with the United Auto Workers and the United Steelworkers. But today, those conflicts are in distant memory. SKF shows respect for the basic intelligence and fairness of its employees. It expects, and receives, the same fair treatment in return. *Business Week* reported that SKF was a tough bargainer, negotiating important changes in union working rules that saved the company millions of dollars. But the company makes concessions too, with the result that year after year, agreements have been reached peaceably, and one union official said of the company negotiator, "He is a fair man. We are completely satisfied with the contracts we have signed with him."

The policy of fairness to employees, and a respect for their dignity as individuals, can be implemented by the junior executive as successfully as by the president of the company.

Admittedly, it isn't easy. You'll have to shift your mental

gears to do it. Instead of thinking negatively ("fight unions"), you'll have to think positively ("treat the employees fairly"). You'll have to think calmly instead of emotionally, and that's difficult to do.

In major industrial corporations, where unions have long been established and accepted, albeit sometimes grudgingly, management has learned to determine its position entirely on the basis of business considerations. Unionization is not regarded as a personal insult to the executives, but merely as one more factor affecting the costs of doing business.

This doesn't lead to passive acceptance of unions, but rather to a calmer way of developing a management strategy. "We fight to reduce our costs in every area of the company," one steel executive declared. "Sometimes, the costs of our raw materials go up. When they do, we try to use less of them. We work constantly to reduce our costs of production. Likewise, we look at the union problem as one of obtaining our labor supply at the best possible price. We must decide whether it will be less expensive to yield to the union demands in the interest of ensuring uninterrupted production. Or will we be better off to take a strike, and if we do, how much will it cost us to settle later on? Of course, there are other considerations, because we want to treat our workers decently, and we must equally have regard for the problems which a strike creates for our customers.

"But basically," the steel man said, "it's dollars and cents with us, not an emotional crusade."

Such an attitude doesn't develop overnight, nor can it be accomplished without the cooperation of executives up and down the line. If top management regards its labor relations in the same calm manner as it treats its sales and production problems, executives at all levels will be guided accordingly. It's up to the senior executives to set the basic policy, and then to communicate it to junior executives and employees alike.

You can do much to develop good relationships with your employees. By your attitude and actions, you can establish your department as a model for the rest of the company to emulate. Good labor relations result in increased production, less product rejects resulting from defective manufacture, and, often, a better safety record as well. All of these are measurable, and they occur when employees feel reasonably contented on the job.

Labor harmony begins with understanding. By your understanding, you demonstrate your skill in an important area of management responsibility.

16

Trial
by Firing

IF YOU COULD somehow devise a way to photograph the image inside the brain of an average employee, you might capture his secret mental picture of the boss.

Your film might show the executive sitting with a broad smile, almost a grin, across his face. In the employee's mind, the boss lounges comfortably behind a large desk, perhaps smoking a long cigar, the traditional symbol of affluence. He is gesturing expansively with his hands. Across the glass-top desk, the meek and frightened employee sees himself sitting on the edge of a straight-backed chair.

"Edwards," the boss booms loudly, "you're fired. I won't put up with the likes of you! Get out!"

In a quiet voice, the employee replies, à la Walter Mitty, "Mr. Foley, now that I'm out, I want to tell you exactly what I think of your blankety-blank company. . . ." Whereupon, in the dream scene, Edwards pours obscene invective on the executive.

In reality, however, dismissals seldom happen that way. Many executives privately admit that firings are their worst ordeal. Some confess they go to almost any lengths, even beyond the point of good judgment, to avoid them. For every employee who was fired unjustly or without proper warning, executives point to others who were fired years after they should have been, simply because the executive feared to commit the unpleasant act.

Your "brain photograph" is out of focus also in its portrayal of the discharged employee. He seldom gives immediate vent to his true feelings. He is more likely to follow the prudent course of restraint, because he knows that his next employer will certainly check his references. He sees little sense in aggravating the situation by telling the boss "exactly what he thinks," even though he is for the first time "free" to do so. So he usually says little or nothing.

The executive wishes he could do the same. He dislikes intensely having to fire an employee. He doesn't relish a "scene." He knows that a terminal interview may produce acid words, shock, and frequently tears. The boss never can be certain whether he should be prepared with a crying towel, body armor, or a pat on the back. In our society, which frowns on public display of emotion, the employee's unpredictable reaction embarrasses and unnerves the executive.

Further, dismissal is, to say the least, an unfriendly act. The executioner does not make a friend of his victim. No matter how well justified the dismissal, staff sympathy will be extended to the underdog, rather than to the company executive who performed the execution. "Hatchet man" is the kindest epithet that he will be called. The executive who wants to be well liked does not enjoy the villain's role that circumstances and his position have assigned to him.

Personal reasons like these, of course, often account for executive reluctance to terminate an unsatisfactory employee. But there are solid business reasons too. When a staff member is fired, shock waves radiate through his department, upsetting the equilibrium, and disturbing his erstwhile associates. Sympathetic vibrations shake other employees, and intensify their own job insecurities. So the executive often leans over backward to avoid damaging the morale of his entire department.

Yet firings are sometimes necessary, despite their unpleasantness and the consequences they may create. During the span of your executive career, you will probably have to fire at least a few people, so you should face the unpleasant fact head-on.

Dismissal from employment is indeed a severe blow to the victim. At the very least, it constitutes criticism of his personal ability, and damages his self-esteem. More likely, it also results in prolonged and demoralizing unemployment, financial hardship, and possibly a sharply reduced standard of living. The executive who has himself been unemployed, at one time or another in his own career, will hesitate to visit such hardships on anyone. Yet sometimes it must be done.

While the employee's responsibility is to himself alone, yours is to your department, and to the entire company. Certainly you do not serve the company's interests by protecting an incompetent. Neither do you help the entire group of employees when you retain a man who is not earning his pay.

For the employee who has failed to perform his duties endangers the jobs of others besides his own. By damaging the business, he weakens the entire organization. The ineffective salesman menaces the steady employment of production workers when his poor sales presentation loses orders to competitors. The incompetent administrator who allows office costs to climb makes it more difficult for the company to compete without raising prices. Keeping a corporate failure on the payroll, because of misplaced kindness on your part, endangers the employment of all.

To him as an individual, you indeed have a moral obligation: the obligation of giving him an opportunity to produce satisfactory work that will justify his salary. He, in turn, has a responsibility: to produce satisfactory work that justifies his salary. If you have given him ample opportunity, but he has failed to keep his end of the bargain, your responsibility is ended. Human decency may induce you to help him further, but such help cannot include keeping him on your staff unproductively.

Before you finally decide to fire a member of your staff, ask yourself if you are acting out of concern for the company's best interests, or out of personal pique and anger? Arbitrary exercises of whim are not untypical. A high executive who told me there were too few firings in industry simultaneously insisted there were too many firings for emotional reasons. He cited careers smashed because employees irritated the boss with their personal idiosyncrasies. These included rocking back and forth in an office chair, or smoking in the presence of The Man. In one case, an employee was fired for wearing tasteless clothes and loud, flashy ties. Although his work was satisfactory in every respect, the annoyance of his conservative boss grew until it exploded, and the employee found himself outside looking in.

In another case, a salesman found himself "on the outs" with his manager, entirely for personality reasons. The salesman was a consistent producer. But outside of business hours, he was reputed to be something of an intellectual, enjoying literary classics and hi-fi music. The sales manager, a self-made, hearty handshaker, imagined in his private thoughts that the lowly salesman regarded him disdainfully. (I personally observed the two men in action over a period of seven months, and saw no such evidence). The manager's dislike grew until finally he found an excuse to fire the salesman.

The company is the loser when dismissals take place for such reasons. An able executive would insist on a factual analysis of the man's performance, fairly balancing his strengths and weaknesses to reach a total judgment before permitting the dismissal to take place. For dismissals create problems as well as solving them.

Even when you're certain an employee is unsatisfactory in some aspects of his work, will his successor likely be any better? Since the perfect employee (or executive) has yet to be found, it is a reasonable assumption that his successor will, in due time, display other shortcomings. Will the company then be better off? If the employee has displayed some valuable attributes in his work, perhaps it would be worthwhile to spend additional time and money to retrain him because of his already known strengths. Or will it be better, and less expensive, to start from the beginning with a new employee, selecting him carefully and training him thoroughly? Such questions should stimulate a more factual appraisal before you make the firing decision.

It's also in order to ask whether you gave the employee proper warning. This isn't a legal obligation, but a good business practice because a "last chance" sometimes produces real improvement.

The key words are "proper warning." Proper criticism is not a vague, general complaint of your dissatisfaction, but a specific description of the employee's failings. Usually, it requires telling the employee what improvement you will require if he's to keep his job. A time limit is usually set.

For a St. Louis architect, the time limit for one of his employees was one month. He had reached the end of his rope with his office receptionist and was about to dismiss her. Repeatedly, he had told her of his dissatisfaction, but to no avail. Finally, he called her in for one last warning.

"Miss Morris," he said, "I'll give you one last chance, but if you haven't improved in thirty days, I'm going to have to let you go."

"Is it too late for me? Have I still got a chance?" the young lady asked.

"Yes, you do have a chance," the architect told her. "But one more complaint about you from a visitor and that's the end. When someone comes to my office, he's my guest. I want you to treat him that way. Take his coat and make him comfortable. Offer him a magazine. Apologize for keeping him waiting if I'm delayed. Keep checking to make sure I haven't forgotten him."

Miss Morris looked nonplussed. "Certainly," she replied. "You never told me these things before. I knew you didn't like my work, but I didn't know why."

You might think that a girl of reasonable intelligence would have known enough to extend these elementary courtesies without being told. But she hadn't.

In any case, Miss Morris went forth and sinned no more. She became the epitome of friendly courtesy and helpfulness to his guests. Her warm smile showed that she was finding new personal pleasure in her work. A few weeks later, when the architect complimented her, she beamed with pride and repeated, "I only wish you had warned me much earlier."

The executive is obliged, for his own sake, to give proper warning. But more than that. He must also ask himself whether the employee's shortcomings are really shortcomings at all. Executives have on occasion fired employees for acts which should instead have brought promotions. The staff member with an independent turn of mind most frequently finds himself the victim of such faulty judgment, usually rendered by an executive who himself is frightened.

In the New York magazine industry, they tell the story of a senior editorial executive who one day felt himself called upon to warn his superiors that the magazine was headed for disaster unless they made drastic changes in its contents. The editorial formula, he declared, was old-fashioned, lacking in interest for today's readers; it urgently needed revitalization. The executives listened intently, and after his impassioned talk, one asked him to write a memorandum summarizing his thoughts. This he did.

A week later, the publisher himself phoned and asked him to stop in to chat. When he entered the office, his memo was lying on the desk, heavily underlined with crayon.

"I'm sure you realize," the publisher said, "that you've

created an impossible situation for yourself here. I really have no choice but to ask you to resign."

The words did not surprise the executive, for the office grapevine had warned him this might happen. He resigned on the spot, and left the company.

The publisher, who himself had been responsible for the outdated editorial policy, had no desire to hear criticism from anyone, especially from within his own ranks. Had he analyzed the situation objectively, he might more properly have thanked the executive for his integrity and loyalty. Even if the publisher was unreceptive to constructive suggestions, one can hardly conclude that the executive should have been terminated as a dangerous cancer on the corporate body.

In truth, the executive had not created an impossible situation for himself, but only for the publisher who had chosen voluntarily to blind himself to reality.

Less than four months later, the publication closed its doors, and departed this life. Only then did other executives recall the prophetic warning of the dismissed man.

The employee who doesn't really care, the executive who has no deep-felt loyalty to his employer, will never create such a situation. It is only the company-minded man, however misguided he may sometimes be, who will typically become involved. Management, understandably, tends to regard him as presumptuous and irritating. Yet, carefully handled, his value is greater to an alert management than a half-dozen conformists who do what they're told, think what they're expected to think, and say what they're expected to say.

Should such a man be fired? Certainly not, if his contributions outweigh the problems he creates. If you're the executive with final decision-making authority in his case, balance the pros and cons carefully before making up your mind.

But the executive or employee who constantly irritates others, who disrupts a harmonious operation by inability to work well with others, is a different story again. If management must constantly concern itself with undoing his damage, he has tipped the scales against himself, and deserves to go.

Sometimes a man faces dismissal because he has failed to perform a job for which he was not hired, is not qualified, and has never wanted to perform. If management, by a poor personnel assignment, has shifted him arbitrarily to another type of work for which he is admittedly untrained and unqualified, then the personnel man deserves to be dismissed instead of the transferred employee. When this type of dismissal impends, it's a good policy to ask why the man can't be assigned to a proper position, instead of losing his services entirely. Sometimes, simply asking the question is enough to produce from nowhere a suitable post for him. It eliminates an unnecessary termination.

But if there are valid reasons for the transfer, the employee has the responsibility to adapt. His previous job may have been eliminated by automation, and management is trying to place him elsewhere. Management must show patience, but if he resists retraining, there is little choice left except to terminate him.

While your decision should not be made emotionally or hurriedly, neither should you use excessive caution. Sometimes, you'll face an open-and-shut case, where clearly you have no alternative except to fire a man.

For instance, if an employee makes an appointment to see you two days in advance, enters your office, and abuses you with a string of four-letter words (as once happened to me), do you really have any choice?

Or what would you do if you three times warned a young secretary not to leave the office for a midmorning coffee break in the downstairs luncheonette, and she then proceeded to do exactly that, adding insult to injury by an additional midafternoon coffee break? To keep such openly defiant employees on your staff would destroy your own authority over your department, and would damage the morale of conscientious employees who were complying with office rules. In such cases, your decision will be easily reached, and should be quickly executed, preferably before sundown.

It is difficult to study such cases of insubordination without concluding that the employees are challenging you to let them get away with it. It's like the little boy walking around the schoolyard with a chip on his shoulder, looking for trouble. I suspect that their insubordinate actions are a sign that, whether or not knowingly, they really want to be fired.

I don't pretend to understand why anyone should want to be fired. But I've known people who courted dismissal. A middle-management executive who worked for me some years was one. He had been doing a poor job, and many warnings failed to produce an improvement. My dissatisfaction continued, and I should have terminated him at that time. Instead, I allowed him to continue, month after month.

I must confess the reasons why I did. He was a bright, able, and extremely likeable individual. He had served the company for many years. I knew that he needed every penny of his high salary to maintain his present standard of living. I worried what would happen to him if he lost his job. So I stalled.

But finally, his work became so clearly unsatisfactory, judged by even minimum standards, that I could delay no longer. Nevertheless, I still experienced considerable inner struggle before I could make up my mind. Searching my soul, I realized that I had delayed because it was all too easy for me to imagine myself in his shoes. With further procrastination clearly impossible, I called him into my office to give him the unpleasant news.

His unexpected reaction startled me. He showed not the slightest bit of perturbation. With utter calm, and an assured pleasantness of manner, he told me: "I'm not surprised. I knew this was coming. As a matter of fact, I really haven't worked very hard for at least a couple of years."

Before I could recover from my shock, he thanked me warmly for my courtesy in keeping him on the payroll for so long. He said cheerful good-byes around the office, and left without a harsh word. A few weeks later, he phoned me to report that he was safely ensconced in another executive position, where, he assured me happily, he would not have to work quite so hard.

This was not the only such incident I have experienced, and it taught me the difference between humane consideration, on the one hand, and being played for a sucker, on the other.

When you have finally made up your mind to dismiss an employee, however long you have taken to decide, you should move quickly. The longer you wait, and certainly if you wait more than a week, the greater the chance that rumors will spread through the office while the necessary papers are processed.

The first step, depending on your company policy, may be securing clearance from your superiors. The next step is to arrange for the personnel department to compute his accrued vacation pay, and other benefits. Does he hold an outstanding petty cash advance? Were credit cards issued to him? (One dismissed executive retained his air travel card for only two weeks after his termination. In that time, he managed to fly from New York to San Francisco, thence to a Miami vacation, before returning home to find a request for the card. He returned it, and told the company to try to collect!) All these routine matters must be disposed of so that his final paycheck is in your hands for presentation at the close of the fateful interview.

Because you can never be sure how an employee will receive the harsh news, you'll want to select carefully the right location for the interview. He may emerge shaken and emotional. If your office is a glassed-in partition in the midst of a busy open area, it's hardly a satisfactory place. Is there a quiet corner office where you can speak in complete privacy, and allow him to leave inconspicuously? Such thoughtfulness will avoid embarrassing displays in the office, and he may appreciate an opportunity to recover his composure before saying good-bye to his associates.

When you give him the word, it may or may not come as a surprise, but it will usually cause shock. It's wise to minimize the shock by avoiding entirely the use of the word "fire." "You're fired," are blunt words. There are gentler ways to say the same thing. "I'm afraid we're going to have to let you go." "It looks as though we've come to a parting of the ways." "I'm sorry to have to tell you that you're out." A little detail; but sometimes it eases the pain of the corporate guillotine. I heard an oil industry executive boast that he could perform an execution so skillfully that the victim never realized he had been fired until after he was out of the office.

Corporations generally display consideration when the victim himself is an executive. The fiction of no friction is carefully maintained. Executives are rarely "fired." They customarily "resign for personal reasons." An executive leaves "for a new position, to be announced shortly." Since his successor is often announced in the same memo, this is minor consolation for his injured pride.

Sometimes executives try to make things easier for themselves by passing the buck, and blaming their superiors for the decision to fire an employee. "I'm sorry, old man; I've gotten the word from on high. I don't like to do this, but I have my orders." This is the cowardly course to follow; seldom does it deceive the victim. If the decision was yours, you should take the responsibility. If the decision actually was made at a higher level, you nevertheless should accept the burden of responsibility, for your superiors have delegated it to you.

A terminal interview is not the place to display your resentment at the victim. It is easy to feel anger, because he has failed you. If you originally had selected him, his failure reflects adversely on your own judgment. The temptation is strong to "tell him off," but the sheer act of dismissal is punishment enough. I've been told of cases where an executive accompanied a dismissal with criticism of a savage and destructive character. In hurt tones, he asked if the employee ever "took the trouble to think before you acted?"

"How could you possibly have made such a stupid decision?" "There's really no excuse for this performance." "Didn't you realize what would happen?" The victim left his office shattered by intemperate and destructive criticism which was grossly disproportionate to the offense.

At some point in the interview, the employee will certainly ask you for a bill of particulars, but think twice before you pour out your long list of grievances. If you do, he will inevitably begin a detailed refutation of every point. The discussion will accomplish nothing except to raise the room temperature. A wiser course is simply to listen quietly, and avoid engaging yourself in argument.

Certainly, you owe it to him to tell the general grounds for his dismissal. But the more you soften them, the better. Gentle, vague words are preferable to a harsh blast, provided that your words are truthful and honest. If, to ease the pain, you falsify, you will do him and the company an injustice which may rebound against you in the future.

Should you, out of paternal kindness, try to help him? Should you specify his shortcomings in sufficient detail so that he may learn from them and avoid difficulty on his next job? Decency and humanity may suggest this course.

The answer I've evolved over the years is this: Try to avoid compounding the bitter hurt. My experience makes me doubt that you'll be able to help him at all.

For him, dismissal means personal failure. Nothing could be more painful. His self-respect has been wounded. His instinct for protection will immediately raise his psychological defenses to preserve himself against further injury. It is quite unlikely that he will be receptive to your specifications of his shortcomings. He will refuse to believe that he has failed. Instead, he will convince himself that you have failed to appreciate him, or have shown poor judgment in rating him adversely. He will hardly be in a mood to be told about his unsatisfactory work, even "for his own good."

Indeed, sometimes a dismissal does benefit the employee, but a discharged person will rarely admit it. If he was clearly miscast in the wrong occupation, firing may compel him to shift into another for which he's better suited.

He's a better judge than you of what's best for him. Too many successful executives can recall incidents early in their career when they were told they were in the wrong occupation. But instead of changing occupations, they changed employers and often found success, while their superiors—the men who fired them—faded into oblivion. You may think you know what's best for the employee, but discretion suggests silence on this point. If you've just fired him, he'll not take kindly to your well-intentioned vocational guidance.

And don't make the mistake of asking his comments on the department from which he is departing. You can't use a fired employee as a management consultant. Instead of counsel, you'll more likely get vitriol.

When the deed is done, the way to terminate the interview is to give the man his final paycheck, wish him well, and say good-bye. The practice of keeping a dismissed employee at work for a final two weeks is fortunately disappearing. It is wasteful to the company, for a man cannot work efficiently after dismissal. And it is cruel to the man himself, for it returns him daily to the scene of his failure. The situation is thoroughly awkward for all concerned. The dismissed man's presence hangs like an albatross around the necks of the remaining employees, increasing their own anxiety and leaving them to grope for something to say, morning after morning, for ten working days. Today, most companies prefer to give him two weeks pay "in lieu of notice." It's better all around.

Hopefully, you won't have many occasions to fire an employee. But when you do, face up to the fact that the victim will not admire you for it, no matter how much consideration you show. All you can do is try to be human while you perform the act.

Living with
Your Secretary

IT'S AN OLD SAW that you spend more of your waking hours with your secretary than with your wife. It's also true that, as an executive, you spend more time with your secretary than with anyone else in the company. If "people problems" develop within your department, they'll probably be first detected by your secretary. When you try to motivate your staff toward better performance, you will do well to begin with your secretary, for she's your best link to the staff.

Your secretary can help you succeed. Or she can destroy your career by improper behavior. The American Management Association asked, "Are you aware of how much an executive's performance—his status and prestige—depends on the way his secretary performs?" Any person who can exercise so much influence on your executive career is worthy of close attention and careful handling.

Your secretary contributes equally to your prestige and your performance. In many companies, a secretary outside your door is the most visible sign that you have become an executive; a secretary is automatically assigned to each executive, whether or not his work load requires one. Higher in the executive hierarchy, your secretary becomes a major status symbol. When you reach vice-presidential level, your secretary may have an office of her own, with her name on the door. At the top, the president may have two secretaries, while the chairman of the board crowns the pinnacle by designating his principal secretary as an executive assistant, and in turn provides her with a secretary.

But changing business conditions and new technology threaten to displace the secretary from her honored position. She may already be well on her way toward becoming as passé as the old-fashioned clerk described by William S. Gilbert in *H.M.S. Pinafore:*

> "As office boy I made such a mark
>   That they gave me the post of a junior clerk.
>   I served the writs with a smile so bland
>   And I copied all the letters in a big round hand.
>   I copied all the letters in a hand so free
>   That now I am the ruler of the Queen's Na-vee!"

The typewriter eliminated the writing clerk; a century later, the punched card wiped out hundreds of thousands of clerical jobs. Soon, your private secretary may also vanish in the same manner. One by one, her traditional duties are disappearing. If the trend continues, her only function may be to serve your morning coffee.

Today, she spends the largest part of her time in handling your correspondence. First, she sits at your elbow to record in shorthand your golden flow of words. Then she returns to her desk, to translate her cryptic scrawl back into English, in a form approximating what you said originally. As a final step, she types it neatly for your signature.

"Miss Amy, please take a letter," are words which have inwardly thrilled every young executive with a sense of his own importance. As the opening scene in a Hollywood movie, they symbolize executive power and status.

But now the electronic age has come to the executive suite in the form of the dictating machine. It may produce explosive effects comparable to those which followed the invention of the steam engine or the cotton gin. For it immediately abolishes a big part of the secretary's job. It keeps her out of your office, except when once or twice daily she enters to pick up your dictation tape. No longer is the time of two people—yours and hers—required to write a letter; only you and the machine are needed. So she sits outside at her typewriter and transcribing machine, her ears glued to a headset. She types your words directly as she hears them. Shorthand, her professional badge of skill, is no longer necessary. Suddenly, your secretary's skill, developed over many years of practice, has become as superfluous as the art of the village blacksmith. This segment of her duties has been downgraded to that of a typist. In some offices, your dictation will be handled not even by your own typist, but by an impersonal institution known as a typing pool.

Answering your telephone is another important job of your secretary. She uses the five-button phone (two outside lines, two interoffice extensions, and a "hold" button) which has been as much a part of the executive scene as the button-down collar on Madison Avenue. But now the telephone company has introduced the Call Director. It has not five buttons but eighteen, and it's correspondingly efficient. With the Call Director, one girl at a single location can answer any of ten or fifteen telephones. No longer do secretaries have to "cover" each other while they lunch; a single receptionist can cover an entire office. Some companies use the Call Director to enable two or three girls to answer and place telephone calls for an entire department. It cuts costs and increases efficiency. But it also erodes still further the traditional duties of the private secretary.

Such electronic equipment wasn't necessary in the days when secretaries of good quality were available in sufficient quantity to meet every executive need. Today, able executive secretaries are almost as scarce as engineers experienced in thermonuclear fusion. The college classroom and the marriage bed have combined to remove large numbers of potential secretaries from the labor market. The girl who, a generation ago, would have become a secretary after her high school graduation, today goes on to college. She must earn a college degree today to maintain the social status which she once automatically acquired with a high school diploma. If perchance, she doesn't enroll in college, she probably has already married, for half of all the girls in the United States who are expected ever to marry now marry before the age of 20.3 years, according to census figures.

You can see the resulting shortage in the classified ads—column after column of enticements to lure the young lady to this company or that. As a result of these factors, the typical secretarial job today remains unfilled for as long as four to eight weeks.

Because competent secretaries are so difficult to find, executives frequently lure them by describing jobs in glowing but exaggerated terms. "Excellent opportunity," "chance for advancement," "pleasant and interesting job," "stimulating diversified work," are phrases used in the classified ads.

And when you finally find a secretary, her skills may not meet even your minimum requirements. One large New York employer was compelled to introduce, at its own expense, a ten-hour course in spelling for new clerks and secretaries! But while the secretary's basic skills may be low, her pay will be high. The result is increased pressure on management to substitute office typing pools and "telephone secretaries" for the private executive secretary. It becomes difficult to justify a private secretary for each executive, simply to maintain his high status, when electronics can do the job better and at lower cost.

You were promised, however, at the time of your promotion, that you'd be allowed to hire your own secretary. While the personnel department searched for candidates, you improvised with temporary help. Now they've located a promising young lady who wants to meet you. She'd like to size you up as a prospective boss, and find out the details of the work she'd be expected to do.

In your interview, you won't need to concern yourself with her skills, her accuracy as a stenographer, or her speed as a typist. She has already passed tests administered by the personnel department. Your task is to determine whether she's the right person for the job, and whether her personality will be compatible with yours.

You describe the position to her. She'll take your dictation, of course, and answer your telephone. She'll make your appointments while screening out unwanted callers or visitors. She'll open your mail and organize your work. She'll keep your files so efficiently that, a week from tomorrow, she'll be able to put her finger quickly on that memo you wrote to your branch manager in Wisconsin Rapids.

She listens intently, and from her questions, it's apparent that she really wants the job. But don't embellish your description of her duties. If the "opportunity for advancement" which you offer her hinges on the unlikely possibility that the elderly office manager may someday retire, this is hardly honest. If the "interesting" work becomes repetitious and boring after two or three weeks, you're likely to lose your woman quickly, because the job wasn't what she had been led to expect.

It's a rule of life that, in general, you get what you ask for. If you attract your secretary by telling her that the job will be easy, the work will be light, the atmosphere will be pleasant, you'll find she expects just that, and no more. When the work load becomes heavy, and you must ask her to stay late, you'll have an unhappy woman on your hands.

So take the opposite tack, and warn her instead that the job will be difficult. You may tell her you'll have a heavy work load, that occasionally she will be expected to work late, that she'll be under constant pressure. Then when the heat is on, she'll be prepared realistically to accept it. If the work load turns out to be lighter than you warned, she'll be pleasantly surprised.

But carry it too far, paint a totally black picture, and she won't take the job. She should be told the pleasant side too. If you are willing to give her considerable responsibility, she should know it beforehand. The woman who likes to think and act for herself will regard it as a plus if you welcome her initiative. If she'll often be "on her own" because of your absences from the office, she will consider this an attractive feature of the job.

The time to establish the rules of the game is at the beginning. If your office hours are nine to five o'clock, you should tell her so firmly before she's hired, not afterwards. I always add at this point, "If you think you'll have trouble getting to the office promptly each morning, you should tell me now, because I would expect you to be at your desk ready for work on time every day."

Although you're hiring a secretary and not an executive, the selection may be more difficult for you than the choice of someone to fill a top position. The reason is that the applicant is a woman and you are a man.

You won't look upon her as you would a male job applicant. You'll quickly notice whether she's comely or homely. No detail of her figure, from neckline to ankle will escape you. The female applicant expects this. Having discovered the rules for survival in a male business world, she has carefully prepared for her interview with you. Her grooming is immaculate; her dress is conservative; her smile is working overtime. She may lack experience in dealing with executives as such, but she is fully able to handle herself with men. If she doesn't know how to cope with you as her prospective boss, she will probably do very nicely by treating you with charm and attention.

While, outwardly, you may appear to be interviewing her

with cold objectivity and businesslike manner, she knows this isn't so, and so do you. One perceptive professional secretary told me that male executives often acted as if they were sizing up opportunities for subsequent dalliance. Sometimes a young executive, hiring a secretary for the first time, mistakes a girl's job-seeking charm as an invitation for an affair.

Your social life is your own business. If you mix it with the company's business, your life will become complicated. I haven't heard of any executives who were asked to resign because of involvement with their secretaries, but I know several promising careers that were halted in their tracks by high jinks after five. You can't successfully combine an executive position with an office affair. The time to establish your relationship correctly is the first moment you meet your new secretary.

By nothing more than the tone of your voice or the look in your eye, you can draw a line between you and your secretary which must not be crossed. That line, unstated but very real, must establish a business relationship between you, nothing more. Your secretary must always realize that she is your employee, not your social acquaintance, however friendly you may be. She may indeed be your social equal in every sense, but in her office relationship, she is your subordinate, not your equal. She is working for you, and with you, in a business enterprise, not a social situation. No matter how friendly you may become, even if your ages are similar, you should always be addressed as Mister. In some offices, executives customarily address their secretaries by their first names, but here, too, if custom is not firmly established, it might be preferable to call her "Miss Smith," rather than "Rosemary," to avoid undue familiarity.

During the many hours you spend working closely with your secretary, she'll inevitably share your moments of triumph and distress, of accomplishment and frustration. Her position at your side stimulates a common bond of understanding. One executive commented that it was a closer bond than he had formed with his wife, for his spouse was far removed from a day-to-day knowledge of his problems at the office.

As such unspoken bonds develop with the passage of time, the dangers of emotional entanglement increase. Frequently, emotional ties grow beneath the surface. Neither person is aware of their existence. They may erupt one day, when a scheduled business lunch is unexpectedly canceled at the last moment, and you invite your secretary to lunch.

The luncheon is an opportunity to show appreciation to your secretary for work well done. It is a courteous and gracious gesture which she will appreciate. But, if after a couple of drinks, the conversation turns to the personal, you're extremely close to that invisible line if indeed you haven't already crossed it. If the conversation leads to an afterwork meeting for cocktails, you've already fundamentally altered your business relationship. From that point, you're on your own, and there's not much point in your reading any books on executive advancement. You'll have enough other problems to occupy your mind.

"There was once a happy time (remember?) when an executive's tensions were eased easily by the view (from his office) of a pretty secretary. Sometimes he even eased his aching feet by taking her out dancing, with the phoned-home excuse of an 'important' client in town," said *McCall's* Magazine recently in discussing various toys to reduce executive tension.

"Perhaps the modern type of tension toy is an improvement, but we still think the old-fashioned kind has merit. We can't believe it has really gone out of style."

But it has. Most observers of the executive scene confirm its demise. Today's corporate environment does not encourage the employment of your secretary as a dancing partner. Nor is dancing with the boss her idea of a dream evening. The executive secretary has her mind on other things. Unlike the bright young girl newly promoted from the typing pool, the professional secretary has goals and motivations different from those of the young beginner. For the young girl, a secretary's position fills an interlude before marriage or motherhood. The older secretary is either already married or has abandoned hope of reaching the altar. She expects to continue working indefinitely, and consequently brings to her job a seriousness of mind and professionalism of attitude. Whether thirty-four or forty-four, or fifty-four, she's referred to as a "career gal." She's a very special type, and requires equally special handling by her boss.

Such a woman craves hard work, and thrives on responsibility. She will cheerfully come early and stay late. The more initiative you allow her, the better she'll like it, and the more valuable to you she'll become. She'll be delighted if you allow her to compose your letters instead of merely using her to transcribe your dictation. The best secretary I ever had could accurately anticipate my responses to much of my incoming correspondence. Although her style of expression was quite different from my own, she had carefully studied my characteristic expressions and sentence structure, and could write a reply that read uncannily like one I might have dictated. Sometimes, when signing the outgoing mail at the day's end, I had to read a letter twice before I could decide whether she or I had originally written it. Because my correspondence was heavy, it was a marvelous time-saver.

But, more important, my secretary relished the opportunity to use her brains and ability. Applying her secretarial skills was not enough to stimulate her, but exercising her judgment provided satisfaction. She, not I, decided which letters to answer, and often, what to say. Occasionally, I would have to rewrite one of her letters, but this was a small price to pay for the overall benefits.

The able executive will seek to develop his secretary into

a genuine assistant. "Make-work" in the form of artificial assignments to keep her busy won't satisfy her. But if you delegate work that will actually relieve your own burden, she'll be delighted, and so will you.

It may take quite a while before your new secretary reaches the point where she's qualified to work independently. She must first learn her job and a good deal about yours too. Her first attempts will falter, and much of her work will have to be done a second time. You'll need patience and understanding until your investment pays off and she can assume greater responsibility.

There are many ways to use all of your secretary's ability instead of only part. She can help organize your time, and schedule your appointments. When you're planning an out-of-town trip, she can arrange your travel schedule, and, subject to your approval, make reservations. She can follow up your various activities to make sure that staff reports are received promptly as they become due. If she is able to perform all these duties for you, you have a good secretary and a valued assistant.

While it's good to give maximum responsibility to your secretary, however, that responsibility should be strictly limited to business matters. Your personal affairs are another thing entirely. There's no harm in occasionally asking your secretary to make a personal phone call for you, or even asking her to do a minor shopping errand, but the less the better. One executive secretary told me she spent one hour a day updating the investment chart of her boss. Each afternoon at four o'clock, after the stock market had closed, she telephoned his broker for final prices, which she then multiplied on a small adding machine. Another girl complained that her duties included balancing the executive's personal checkbook each month. Still another lamented that she was expected in mid-December to purchase a complete collection of Christmas gifts for the wife and children of her boss.

Each of these executive secretaries performed the assigned chores with a smile, but inwardly they resented the imposition. It was not why they were hired, they said; the boss should have done the tasks himself.

The only thing that might have been worse, one told me, was doing chores for the wife of the boss. That happens too. In one company, an executive gave his secretary the afternoon off so that she could go to his home and baby-sit for his seven-month-old son. His superior never found out. Fortunately for him, when his secretary finally quit in disgust, she never divulged to anyone the real reason why.

It's quite proper to make the most of your assistant, but for the sake of the company, not for your personal needs. Chattel slavery having been abolished in 1865, your secretary hasn't been assigned to you as a personal serf, and she deserves better than to be treated as one.

Nor should she be made into an office informer, even if she volunteers to play the part. She may enjoy the opportunity of passing on to you rumors, tidbits, and gossip about your staff. Because she has your ear, and can command your attention at all times, she is in a position to influence your opinions of your subordinates. The woman who seeks power and influence particularly enjoys this role, if you allow her to play at it.

Because the state of office morale is more readily visible to your secretary than to you, you'll be tempted to encourage her amateur detective work.

But what is proper behavior for your secretary? What is business information and what is malicious gossip? What is proper observation and what is improper snooping? What is objective description and what is character assassination? Sometimes the line is not easily drawn.

You can hardly decline to listen to her "intelligence reports" and it would be unwise to do so. Sometimes, she'll pass along new information you'll immediately want to check on for yourself. But don't encourage her by asking further questions about this employee or that. The staff soon will regard her snooping (and yours) with distaste.

It's another thing entirely to use your secretary as an open-and-aboveboard listening post. Employees may find it easier to say things to her than to you, although their remarks are intended for your ears. In such cases, you should instruct her to tell the employee frankly that she will pass the information on to you. Once when my work kept me away from the city for lengthy periods, I suggested to the staff that they tell my secretary any information they wanted me to know. They did so, and apparently it was habit-forming, for they continued to keep her informed long after I was back at my desk. It gave me still another channel of communication, to supplement my own direct face-to-face contacts, and everyone seemed to prefer it to clandestine snooping.

The big danger in using your secretary as an office informer is that she will filter information through the screen of her own likes and dislikes. If you yourself don't know what's going on in the department, she can prejudice you against a particular employee by reporting a series of damaging "facts." They may be pulled out of context unfairly; or she may have omitted favorable information which would counterbalance the negatives. You can hardly avoid being influenced by reports of this kind. Yet the man who succumbs is in effect delegating to his secretary a responsibility which he should not delegate to anyone. His secretary won her position by her secretarial skills, not by her ability to evaluate other employees. If you need to keep an "office snoop," you've cut yourself off from firsthand contact with your own staff.

The role of the executive-secretary-turned-office-informer comes into being only when the executive finds it necessary to rely on someone else to keep him informed. To eliminate the need for informers, therefore, keep close enough to your staff so that you know what's on their minds without benefit of middleman. By so doing, you cut the ground away from the secretary who is only too eager to do your listening for you.

If you don't want your secretary to be an informer, however, there will be times when you'll need to make her a scapegoat. The situation may arise when you forget to write an important letter to a customer. He calls on the phone, asking what happened. To cover up your own error, you tell him, "I'm sorry, Mr. Sabagh, I dictated the letter, but my secretary must have slipped and failed to get it out. I'll talk to her and have her get it out immediately."

Your secretary has been standing by, listening to your end of the telephone conversation. Her face reddens. She knows very well what happened. You, not she, forgot to write the letter. But she's getting the blame.

You won't often forget to write an important letter. When you do, the right thing to do is to apologize for your own error and promptly correct it. There are times, however, when it will be expedient to place the blame on your secretary's shoulders. A customer who would be annoyed or insulted by your failure will be more inclined to accept the inconvenience if it is explained as a secretary's mistake.

When this happens, it's best to be completely candid with your secretary. You may explain to her that you know the error was yours, not hers, and that you felt it necessary to "pass the buck" to her to pacify a customer who would otherwise be irritated. Perhaps you may tell her that such a situation increases her value to you, because it retained a valued business relationship. From an ethical viewpoint, no one was hurt by your "white lie" and it does not, for that reason, seem improper to me.

The experienced professional secretary will understand why your action was necessary. With her the job comes first. She would willingly endure almost anything to meet its demands. Her job is more than a job. It is her *raison d'être,* the center around which her life revolves. It is more than an opportunity to earn her daily bread, for it provides an outlet for her drives, her dreams, her ambitions, her emotional needs. In the words of the women's magazines, she seeks fulfillment in her job for many of her emotional needs. These needs go beyond the desire to feel important and to be needed by her superior. An electronics executive gave his secretary the title of executive assistant, and the young lady promptly reacted as if she had been granted all the power and authority of the executive himself. That she was ill equipped to exercise it didn't dampen her enthusiasm in the slightest.

Such a woman may try to establish an unhealthy emotional relationship with the executive. I am not suggesting a love affair, but rather a possessive relationship. She may come to look upon you as "her man" in the office, her personal property and responsibility. And if you allow it to happen, your secretary will soon act as if she held your job. She'll utilize her position to keep your staff members at arm's length from you, compelling them to deal with her instead of with you.

The possessive woman begins imperceptibly. Offering gentle suggestions, she may seek to guide your activity along her own predetermined lines. If you don't stop her, she may soon be telling you, pleasantly but firmly, what to do next, whom you should see, and "if I were you, Mr. Soderholm. . . ." She'll push more and more strongly to dominate you unless you ring the bell and call a halt.

I allowed this to happen to me. In one situation, I wasn't sufficiently aware to realize at an early stage what was going on. When my secretary's activity became obvious, I had the unpleasant task of calling her in and having to tell her candidly that she was working for me, and not the other way around. The situation would never have developed, had I been on my toes.

It's better to nip such attempts in the bud before the habit pattern has become formed. The first time your secretary oversteps herself, you may say quietly, "Thank you, Miss Amy, but that's something *I'll* have to decide." She'll get the idea; if not the first time, then the second. Try not to put it more strongly, such as a blunt "That's none of your business," for that may stir up her hostility and leave you worse off than before. You want her ideas, her assistance, her enthusiasm; you don't want her domination. If you're uncertain which is which, step backward, and look at the situation in a cold, businesslike manner. Is she offering suggestions to help you do a better job? If so, that's fine. But if she's offering them to gain a feeling of superiority over you, stop and think twice before you accept them.

The manner in which you receive her suggestions is also important. If you accept them because they're helpful, that's good. If you accept them to please her, or to make her feel important, you're probably making a mistake. Treating her courteously and considerately is not the same as trying to provide her with emotional fulfillment. It isn't your job to do so. If she expects it, she's making improper demands on you which you neither can nor should try to meet.

Frequently, an executive complains of the opposite problem, that his secretary takes little responsibility, and isn't smart enough to be given any. Too often, it develops that he himself is too disorganized to delegate work to her. I've never forgotten my initial shock at seeing the marketing director of a $130,000,000 corporation negotiate over the telephone for theater tickets for an out-of-town customer. He hadn't learned the difference between the duties of a high-paid marketing director and those of a low-paid secretary, so I shouldn't have been surprised.

Not every executive has learned to delegate to his secretary what should be delegated, and not every executive has learned how clearly his secretary's performance mirrors his own. Your secretary reflects you. If you are disorganized, she will probably be too. If you want to convey warmth and friendliness, it's up to you to see to it that your secretary is warm and friendly. Her personality provides visitors with their first impression of you.

If she's surly or officious to callers, it's probably because you don't care. Perhaps she acts discourteously because she's taken a cue from you.

You'll make the most of your valued secretary if you work with her in a thoroughly businesslike way. A pleasant, efficient, and down-to-earth secretary will ease your executive problems. More than that, she will help build your image as a pleasant, efficient, and down-to-earth executive. That image will be a valuable asset when senior management sizes you up for promotion.

18

....

On the Path
to Glory

YOUR NEXT PROMOTION will probably come more quickly than did your last, for, as an executive, you are exposed to closer scrutiny by your superiors than when you were a member of "the ranks."

I assume, of course, that the exposure shows you in a favorable light. If it doesn't, you'll stay right where you are. The corporate scene is full of men who reached their peak while still in junior posts, and moved no further. Promotions passed them by, and the years rolled on until baldness and gray hair made their very title of "junior executive" an incongruity.

Every management executive can point to one or more such men on his staff. They meet the requirements of the job, but no more. Their youthful ambitions of high corporate position have crashed against the rocks of reality. They've settled back into their little offices to serve out their time until retirement. Age has nothing to do with it; I've known men who reached their peak before the age of twenty-five.

There's nothing wrong with having such men in your department. Properly placed where their limited abilities can be used to the fullest, they're an asset to their company. They do their work well, and they cause no difficulties for their superiors. What they lack is the ability to take over a job at the next higher level.

Management of a function isn't the same as performing the function. For example, a salesman's duties change radically when he is promoted to sales manager. Instead of persuading customers to buy, he now has the responsibility for establishing sales territories, setting quotas, providing promotional material, and so on. Likewise, the accountant who kept the company's books would find his duties changed if he were upped to the post of controller. In the higher position, he'd be concerned with putting the figures to work, establishing cost reduction plans, and dealing with bankers in anticipation of the company's credit requirements.

The man who seeks promotion must be technically qualified for the higher post. And, above all, he must have relentless drive. In the words of one company president, "I look for a man who acts as if he's always sitting on top of a firecracker." The man with drive is the fellow who's always searching for new ideas and new ways to do things. He's the man who's nicknamed "Go-go-go" (what they called Matthew J. Culligan, who climaxed a brilliant executive career in his early forties by becoming chairman of the board of the Curtis Publishing Company). He's the man who constantly comes up with suggestions, and finds many of them accepted.

And he works his tail off. I saw that for myself as a member of the Young Presidents' Organization. This is a group of men who became presidents of million-dollar companies before the age of forty.

Several times a year, the young presidents schedule regional seminars which last for three or four days. They jam their programs from morning to night with work sessions on management problems. Usually only one afternoon is reserved for relaxation, most often spent on the golf course.

I recognized the educational value of the seminars, but several YPO'ers added an unexpected reason why they came.

"This is the only time I get away from the office," one president told me. "I never take a vacation, so I try to come to a couple of the seminars each year. It gives me a change of scene, and my wife looks forward to coming with me."

The YPO'ers considered their hard-driving sessions a relaxation. For many, it was their only vacation. Even on "vacation," they were hard at work.

The discovery shouldn't have come as a surprise to me. Without this driving force, how could a man become president of a million-dollar company before his fortieth birthday? (The only exception is the new president who can say to the chairman of the board, "Thank you very much for the honor, Dad.")

The burning drive of the ambitious young executive doesn't always show itself outwardly. His speech may be soft and gentle, concealing his inner fire. By no means is he always, or even frequently, a "what-makes-Sammy-run" type. But in his own quiet way, he manages to let his boss know that he has his eye on bigger things. Sometimes he does it subtly; on other occasions, he makes his goal as clear as the junior executive who responded to a pat-on-the-back from his boss by saying: "Thank you very much, Mr. Cooper. But quite truthfully, I'm not satisfied in this job. If I don't get something better by this time next year, I'm going to have to leave." Faced with the possible loss of a valued employee, Mr. Cooper promoted him within seven months.

A surprising number of young executives don't have this drive. Perhaps because they fear failure in a bigger job, they're content to stay where they are. They avoid risks. They perform their present duties well, so why chance disaster? If a promotion comes to them from on high, fine, but they'll lift not a finger to seek it. Since corporate miracles occur rather infrequently these days, they usually stay where they are, in junior posts, and lament their unappreciative bosses.

It's already too late in your life to acquire this drive.

Either you have it or you don't. It's part of your basic pattern of living, and you acquire it—or fail to acquire it— in your childhood. You may have resented domination by a parent. To escape domination in your business life, you have struggled to reach the top. Perhaps you wanted to escape the frustrations of service in the lower ranks. The successful executive is often a man who resents, consciously or unconsciously, the corporate hierarchy over him. He regards his superiors as opponents, for too often they turn down his ideas. His solution is to free himself from bosses by becoming one himself. Inner needs like these kindle his fire of ambition even though, outwardly, he talks of seeking the money, honor, and prestige of corporate power.

In other cases, the executive's childhood was marked by poverty and privation. Early, he formed the habit of driving himself unmercifully. First, it was to earn money to feed his family; then it was to ensure himself against poverty in the future. But now that he has achieved financial security, he drives himself onward as hard as ever. He is motivated by his "poorhouse neurosis." (He fears he'll end in the county poorhouse if he stops pushing.)

This has been the life story of a prominent Cleveland industrialist. His name appears engraved in stone over the entrances to hospitals, college buildings, and research institutes he has endowed, for his benefactions always include the stipulation that the buildings be named in his honor.

His origins, in the Horatio Alger tradition, were humble. As a young child, many times he went hungry while his father, an unskilled factory worker, knocked on factory gates in vain search of a job. The young child did not understand why there was no food to eat, but somehow he blamed it all on his father. He promised himself that when he grew up, he would never allow his children to go hungry.

He worked hard. One job was not enough. He held two, working night and day. He skimped and saved while he educated himself. His hardships compounded his childhood fears of suffering, and he drove himself relentlessly. By the age of eighteen, his ambition was already sharply focused. His life goal was to earn ten thousand dollars a year.

The year was 1913. At that time, ten thousand dollars a year was a princely sum. It was before the days of the income tax, and the dollar's purchasing power was much greater than it is today. Ten thousand dollars a year! It was huge beyond realistic expectations for even an ambitious young man.

Yet, somehow, the Clevelander managed to earn it by the time he was twenty-three. He had taken his modest accumulated savings, opened a small business, and brought it to surprising success. Every dollar earned was quickly reinvested, and every waking hour was spent working for tomorrow. The days of hunger were past, but the inward fear lingered on.

His burning race for security flamed brighter instead of dimming. Now he set his ambition to acquire wealth of one hundred thousand dollars. He must be a rich man; if he accumulated such wealth, he reasoned, he would be safe from privation for the rest of his life.

In due time, this goal, too, was achieved, and before the young man had passed his thirty-fifth birthday. Now his wealth was amassed by shrewd investments and astute decisions rather than by long hours of toil.

At this point, you would think that the executive might have relaxed and begun to enjoy his riches. His childhood ambitions had been met and surpassed. The fear of poverty had been eliminated for the rest of his days.

But his compulsion did not diminish. His relentless drive impelled him onward. He moved to an oak-paneled suite, but still he, not his secretary, unlocked the office door a few minutes after eight o'clock each morning. Now he reached for a new goal: to acquire one million dollars. In due time, this also was achieved. And this too was superseded by still another ambition: to endow each of his children with a trust fund of one million dollars "so that they'll never have to go hungry."

With each changing season, he advanced closer to this

objective. By the time he reached his mid-fifties, the trust funds were properly established and adequately financed. Now he lived in a magnificent home, surrounded by ostentatious luxury, but the insecurity that began in young boyhood still drove him forward.

What goal could he set now? His immoderate self-demands had already been achieved. His need to work had been eliminated. Two generations of his family, besides his own, had been provided for beyond their dreams.

At the moment, he has turned to philanthropy, and is providing generous endowments to several colleges. In 1964, if you asked him why he continues in his sixty-ninth year to drive himself as rigorously as he did a half-century before, he would tell you that he wants to help worthwhile causes and to repay the debt to the society which rewarded him so generously.

But his life story demonstrates that this isn't his real reason. Barely concealed beneath the surface is his true motivation which began in early childhood. The search for security continued to dominate his life long after the poverty which caused it had disappeared.

The industrialist's life epitomizes the lifelong intense thrust which companies seek in the young executive. The corporation which hires more college graduates each year than any other, the American Telephone & Telegraph Company, looks for "self-starters" more than anything else. The Bell System recently studied the executive careers of 17,000 of its executives, comparing their performance to their college records. A.T.&T. reached the conclusion that scholastic achievement is the most important single indicator for predicting success in their company.

Frederick R. Kappel, chairman of the board, explained why in a frank talk to a group of Westminster College students:

When you hire a man of high intelligence but low grades, in effect you have to bet that a drive he hasn't yet shown *will* show after he goes to work. If, on the other hand, you are considering a high scholarship man, your bet is that a drive already demonstrated will be sustained.

As we look for career managers, why should we spend a large part of our effort searching among men who have made a career of just getting by? The proper goal of a business can't be just to get by. No enterprise with that object in life will be able to do what the times demand. But if we should content ourselves with get-by people, that is the way they would shape the business.

You won't be hired by the Bell System unless you have demonstrated inner drive, and rightly so. You won't be promoted anywhere unless ambition is in your bloodstream. Charles Revson once told an associate, "I can't make executives; they've got to make themselves."

Critics of the corporate scene have repeatedly charged that only the "organization man," not the rugged individualist, can move ahead as an executive. It is certainly true that if you are constantly at odds with your associates, you will likely be eliminated by senior management. They will be unwilling to pay the price of internal disharmony which your continued presence will demand. If that's what the critics mean by elimination of the rugged individualist, they are absolutely correct.

But individuality itself is another matter. Corporations want it, and many of them encourage it. This is not the individuality of the antagonistic person, but the creative uniqueness of the executive who brings originality and freshness to the solution of business problems.

The Standard Oil Company (New Jersey) faced squarely the matter of corporate conformity when its Social Science Research Division launched a six-year research project to identify employees who would be likely to perform successfully in management positions. Jersey, as the company is known, was particularly concerned lest its test program eliminate nonconformists from executive positions in the future.

In its summary report, called "Early Identification of Management Potential," the division summarized its conclusion as follows:

The description of the methods and procedures used in this study may cause concern that their future application would select only conformists, men who think alike and act alike. This is not the case. The evidence is that successful managers in Jersey do not conform to any set pattern. If they did, the research problems in this project would have been much simpler. When groups are described as being alike, the reference is to levels of ability and general personal and background characteristics rather than to specifics. The test battery includes several different tools and there are many kinds of questions in each of them. Thus a man can get a high score on the combined test by a number of different avenues and for many different reasons just as he can advance in the organization for a variety of reasons. There is not just one pattern alone—a pattern of conformity.

Two recent reports of other research are pertinent to this problem of conformity. One researcher, Ghiselli, pointed out that "uniqueness of response" was the best single predictor of management success. Another, Dalton in *Men Who Manage*, traced the problem of conformity back through history and found that critics of various social systems have been discussing it for centuries. He concludes that man's adaptation to the situation in which he finds himself is not the same as the complete relinquishment of independence of thought and action. Dalton summarizes as follows: "Those who mistake surface conformity in organizations for *total* conformity and the death of originality, should refocus to concern themselves with the ethics of protective coloration among thinking animals."*

---

* Summary Report of the Early Identification of Management Potential Research Project in Standard Oil Company (New Jersey) and Affiliated Companies. Prepared by Social Science Research Division, Employee Relations Department, Standard Oil Company (N.J.), August, 1961. Reprinted by permission.

The Jersey study makes a distinction between surface conformity and total conformity. I define surface conformity as the ability to get along amicably with your associates, playing by the rules of the game. At the same time, you retain your independence of mind, bringing your judgment to bear on business problems without regard to what "the others" think. A total conformist, on the other hand, avoids original thinking and will not propose solutions unless they meet the test of orthodoxy. For him, the yardstick is whether his idea will win the approval of his colleagues, and only secondarily whether it will help the company. Unfortunately, there are many total conformists in executive posts, but, fortunately, they don't often win promotions. Competitive business pressures demand individualists to solve complex management problems. The total conformist just doesn't have what it takes.

Besides individuality, management places a high value on objectivity. This is the ability to look at any situation and appraise it utterly devoid of emotion. It's a quality essential to a successful executive, and your supervisor will be looking for it when he evaluates you for promotion.

Objectivity means looking at facts, not feelings. It means looking at what is, rather than at what you'd like things to be. It means the ability to size up a situation coldly and analytically, weighing the facts without prejudice.

You demonstrate objectivity when you evaluate an employee's strengths and shortcomings, regardless of your personal feelings toward him. You demonstrate it when you analyze your own project that failed, neither minimizing nor exaggerating your own errors of judgment.

Since you're a human being, and not an electronic computer, you'll never be able to dispense with your emotions. The objective executive doesn't try to eliminate them; he merely pushes them aside to keep them from getting in the way of his business decisions. He may personally like a particular member of his staff, but he won't let his office friend-

ship stand in the way of getting rid of him if it becomes necessary. Or the executive may be expansion-oriented, deriving
satisfaction from the constant opening of new factories. But
if business conditions so indicate, he won't hesitate to contract
rapidly, close down obsolete plants, and sell them off. He'll
regard it simply as a business decision which unfortunately
had to be made, not as a personal defeat.

To win recognition as a promising executive and to be
earmarked for promotion, it goes without saying that you'll
have to possess considerable brainpower. Unlike objectivity,
which can be acquired, intelligence seems to be inborn.
Today's business leaders require it in increasing degree.

Intelligence is the ability to think through a problem, and
to come up with solutions. If you're smart, you'll look at the
same set of facts that your fellow executives have, but you'll
see something in them that nobody else does. You'll break
down a complex situation into its components, sift through
each, and then put the pieces back together again in a way
that will mean hitherto unseen profits for management. You'll
connect two observations in a novel way, and propose a new
product as a result.

The air freight manager of a major United States airline
showed creative intelligence when he developed a new way to
promote shipment by air freight. Because air freight is more
costly per pound than rail or truck shipment, the airlines had
previously emphasized the advantages of speedy delivery. The
manager noted that air freight made possible the overnight
delivery of any item anywhere in the United States. Therefore
it eliminated the necessity for companies to maintain local
inventories to ensure prompt delivery. With the need for warehouses gone, companies could reduce or eliminate fixed
expenses for real estate, buildings, and personnel, as well as
the cost of the inventories themselves. Products could be
shipped directly from factory to local customer overnight.
Savings which would result from elimination of warehouses
more than offset the extra expense of air shipments.

This sound approach produced a sizable increase in air freight business, the result of intelligent analysis by an able executive. If you demonstrate comparable ability, even on a modest scale, you may be certain your superiors will notice it quickly.

Another case where intelligent thought brought great rewards to a corporation happened during the late fifties.

At that time, television set manufacturers were seeking new markets for their products. Saturation of the one-set-per-home market was approaching, so they turned to the portable market. They used simplified components, lighter-weight cases, and new manufacturing techniques to develop TV sets that could be carried to another room or even to the backyard. The screens were big, from sixteen to twenty-one inches, and the pictures were bright and clear.

But across the Pacific in Japan, executives added up the same set of marketing facts and reached entirely different conclusions. They reasoned that a segment of the American public was more interested in a truly portable TV set than in retaining the customary large screen picture. Backing their judgment with a substantial investment, they developed a portable set reduced to almost the size of an ordinary telephone, with a post-card size picture. It was difficult to manufacture; extreme precision was required. They set the price accordingly, considerably higher than a large-screen American set.

Their bold judgment proved correct, and the set sold extremely well. Thoughtful market analysis and intelligent judgment brought high rewards. This is the kind of intelligence that companies welcome, and the executive who displays it will quickly stand out in any organization.

I don't know the identity of the air freight executive who developed the new marketing policy, or the electronics executive who suggested the small TV set. These men probably were able men, but not necessarily of the caliber of Leonardo da Vinci, whose massive talents made him simultaneously a great painter, a master sculptor, an inventor, an architect, and a military engineer as well. A genius like Leonardo appears perhaps once or twice in a century. The talents of most of us are much more limited. It may well be that the two executives possessed ability only in narrow areas. Had they been assigned to work on a complex financial problem, they might have failed completely.

Intelligence itself isn't enough, therefore, to win you advancement from your present post. Your thinking ability must be of the type that your position and the times require. For instance, in the early postwar period, a whole breed of promoters came to prominence in American industry. Rising rapidly from obscurity, they took over old, well-established corporations, and then moved ahead by complex mergers, acquisitions, and financing to achieve control of entire industrial empires. They displayed amazing talent for manipulation, consolidation, and pyramiding. Their financial judgments were shrewd in the extreme.

Most of them, however, never involved themselves in the actual operations and management of the companies whose control they had acquired. At the peak of their power, about 1960, a leading business magazine praised their ability to manipulate, but wondered in the same breath whether they would be able to manage successfully even one of the companies they now dominated.

The 1962 break in the stock market was the beginning of the end for some of the best-known corporate savages. All of their brains and ability could not hold together their paper empires. The lesson was clear that they were not Tarzan-like supermen but only mortal individuals whose particular talents flourished under a particular set of circumstances.

Similarly, the current condition of your company may control your future. You may have earned a fine reputation as a production man, but, in your company, the primary need right now is for more sales, rather than for more production. The management struggling to market its products against fierce competition is unlikely to promote a production man to a top post, however well qualified you might be.

Or conversely, you may have an excellent record as sales manager, but the nature of your business involves the government, either as a customer or legal foe in antitrust proceedings. A lawyer is then more likely to receive preferred consideration for promotion to a senior management post. Your specialized sales experience isn't needed at the top. There's not much you can do about it except to try to find a better spot elsewhere.

Your chances for promotion are best if your specialty is general management, according to *Dun's Review & Modern Industry,* which surveyed the 250 largest United States corporations. The magazine found that 18.5 percent of the companies were headed by men who came up through general management, rather than a particular specialty. This was the largest single source of company presidents.

Dean Howard W. Johnson of M.I.T.'s School of Industrial Management, in discussing a hypothetical situation in the *Harvard Business Review,* explained why:

> Our candidates seem to have mastered their own specialties rather well, but don't have much experience with over-all company problems. This, of course, is not an uncommon predicament— having men who have proven themselves in a given field but who wear the blinders of their own specialty. They tend to see that specialty alone, and give it more priority than perhaps it deserves in the broader picture. The fellows in this case do need broadening; they ought to understand more about the other parts of the business.*

The Dean went on to discuss the problem of acquiring well-rounded management experience in a period of increasing specialization.

* Reprinted by permission of the *Harvard Business Review* from

This is a critical question for all of American business, especially for industries in which there is a tendency for men to grow up in a specific line. Of course, no man can be expert at everything—he's the expert at nothing. It's important that everyone moving up in an organization master some field. But it's also important that a man *understand* other kinds of assumptions and take them into account when making decisions.

As a man begins to prove himself, the worst thing a company can do is to keep him in one narrow groove. He should be given other kinds of assignments, task force projects, and so on. One of the major values in community activities is the opportunity to see the way other people are thinking about serious problems.

You'll do well to range widely through the company on the way up the ladder. The critical time for this phase is at the beginning of your career. You can become acquainted with executives from other departments and learn their problems. If company policy permits it, you can visit the factory to observe production methods. You can lunch with company salesmen, accountants, and lawyers. A knowledge of their activities will be invaluable to you.

As a matter of fact, it was by just such a method that I launched my own career almost a quarter of a century ago. I had begun working as a page boy in a radio broadcasting network, while attending college at night. A page boy is at the very bottom of the network's social scale. He wears a uniform like the doorman and the elevator operator. His job is to usher guests into the studios, to run errands, and to deliver morning coffee to the executives.

During my lunch hour, I made it a practice to visit various departments of the network to find out what part each played in the total company. It always seemed to surprise the executives that a young page boy showed serious interest in their activities. They were delighted to answer my questions and to introduce me, albeit superficially, to their problems. The immediate consequence of these visits was a promotion to one of the departments I had visited. But the longer-range result was a broad familiarity with the company which served me well in later years.

A friend of mine won advancement by displaying a broad view of his company at a much higher level. He was an attorney in the corporate legal department, responsible for negotiating complex leasing and financing agreements.

If you've ever had occasion to deal with company lawyers, you know they usually give all the reasons why you *can't* follow your planned course of action. Armed with law and judicial precedent, they emphasize the hazards that will ensue if you follow a certain direction. This lawyer did too, but, unlike the others, he proceeded to outline alternate courses which management could safely follow to accomplish its objectives. He employed his legal skill as a tool of management, rather than as a tool of obstruction in the interests of supposed corporate safety.

It was this quality which won him promotion to the post of general manager of an entire corporate division. Significantly, his new job offered him little opportunity to apply his years of legal experience. His legal career had ended, and he began a new one as a general executive; his broad management thinking had earned him the post.

Nor is a broad outlook and excellent qualifications enough. You also must be in the right place at the right time. In one of the leading chemical companies, Harry Thompson, the promotion manager of the textile fibers department, was called in suddenly and told that the advertising manager had just resigned. To economize, management decided to consolidate the two positions and offered Mr. Thompson the post as an addition to his present duties. Only a slight pay increase was involved, but Mr. Thompson seized the opportunity; the responsibilities of his new post were greater than those of his present one.

Mr. Thompson did a fine job, considerably better than his departed predecessor. Two years later, when business conditions had improved, and the department had expanded, Mr.

Thompson appointed a promotion manager under him while he retained the advertising post. The transition was complete, and he ended up with a much bigger job.

Don't let this give you the idea that it's easy to climb the executive ladder. You may have all the desirable characteristics I've outlined, and still not make it, for reasons completely beyond your control.

For one thing, your age may be against you. Most companies seek men between forty and fifty for top management jobs. For middle management, the preferred age level is between thirty and forty. If you are too old, or too young, for the next level above you, you may be frozen where you are.

This practice tends to create an identical age group among executives at each level in the organization. At the top, all the vice-presidents will be of the same age, headed for almost simultaneous retirement. When that day comes management will regret it, but meanwhile, the age policy may halt you in your tracks.

Or your personality may hold you back from advancement. Each corporation tends to recruit a different personality type, depending on its needs. If you are in the wrong company, you will soon discover you are a corporate misfit, unlikely to advance further.

A bank, for example, tends to staff itself with careful, precise, conservative individuals, men accustomed to weighing each move slowly and cautiously. Psychologically, they find it easier to say "no" than to say "yes." In such an environment, a dynamic young man would soon stand out unfavorably.

A food manufacturer, accustomed to battling for shelf space in the supermarket, attracts a different type of personnel: men who are quicker to respond, more aggressive in temperament, and thoroughly at home in a highly competitive atmosphere.

The giant utility corporations select men who, above all,

are team workers. In these companies, no one individual, often not even the president himself, makes decisions of major significance. Almost every decision in such companies causes such large and far-reaching consequences that prolonged collective discussion must precede it.

If you have aggressive drives for authority and responsibility, the likelihood is that you won't be very happy in the utility company, even if you succeed in getting the job. If you are slower moving, more reluctant to make decisions, you won't fit very well into the food company. Management will measure your performance by the same standards they have applied to their existing staffs. (Why should they suddenly change for you?) By this yardstick, you are doomed to failure even before you begin.

Don't bang your head against the wall. It's difficult enough to win a promotion on your own merits. But if your company doesn't want or need your abilities, you don't belong there. It's time to begin looking for a new job.

19

Job Hunting
and Head
Hunting

So YOU JOIN the legion of executive job hunters. The ranks of this vast army constantly empty and are refilled every three to six months by perhaps 75,000 executives, men whose annual salaries have exceeded $20,000.

The average survival time in the executive jungle is short. Rare is the executive who has spent most of his working career with a single company. One survey of a group of middle-management executives showed that 41 percent survived in their last jobs for less than three years, and three out of every four switched jobs before they reached the ten-year gold-watch mark.

When executives leave their jobs, they become almost invisible. Their protective coloration conceals them from attention and the only places you can spot them are public buildings and railroad stations, where they huddle in telephone booths with a list of prospects to call and a supply of dimes neatly laid out on the small shelf in front of them. In midmorning, in any major city, it's surprising to discover how many there are. You will also find them in the long waiting lines at the unemployment compensation office. They are immaculately dressed and read the newspaper while they wait to sign their claim for their weekly benefit check. Only their slightly belligerent manner reveals that they are men who are unaccustomed to waiting in line for anything.

Now you find yourself on the hunt with them. You are accustomed to performing useful work, exercising authority, and enjoying the status and glory of an important position. Now you suddenly discover that unemployment is a severe psychological trial.

Stripped of your business cards, you feel adrift. You still carry an attaché case, but now it contains your résumé and a cheese sandwich instead of your business papers. For your five-button telephone, you have substituted the two-nickel coin booth. If you previously measured your own worth by the importance of your job, you now feel unwanted without one. As you pound the pavements between appointments, you wonder where your next employment will come from.

Everything seems against you. It's the wrong time of the year to be looking. If it's spring or summer, people tell you that things will be quiet until vacations are over in the fall. If you join the ranks of the jobless during the fall, you may hear that hiring decisions won't be made until new budgets are approved after the first of the year. If it's the winter holiday season when everyone else is preoccupied with office parties, gifts, and celebrations, no one may be interested in talking with you seriously. At any time of the twelve months, current business conditions may be offered as a reason for not seeing you. It's enough to shake any man's self-confidence.

But the choice of time and circumstances was not yours, so there is little point in regretting your real or imagined misfortunes. If ever there was a time to think positively, this is it. Whatever the month when you are seeking a position, at that same time certain companies are seeking the right person to fill particular openings. Good positions are never easy to find, but some always exist. Your problem is to locate one quickly, and then sell yourself into it.

Several reasons explain why executives change jobs so often. Whether they are fired, are asked to "resign," or voluntarily leave, isn't always significant. A man may elect to leave voluntarily because he senses that, if he doesn't, he'll be fired within a few months.

Whatever the timing, however, the major reason for change is that he wants more responsibility. Executives start looking elsewhere when they've reached, or think they have reached, a dead end. Considering their individualistic personality, it's not surprising that they should thirst for bigger jobs.

The second factor that drives executives out of their jobs is disagreement with management policies. Put bluntly, this means they haven't been able to get along with their superiors, even though there may be good reasons for their disagreements. The very aggressiveness that makes an executive successful often makes him a poor team player. He engages in personality clashes with other senior executives, sometimes because they want the same top position he wants.

A third reason for the increasing number of executive changes is the technological revolution which causes managements to seek new skills and experience. The old ways have become obsolete, along with the veteran executives who practiced them. Today's forty-year-old, who looks forward to another quarter-century of employment before his retirement, will almost certainly find it necessary to learn a new occupation before his working days are over.

And a fourth reason is the rash of corporate mergers, reorganizations, and consolidations, the symptoms of an ever-changing economy.

If any of these factors have jeopardized your present position, and your superior has suggested that you look elsewhere while remaining on the company payroll, you have the best of all possible worlds. You are free to seek a new position from the privileged sanctuary of your present employment.

Your income continues while you search, but even more important, you are more desirable to the "head hunters," those who are looking for personnel to fill current executive openings. One recruiter estimates that 90 percent of men hired for top positions are employed elsewhere at the time. Another says that it's one hundred times harder for a man to get a job when he is out of work, no matter how high a position he may have held. Companies often ask, "If he's so good, why is he out of a job?" The reason could have been a corporate merger or reorganization, but nothing influences them as much as the fact that right now, today, he is not employed.

If you have decided to look for greener pastures while you are still "happily" employed, and without the knowledge of your superior, your search will be made more difficult by the need for secrecy. Open search is impossible, for a "leak" to your employer would quickly terminate your present position. Only discreet contacts may safely be made; blind newspaper ads may not be answered, for they may have been placed by your own employer. Competitive firms may be approached only with trepidation, for fear of some unknown personal connection between their executives and your company.

Despite all these handicaps, however, your quiet efforts may in due time produce an offer of a better position at a higher salary. If the opportunity is clearly superior to the job you now have, your choice is easy. But perhaps the new post offers an uncertain future. Or the position may pay a higher salary, but the company itself is in financial trouble. If you are undecided, a frank talk with your present superior may be worthwhile. You may find out during the interview exactly where you stand, and thus be able to make an intelligent choice between two alternatives. But your offer had better be firm and definite before you speak with him. Otherwise, he may call your bluff and invite you to take the other job. If it exists only in your imagination, you're out of work before you wanted to be.

The wisest course is to tell him the details of the other offer, where it is, what it is, and how much the job will pay.

Tell him why you are considering it. Does it offer greater opportunity? Have you been offered higher salary? Then ask what opportunities you have if you remain, and what your compensation would be.

Your superior may respond to these questions by asking one of his own, "What would you really like to do?" Your answer should be well prepared. If you really would prefer to stay, you should say so. He may then try to obtain a pay increase for you, or even a promotion to larger responsibilities.

And if you really want to stay, don't use the offer as a lever to pry an increase out of the boss. Threaten to leave unless you get more money, and he'll certainly invite you to leave. No executive wants to be pressured. If you happen to be indispensable at the moment, he may award you the raise, but only long enough to train a replacement to take over your work. Then he'll no longer "require your services."

Few executives handle themselves well in job hunting situations. For one thing, they fail to make a realistic appraisal of their worth in today's job market. All executives believe they are underpaid and overworked. Your job hunt will become easier if you can assess accurately the current supply and demand, and the going market price, for someone with your capabilities.

When executives decide to look elsewhere, or when they receive the signal to begin searching, they frantically contact friends and associates almost at random. Then they visit employment agencies and executive searchers. Next they send a slew of letters to firms which competed with their former employer. When their initial burst of energy exhausts itself and their contact list is fully tapped, they stay at home, discouraged and tense, waiting for a letter or phone call which may not come for months, if at all.

Your own search should be more carefully planned and better executed. You should anticipate disappointments, and steel yourself against them.

Some prospective employers, for instance, may exclude you from serious consideration because you're too young. ("You're only twenty-seven, and we prefer middle-management executives in their thirties.") Others will exclude you because you're too old. ("The man you'd report to is only thirty-eight. I can't put a forty-five-year-old in there.") Or your asking salary may be too high, or too low, in terms of related jobs in the organization.

You must be prepared to encounter such barriers, but my advice is to ignore them, because you can't change them. Somewhere, you'll locate a company that seeks an exceptionally young executive, or an older man, or a lower priced man, or is willing to pay a premium to attract a man of exceptional experience. Your campaign must make yourself known to so many prospective employers that you'll find the one who wants a man exactly like you.

Nor will it help if you hear today of an opening which was filled yesterday. This too is an inescapable part of the hunt. Only a large-scale approach, pushed as rapidly as your energies will permit, will minimize lost opportunities. If you write only a few letters, and contact only a few people, you limit your opportunities to that extent. On the other hand, a wider and deeper search will help you find the right position and more quickly. If you attract two offers instead of one, you'll also acquire bargaining power, or leverage, which you can apply in either situation to secure more attractive terms.

Your job hunt is a marketing problem. You are the product. You are also the product manager, responsible for locating your "customers" and selling them. A market analysis will define who potentially needs your services, and a sales analysis will define the best techniques for selling them. You may need a new job so desperately that you don't have time to plan carefully. The experience of successful job hunters, however, testifies that a few days of intensive planning at the beginning of your search will invariably bring results sooner.

It will also eliminate the errors which executives commonly make.

The first of these errors is inadequate self-appraisal. As I pointed out earlier, an executive's job has parallels in many companies. Yet, too often, unemployed executives regard themselves as qualified to perform only the identical job in a similar company. Such an approach is needlessly limiting. It prevents the executive from seeking other opportunities for which he is qualified.

A top-to-bottom study of your own industry will locate many possibilities of different jobs which you could perform. If you have headed a production department in an agricultural implements firm, for instance, your experience might qualify you to sell agricultural implements, service them, handle inventory of replacement parts, or to become purchasing agent for an agricultural implements firm.

You may prefer to stay in the same industry, doing work closely akin to your last post. This is quite understandable; we feel most comfortable doing what we know best. But don't let your preference deter you from pursuing an opportunity in whatever industry it may develop.

Outside of your own industry, your skills may be useful in others. The production executive may qualify for a similar post in any company that manufactures products on an assembly line. The financial executive from the agricultural implements industry may similarly apply his talents in a financial post in many other industries. By the time you complete your study of job opportunities, the picture will look much more encouraging than when you thought only in terms of an identical job elsewhere.

However, a word of caution is in order. You will find it easier to convince yourself than to convince a prospective employer in another industry that you are qualified. A paint manufacturer may perhaps insist that your experience in the chemical industry does not qualify you to work for his company. On Madison Avenue, they tell the apocryphal story of the advertising agency which had just landed a large cigarette account and sought an experienced account executive. The product was a filter-tip, mentholated, king-size cigarette, packaged in a flip-top box. The best qualified candidate, so the story goes, almost got the job because of his experience with another filter-tip, mentholated, king-size cigarette. He lost his chance because he had no experience with filter-tip, mentholated, king-size cigarettes *in a flip-top box!* That's carrying the experience factor further than most employers will do, but undoubtedly some will rule you out because your experience isn't right, and you won't be able to convince them otherwise. It will be more profitable to expend your energies elsewhere.

Since you can't conduct your entire job-hunting campaign in a single month, or even in several months, you should plan an orderly sequence of activities. Assign priorities to each category on your list. At the top, to be tackled first, will be comparable positions in your present field; at the bottom will be positions of possibly lower skill in diverse fields. You may not really wish to pursue the latter, and if you quickly develop for yourself an attractive offer, you won't have to. On the other hand, because good executive positions are rarely found with ease, it is possible that you may reach the bottom of your priority list before you receive a job offer. A good rule is, "Hope for the best, but prepare for the worst."

After your preferences have been carefully listed, your next step is to select individual companies for hot pursuit.

Every industry in America is classified, catalogued, and rated in one reference book or another. Your public library, or trade association, will be glad to help you obtain complete lists. Some sources arrange companies by volume of sales and assets; others classify on a state and city basis. In some cities and for certain categories, the classified telephone directories may be helpful. Several directories identify principal executives by personal name. Whatever information you want, almost certainly you will be able to find it somewhere, and probably without too much searching either.

The directories will also help you avoid the error of insufficient pursuit. For example, a construction executive may contact five or ten large construction companies, but if he gets no affirmative response, he discontinues further efforts in that field. He presumes that further search among smaller companies in the field would be useless, because the largest companies have no immediate offerings. This isn't necessarily so. If you want to work in a particular industry, you should contact every employer in that field, large or small.

And who is the decision-maker in each company? Without first identifying him in each case, you can't know to whom to sell yourself. Is it the personnel director? Probably not, for, in most companies, his hiring responsibility is limited to lower-level positions paying less than $10,000. More likely, a production executive should apply to the vice-president in charge of production; a sales manager to the vice-president in charge of sales, and so on.

The third commonly made error is excessive dependence on friends. Of course, you may ask your friends for help, and many will be pleased to assist you. I know of cases where personal friends extended themselves above and beyond the call of duty to assist an unemployed executive, personally calling their own contacts on an applicant's behalf.

If they can't or won't assist you directly, perhaps they have personal contacts to whom they will be willing to refer you. Perhaps they will make a phone call or write a letter on your behalf. They may grant you permission to use their names to secure interviews that would otherwise be unobtainable. One applicant pyramided four original contacts into enough interviews to keep him fully occupied for five weeks. He stopped only when one resulted in exactly the position he sought. Until that final moment, he continued to ask each contact in turn for further contacts, and his exposure to job situations multiplied accordingly.

But there is a limit to how much friends can reasonably be expected to do for you. They may not wish to exert themselves on your behalf; many a fair-weather friend and summer soldier has faded away on being asked to assist. Sometimes, even if they would like to help you, they may nevertheless prove reluctant, for fear of being held responsible if you fail.

"If I select a total stranger for a job," a retail executive commented, "and the man doesn't work out, management will understand that mistakes sometimes happen. Nobody is 100 percent perfect in making personnel selections. But if I select a friend who doesn't work out, management will say personal friendship influenced my judgment. So I never endorse or hire anyone whom I know personally."

Seek assistance, therefore, from whichever friends may care to extend it, but don't place on their shoulders the burden of finding you a new job.

Another error is to halt in the middle of your search when you come under consideration for a promising opening. After a good first interview, the job looks within reach, so you decide that further efforts are unnecessary. You may hole up at home and wait, meanwhile discontinuing other efforts.

But important executive positions are rarely filled in a hurry. Even if you are the right candidate, budget approvals must be obtained. Sometimes, the job itself must first be formally defined. All this takes time. At the end, you may find yourself out of the running because the specifications change, or because the company decides to hire no one at all. Your morale will hit rock bottom, because you've lost precious weeks during which you could have been looking elsewhere. The conclusion is inescapable that no matter how close you appear to be to landing the job, your search should continue right up to the time you actually get it. The ex-executive cannot afford the luxury of procrastination.

The fifth common error is premature or clumsy discussion of salary. Executives accustomed to handling company budgets frequently mishandle their own compensation. They make financial demands before the position itself is discussed. They set their minimum demand above the peak of their previous position, although that figure was attained only after years of service with a single employer. Or they ask a salary grossly out of line with their economic worth on the job market. Any one of these errors can eliminate a candidate from serious consideration.

Salary discussions should be reserved for the final stage of discussions. They make sense only after the position has been defined clearly and its economic worth reasonably estimated. It's proper, if you're asked (but only if you're asked), to state your previous salary, but not to demand that amount as your starting minimum. One applicant, when queried, made a practice of replying, "My last salary was twenty thousand, but of course that was for a different position. Naturally, I don't know what this job is worth to you. I'm sure you have a budget, which sets a salary compared to the positions above it, and those below it. I don't know what those figures are, but I'm sure that if you decide you want me, we can work this out to everyone's satisfaction."

This is a realistic approach. The candidate answered the specific question asked, but he did not eliminate himself from consideration by rigidity. If management were intending to pay only ten thousand dollars, they would probably reject him as overqualified, but he wouldn't want a job at half his former earnings anyway.

Nor should you fear being taken advantage of by divulging your previous earnings. The employer can probably find it out in any case, either from your former company, or by shrewd estimation. Companies operating under budgets usually provide a "spread" between highest and lowest pay for any job of between 20 percent and 40 percent. Regardless of what you were earning previously, they won't vary their budget figure up or down by more than this range.

The best rule about salary discussions is to avoid the subject entirely until an employer raises it. Even then, the less you say, and the more flexibility you show, the better.

Like any salesman offering a product, you will need a selling tool. Your résumé is not a mere factual statement of information, as so many applicants apparently believe. Rather, it is your prime sales promotion for yourself. Therefore, it must sell your services, not merely state them.

Your résumé can list your years of experience either chronologically, or functionally. The functional résumé selects basic areas of experience, and itemizes your experience in each, regardless of the position in which it was obtained. Either is suitable, but your presentation must be aimed at the possible needs of the employer who reads it. If you simultaneously pursue several types of jobs in a single industry, you may need several different adaptations of your basic résumé. If your search leads you to several different industries, you'll minimize the particular industry in which your experience was acquired, and emphasize the functions you performed which are common to the other industries. Pinpointing your "sales literature" in this fashion will multiply the effectiveness of your search.

The first objective of your campaign is not to get a job but to get an interview. Many techniques will secure employment interviews, but I don't know of any way to get a job without a prior interview. The practical significance is that your campaign must convince prospective employers that an interview with you will be worthwhile. Only after you have won an invitation to meet with the employer can you pursue the job itself.

Successful job hunting may involve four different methods of obtaining interviews. Not all of the four may be suitable for you. Advertising is the first. In certain industries, employers customarily look to advertising in trade publications when they need specialized talents. If you're uncertain whether this is the practice in your industry, check whether many job-wanted ads are already appearing in the trade publications. The more there are, the more likely it's a good place to advertise. Don't make the mistake of placing your ad where few others appear, on the theory that yours will stand out more prominently. It will undoubtedly stand out, but it's less likely to be read by those looking for help. And if you decide to advertise yourself, repeat your ad a number of times; repetition adds impact. If you wait for possible responses before repeating your insertion order, you'll miss a week or two. Much better results will come from two or three successive insertions.

Your ad may produce one or two serious inquiries (you need only one definite job offer to solve your problem), but since results are impossible to predict, other methods should be followed also.

Unemployed executives immediately think of the "head hunters," the corps of executive recruiters who are retained by the nation's corporations to ferret out qualified candidates for management posts. They have, according to rumor, jobs immediately available.

And indeed they do. The magazine *Dun's Review & Modern Industry* published a full-page list of executive posts paying between $30,000 and $125,000 annually. All were either vacant at the time the article was published, or else had just been filled by an executive recruiting organization.

Why should so many top positions remain unfilled while simultaneously, outstanding men are searching unsuccessfully? In the answer may be found the importance of executive search firms.

If corporations merely needed any qualified executive, they would not require outside assistance. But for major positions of importance, they seek to minimize their risks by

finding candidates with exactly the right combination of qualifications. Like the filter-tip, mentholated, king-size, flip-top
box candidate, their men must possess heavy experience in
problems closely akin to those they will face. In the technical
industries, perhaps only half a dozen qualified candidates may
exist in the entire nation. The executive search firm is paid to
locate those six. It is overwhelmingly probable that all of
them will be currently employed. At any given moment, you
may well fit a particular set of qualifications for an open
position, but statistically the odds are against you.

This doesn't mean you should avoid the head hunters, for
tomorrow, one of them may receive a search assignment that
fits you exactly. If that happens, you want to be in their files.

There's no sure way to get into their files, but there is a
way to try. Write them a brief and direct letter, enclose your
résumé, and request an interview. Their names are listed in
various management directories. A referral by someone who
knows them personally will always help. Many recruitment
firms won't respond to your letter, which is understandable
considering the thousands of applications they receive. If,
however, your experience seems unusually impressive, or
represents an unusual combination of proved talents, one or
more may invite you for an interview. Don't get your hopes
up, for the odds are that the most you may expect, even after
a successful interview, is placement in their files in the form of
an IBM punched card. Perhaps within weeks, but more likely,
a few years later, your card will automatically pop out of the
file when the machine is asked to produce men with a particular set of qualifications.

Unless you are unusually fortunate with these methods,
you will probably also want to use the mails for the major
part of your efforts. Countless executives have found letter
writing effective, because it enables them to tell their story to
many companies at the same time. A mail campaign will
multiply your chances of reaching a prospective employer who

today may happen to be searching for someone with just the experience and talents you offer. If you were forced to rely on personal contact alone, many months might elapse before you reached him, and by that time the job would already have been filled.

So you'll have to ask your good wife, or someone else with typing ability, to sit down and type the letter that will accompany your résumé. While the résumé may be reproduced mechanically, your letter must be individually typewritten and addressed. The contents will depend on your particular situation. The letter should be brief; your enclosed résumé tells your story in full. It should be a selling letter, not an informal letter; as the old salesman remarked, nobody ever got an order without asking for it. It should seek an interview; not a job.

Some applicants ask in their letters if they may telephone to make an appointment. Or they proceed to follow up by phone, even without asking. It's a waste of your time and the time of the prospective employer. If your qualifications interest him, he'll want to see you; if not, your phone call becomes a nuisance and sometimes an embarrassment. My advice is to save your dimes and use them to buy more postage stamps to send more letters.

Of course, the effectiveness of your campaign will depend on your letter as well as your qualifications. Several acquaintances who conducted such campaigns checked their personal records, and reported that their average response ran something like this: For every hundred letters and résumés they mailed, they averaged forty replies. Between thirty and thirty-five of these forty were totally negative; "nothing available now." A few replies indicated that no opening currently existed, but that one might be expected soon, and the applicant would be contacted at the appropriate time. Two or three of the forty said they would like to interview the applicant for possible future consideration, although no openings existed presently. And—the heart of the matter—one or two asked the candidate to phone for an immediate interview in connection with an opening. Two hundred letters will produce twice as many interviews as one hundred. An executive I know sent 746 letters by actual count during a four-month period, before he landed a job.

No one can predict the duration of your unemployment. It is entirely possible that one hundred or several hundred letters may fail to produce a single employment offer. If that happens to you, your timing may have been unlucky. Go back to the beginning of your list, and try again, with another version of your letter and résumé. Several executives I know succeeded on their second try, because, the second time, several of their target companies happened to be in the market for their talents.

When you finally receive an invitation for an interview, move quickly into high gear. During the day or two before your appointment, search out every bit of available information about the company. The public library will certainly help you, along with the trade press, trade association, and personal contacts. If the company is publicly owned, you may easily obtain a copy of its annual report, with a description of its corporate structure, new products, and expansion plans, as well as its financial figures. Various credit services, whose reports may become available to you through personal contacts, even provide brief biographies of officers and principal executives of the company. One of the men described may be the man who will interview you. You'll have an advantage if you know his background, age, experience, and education, so that you may make some passing reference to it during the interview. Your genuine interest in the company will show through.

The easiest way to make your interview successful is to remember the things you looked for when you were on the other side of the desk. Listening is one of them. If your interviewer takes twenty or thirty minutes to describe the position, don't interrupt him. Listen carefully; absorb all you can, and when he's finally talked out, show by your comments that you understand what he said. Show him that you really want the job; after months of unemployment, your disposition may be to play "hard to get," but it's a mistake. He will welcome your enthusiasm. Above all, tell the truth. If you were fired from your last job, say so honestly, without embarrassment and without defensiveness. What executive hasn't been fired at one time or another?

Telling the truth, however, isn't the same as emotional blabbering. If you describe the circumstances in gory detail, you will certainly bore him, and you may irritate him as well. It's better to distill into a few sentences the reason why it happened, and let it go at that.

Your best bet is to play it straight. Don't try to outsmart the employer, because it won't work. Your voice and manner will tell far more than your words. Even if you say the right words, they'll probably come out with the wrong tone of voice, easily detectable by a skilled interviewer.

After you leave his office, the waiting seems without end. Finally, three weeks and two interviews later, the phone call comes while you're at home reading the morning paper.

"Mr. Wright, this is Mr. Ricaud at Consolidated. I've got some good news for you. You've got the job! When would you like to come in, and fill out the papers to get started?"

You catch your breath, and make an appointment for tomorrow morning. (You'd like to go in this afternoon, but you delay twenty-four hours so as not to appear frantically anxious.)

The job is yours! You're an executive again! Monday morning, you'll begin work by meeting your new staff and getting acquainted. You are entering the jungle again, but this time, you know the rules for survival. Good luck to you!

Index